FULL OF FAIR HOPE

A HISTORY OF ST. MARY'S MISSION

RED LAKE, MINNESOTA

Owen Lindblad, OSB

PRINTED IN THE USA BY: Park Press Quality Printing, Inc.
Waite Park, MN 56387

BOOK AND COVER DESIGN: Placid Stuckenschneider, OSB

LIBRARY OF CONGRESS NO: 97-092645

ADDITIONAL COPIES: St. Mary's Mission
P.O. Box 189
Redlake, MN 56671

office of the bishop · p.o. box 610
crookston, minnesota 56719

TEL: (218) 281-4533   FAX: (218) 281-3328

March 24, 1997

The history of St. Mary's Mission and the Mission School at Red Lake is intimately connected with the history of Catholicism in northwestern Minnesota, which makes up the Diocese of Crookston.

In fact, the first window of the Bishop's Chapel at the Chancery in Crookston contains the name of Father Lautischar, who is mentioned early in this history. Near his name is the scene of an Indian dwelling in the midst of pine trees. The year "1858" also appears in the window, the year of Fr. Lautischar's tragic death on December 3.

This history of St. Mary's Mission is a wonderfully detailed account of the beginning and growth of the Mission, which still serves the Indian People of Red Lake Reservation. The trials and difficulties of ministering at the Mission are well described, but always in a spirit "full of fair hope." In that same spirit, the successes and joys of ministering at the Mission are also told. The Benedictine presence at the Mission--Brothers, Sisters, Priests--is one of the glories of Catholicism in this part of the Catholic world.

I sincerely thank and congratulate Sister Owen Lindblad, OSB, for this thoroughly researched history, a labor of great love. It represents four years of dedicated and painstaking work.

The history of the Mission still goes on. I pray that it will always go on for the glory of God and the spiritual benefit of the Indian People, our brothers and sisters within the Body of Christ, which is the Church.

(Most Rev.) Victor H. Balke
Bishop of Crookston

+Victor H. Balke
Bishop of Crookston

iii

June 5, 1997

This history is about a people, a place, and a past. It is
about the AHNISHINABAE-OJIBWE people of Red Lake, Minnesota,
since 1858 with a focus on St. Mary's Mission.

I have lived with and served the people as a pastor for
the past six years. I have come to respect the people of Red
Lake as my brothers and sisters. Many of the people have
accepted me as their friend. For this, I am grateful.
Miigwech!

As I have baptized the children, witnessed the marriage
vows of the adults, visited the sick, served persons in their
needs, shared their love, and buried those who died, I have
come to feel a real part of this people in this place along
with their past.

Red Lake, surrounded by its beaches and forests, is a
beautiful part of Mother Earth to be reverenced, cared for,
and cherished. In learning from our Ojibwe people, I have
come to appreciate that all parts of the universe and earth
that the Creator has made are intimately related--the people
of the earth, the animals, the birds, the fish, the trees, the
flowers, the soil, the rocks, the air, the water, the sun, the
moon and the galaxies.

In learning more and more of your history, I have come to
realize both the agony and the glory of the Ojibwe people

through many years of your history. I am
happy to have been a recent participant
during the last few years of your past.

My wish and prayer for you is that
the "PEOPLE" of this "PLACE" have a
future filled with "PROMISE."

With respect and love,

Father Bill

Father Bill Mehrkens
Red Lake, Minnesota

iv

ACKNOWLEDGMENTS

Gathering information and writing this book has been like preparing for the birth of a child. Much care and loving attention is given in the months (in this case, years) of preparation to assure the safe deliverance of a healthy, vibrant, happy child. The child arrives at last, the product of careful nurturing by her parents, but also bearing the imprint of a long line of successive generations from whom she receives individual characteristics. The future lies with this new child. Her soul is pure potential.

With this analogy and in this context I am privileged to present *Full of Fair Hope: A History of St. Mary's Mission Red Lake, Minnesota*. The process of writing has been one of birthing, and much credit is due to many who have helped "parent" and "nurture" this child to life. Gratitude enfolds these many from the old, old stories researched and told, to the people who added editorial and historical credence, to those whose encouragement and support undergird the entire process.

Gratitude, therefore, goes first of all to Father Bill Mehrkens and St. Mary's Pastoral Council who commissioned the work and who confidently upheld it. All those who work at St. Mary's Mission and the many parishioners and Mission friends who have waited patiently for the "child to be born" provided me with the motivation to persevere. Archivists Jody Beaulieu, Sister Ruth Boedigheimer of St. Benedict's Monastery, and Father Vincent Tegeder from St. John's Abbey graciously granted me access to innumerable, precious sources of information without which the book could not have been written. Photos used throughout are generously supplied by these same sources, unless otherwise indicated.

The "kernel" or "pith" of the book also belongs to more than eighty people from Red Lake, St. John's Abbey, and St. Benedict's Monastery who granted me interviews. Without their stories (many of which could fill a second volume!), *Full of Fair Hope* would shine less brightly.

Readers of the manuscript kept me "on track" and alert throughout to such matters as clarity, cohesion, accuracy, and content. I am indebted to Judy Roy and Stephanie Cobenais, Father Meinrad Dindorf, OSB, Brother Douglas Mullin, OSB, and a group of parishoners who met regularly to read the chapters: William and Joan Strong, Veronica Hegstrom, Leonard and Vi Donnell, Melvina Johnson, Betty Beaulieu, Aloysius Thunder, Jody Beaulieu, Ruth Fevig, Gary Fuller, and Donna Whitefeather.

My Benedictine community at St. Joseph, Minnesota, provided me with the necessary time and quiet space to work. I am grateful for this as well as to the sisters who generously pondered my writing, including Sisters Mara Faulkner, Carol Berg, Sheila Rausch, Arleen Hynes and Olivia Forster.

I am deeply grateful to Brother Placid Stuckenschneider, OSB, whose creative talents helped give this book its particular artistic form; to Sister Marina Schlangen, OSB, who worked untiringly to raise funds for its publication; to my dear friend Sister Philip Zimmer, OSB, who saw me confidently through the "birthing" process; to Bishop Victor Balke of Crookston whose words were like balm to usher this "newborn" into existence; and, finally, to those friends whose financial contributions helped make the book a reality:

Toshimi Horiuchi, Sendai, Japan
William Clemens, St. Cloud, MN
First National Bank of Bemidji
Paul & Jackie Welle, Bemidji, MN

Miigwech!!

CONTENTS

While little is actually known about the personal significance of the painted rawhide shield with eagle feathers, both being used as practical in battle or as a decorative symbol in dancing ceremonies of the Native American Indian, here we use it to lead into each chapter.

At the end of most chapters, there is a reproduction of a broad solid beaded shoulder piece design from which hung an ornate Cavalier bag. The floral pattern is typical of the Ojibwe beadwork.

INTRODUCTION

One cold, wintry night, the feast of Epiphany 1855, Father Francis Xavier Pierz, missionary to the Indian people of northern Minnesota, witnessed an extraordinary phenomenon which not only moved his heart and shaped his ministry but helped establish a milieu for the growth of faith among the people living in the light of this event. He wrote:

> . . . *there appeared with the rising of the full moon the sign of the Holy Cross in a wonderful, heavenly, glittering light so that the cross-beam seemed to rest on the earth. For about an hour, as the moon arose higher in the sky, the cross grew bigger and bigger, both in length and width, the base always standing on the earth. The three upper extremities of the cross seemed to be bathed in the yellow rays of the sun, giving it a very striking appearance. On each side of the cross a glittering line of light could be seen; and the whole apparition was encircled by a magnificent rainbow, as with a beautifully colored halo.* (A Century of Missionary Work Among the Red Lake Chippewa Indians *by Alban Fruth, OSB*)

Father Pierz testified that "more than a hundred people" witnessed the appearance of this cross over the north woods of Minnesota. What could it mean but BLESSING and GRACE poured out in abundance over this particular land and people; a munificent REVELATION of God's love for all creation?

Three years after this vision, a young missioner presented himself to Father Pierz for service among the Indian people of Red Lake. The enthusiastic priest, Father Lawrence Lautischar, eagerly wrote home to his friends in Austria about the new mission which Pierz had declared "full of fair hope."

One must begin here, in the light and hope of those first days, to record the story of God's manifestation to the people of this place. Led here by some inner call, some star perhaps, they had entered this luminous land from the East long before over difficult paths.

It is important, I believe, to realize the whole of the story from these earliest days, to know the journey made in light and in darkness. It is a story to be shared among the elders and the children and passed on like life itself.

Today, 1997, as the last shining new window is placed in St. Mary's Church, allowing the light to diffuse and reflect through this refurbished place of worship, the people rejoice. Well may that be. Father Pierz saw new life bursting into bloom over the land in a thousand rainbow colors. Those who follow see the same vision.

It is time for rejoicing. This book is meant to help you do so. *Full of Fair Hope* attempts to record as faithfully as possible the story of the Catholic Mission at Red Lake, of the people that make it up, both in the past and now, in the present.

CHAPTER 1

BEGINNINGS (TO 1858)

THE RED LAKE OJIBWE (less properly called Chippewa in American standardized usage) take their roots from the Algonquian-speaking Indians of the Atlantic coast who, for several thousand years, enjoyed a rich and diverse culture with deep spiritual roots along the eastern seaboard. During the course of some 500 years, groups migrated westward along the St. Lawrence

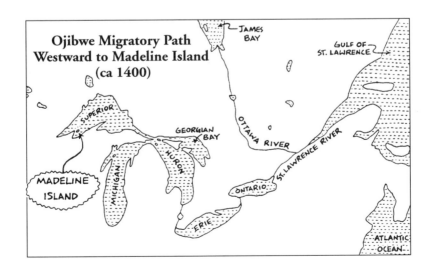

Ojibwe Migratory Path Westward to Madeline Island (ca 1400)

River and into the Great Lakes region, possibly for reasons of overcrowding, disease, factions among tribes, or, according to the people's
creation story, to enter upon a spiritual renewal by returning to the
West from which they believed their ancestors had sprung.

The tribal name "Ojibwe" itself may be derived from a root meaning "to pucker," and referred to a type of moccasin formerly used by
this tribe, made of a single piece of leather with a puckered seam up
the front. An earlier term used by the people themselves is Anishinabe, meaning "original" or "first people."

By the late 1300s, some migrating Ojibwe had settled in the vicinity
of Chequamegon Bay on the southern sand point or peninsula of Lake
Superior of what is now the Bayfield-Washburn, Wisconsin area. They
claimed the Island of LaPointe, later called Madeline, about two miles
across the bay, as their spiritual and central base. Here they built their
Midewiwin lodge for the practice of their ancient traditions and as a
place to gather annually to solemnize their sacred rites.

It was the ancient myths handed down in story form from one generation to the next that gave the people their distinct value and ultimate
spiritual meaning for their lives. These could not be expressed in any
abstract terms. It was said that Mide manido (Grand Medicine spirit)
had placed the Anishinabe on the earth as the last form of created life.
For the people, tribal words themselves held the power to express spiritual energies which helped them live in healing harmony with the natural world.[1] This "code" of sacred ways and teachings formed the
Midewiwin expression.

The tribal family, clan, or "totem" (pronounced "dodaim" in Ojibwe),
formed the basic ingredient of the Midewiwin way of life as well as the
basic political and economic unit of the Anishinabe. In this system,
equal justice, voice, law and order were built in, providing security and
identity for all members. Each clan was designated by the name of an
animal, and given a function with which to serve the people. The
greater part of the settlement at LaPointe belonged to five principal
totems: the crane and loon which served in the chieftainship role; the
marten as protectors and warriors; the bear as police force and as people with special knowledge of medicinal plants; and the catfish as intel-
lectuals and philosophers. Each totem descended in the male line, and

intermarriages never took place between persons of the same symbol or family.

In the traditional way, the people held all things in common ownership. Because they considered hunting, fishing and even fighting dignified endeavors, they regarded LaPointe as an ideal place to carry out these tasks. The island served as a stronghold from which the Ojibwe engaged in conflicts with the Dakota (Sioux) and the Fox for dominance of the area. The soil and climate of the island were conducive to agriculture, and here the people raised corn, pumpkin, and squash long before any contact with the white race. They engaged in other activities, including berry picking, harvesting wild rice, gathering medicinal herbs, making maple sugar, and crafting birch bark canoes for water travel. Men and women cooperated in these industrial tasks.

This traditional way of life remained basically undisturbed in the northern forest and lake area until the late 1500s when the white race began exploring the riches of this country.

By the late 1600s, small French groups had made their way from Quebec to Hudson Bay, to western Lake Superior and Green Bay. They founded missions, forts, and trading posts along the way in the interest of French economy and religion.

The jovial, friendly ways of the French voyageurs and traders who traveled the lakes and rivers by canoe appealed to the Indian. These men brought gifts of metal tools, colored cloth and beads to exchange with the Indians for the furs of otter, fox and beaver. Many of the white traders and hunters married Indian women and lived in one-room log or frame cabins which gradually replaced the native traditional dome-shaped lodge or "wigiwam." The women provided their own specialized knowledge of woodland living, travel and language for the men to use.

As the white race pushed further westward, the Ojibwe were also "pushed" deeper into a competitive arena for food and land – even among themselves and with neighboring Indian tribes. All had to seek furs and fish and corn as "gifts" for these white foreigners who began offering firearms and fire water (liquor) as a means of opening "negotiations" with the Indians for the exchange of land or goods.

Thus the traditional culture, living harmoniously in cyclic fashion around the seasons and nourished by the bounty and beauty of the land, was interrupted by an all-consuming and often violent demand for increasing commerce and colonization. New creeds and laws crowded and confused the people's lives until most tribal dreams and visions and sacred songs were lost and the security of centuries vanished.

By 1640, French Jesuit missionaries had visited most of the Indian people around Lake Superior. These men were called Mukadayikonayayg, or "Black Robe(s)" by the Ojibwe. The goal of the missionaries was to bring the message of Jesus Christ to the Indian people. Following evangelization, baptism was important as evidence of repentance and faith and incorporation into the Christian religion. In one instance, in 1641, the French government presented an Indian, Charles Tsondatsaa, with a gun to celebrate his baptism, thus making Christianity "worth the trouble to acquire . . . "[2] Refusing to accept Christianity meant one could not pass on to join one's ancestors in the spirit world but would instead burn forever in a place beneath the earth – a terrifying idea to the Indians.

The "Black Robes" had the custom of waving a cross over their heads as they arrived at Indian villages and clutching a black book to their hearts. The Ojibwe referred to these priests as "men of the waving stick" and often regarded them as powerful shamans, or religious practitioners. They were reluctant to relinquish their own ancient beliefs not because they were, as some white men considered them, "ignorant children," or even "savages," but because their view of the world and their rituals had served them well up until this time.

It was difficult, for instance, for the people to fathom a concept of inward sin or guilt, and they could not understand how misdemeanors – or mistakes – required punishment. Therefore, it didn't make sense that someone, namely Christ, should die for sins. (It was a practice among Ojibwe to give natural gifts; they did not value human sacrifice.) The notion of heaven and hell, of separation from loved ones, contradicted their deep tradition concerning personal worth and family solidarity. Their spontaneity in communing with God freely and in harmony with nature appeared to them threatened by the construction of places for formal, organized worship (churches) which supposedly "contained" Gijie manido ("kind spirit," a term used by the missionaries to denominate God).

The missionaries, for their part, however, were men of their time and place and tended to evaluate the Indian on the basis of white European Christian culture. Many admired the way the Ojibwe tried to live in harmony with creation, and many attempted to learn the Ojibwe language, an oral tradition with no lexicon, and in some cases to incorporate the Christian message with Ojibwe tradition. But evangelical zeal was often accompanied by insensitivity and neglect of the social, cultural, and religious heritage of the native people. Overall, the Ojibwe found the "Black Robes" less respectful of their way of life than the French traders.

The missionary priests often lived at the fur trading posts. In 1665, Jesuit missionary Claude Allouez visited the Ojibwe village at LaPointe on the shores of Chequamegon Bay. He wrote: "This quarter of the lake where we have stopped, is between two large villages, and as it was the centre of all the nations of these countries, because fish are abundant there, which forms the principal subsistence of this people. We have erected there a small chapel of bark."[3] Further, a report from the *Jesuit Relations in America* for 1670 stated that the Indians were working in the fur trade at LaPointe as well as hunting, fishing and cultivating extensive gardens.

Allouez visited the mission at LaPointe from his Jesuit headquarters at Sault Ste. Marie until 1671, when the little chapel was abandoned. Catholic missionaries did not reside here again until around 1835, when Jesuit Frederic Baraga founded the Mission of St. Joseph on the Island of LaPointe, or Madeline, where a trading post had been established in 1825 for the fur trade.

Missionaries often stated that they found much with which to compliment the Ojibwe character, especially intelligence, memory, and spiritual maturity. Historian William Watts Folwell writes in his study of the Ojibwe: "The Indian was intensely, even devoutly, religious."[4] The Ojibwe were admired also for their generosity and for the honor with which they gave and kept their word. They lived their lives in harmony with the natural elements and intuitively expressed gratitude to their Creator: "Miigwech!" (thank you) for the berries, the fish, the seasons.[5]

Among many missionary priests there emerged a spirit of competition as to who might pierce the farthest into the western wilderness bearing the Christian message. Great emphasis was placed on physical and spiritual endurance. A "successful" missioner was often identified by the number of baptisms he administered. But for the Indian, baptism was sometimes viewed as a talisman to ward off diseases (an evil contagious intrusion spread by the Europeans for which the Indian had no immunity) or, simply, as stated above, a guarantee of joining their ancestors in the spirit world. At more than one deathbed conversion, an Indian's clansmen might ask for baptism to make sure they would be with their loved one wherever it was these Christians met in the afterlife.[6]

According to traditional Midewiwin teachings, the Ojibwe embraced their place in the universe and held sacred special rituals and ceremonials, objects hand-made or painted, herbs and medicines, and even the routines of daily life, all of which helped them live rightly. In the ceremony of the sacred pipe, for instance, persons were aided in finding the divine Presence within but also in realizing that each person as well as the whole world was mysteriously and entirely united in the Creator.

They found spiritual renewal in solitude retreats, fasting, vision quests, dreams and dances. The deep throb of the drum reverberating through the earth and the feet of the dancers was the very heartbeat of manido. In the words of one Indian person today, "Our religion is our way of life, and one of the ways we experience it is through dance."[7]

The Europeans did not comprehend the complexities of the Midewiwin beliefs and teachings and accused the Mide of devil worship and even of cannibalism. Fear developed among confused and rival factions of Christian Ojibwe and Midewiwin followers on the Island of LaPointe so that by the late 1600s, the Midewiwin Lodge and great settlement established there began to break up. Stories circulated among the people of a "haunted" or "contaminated" island, which finally drove them to abandon the place.[8] Other contributing factors causing the people's dispersal at this time included ongoing attacks by the Dakotas, a mounting pressure from French, and later, English, settlers, and the developing alliances with fur traders.

Tribal groups of Ojibwe migrated inland and fanned out into what is now Wisconsin, Minnesota, the Dakotas, and Canada, living along canoe routes or on the lakes and plains.

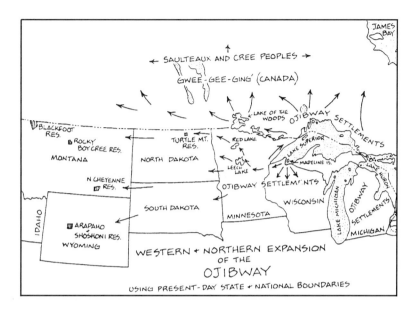

With the establishment of trading posts over the Great Lakes and Upper Mississippi region, more enthusiastic French missionaries and explorers arrived. In 1673, Jesuits Claude D'Ablon and Jacques Marquette, followed by Franciscan Father Louis Hennepin, came to the area.

Jesuit missionary effort expanded vigorously until about 1700. These priests produced the first dictionaries containing native dialects. They made it a point to acquaint themselves with local native customs which could enhance the gospel acceptance. These included gift giving, family and group loyalty, and personal friendship.

The missions also exerted strong social and political influences in allying various Indian groups with French interest. In an attempt to curb nomadic tendencies and develop a sedentary, more "Frenchified" lifestyle, Indian families were at first encouraged to live in permanent mission settlements. But as the people continued to leave for the winter to hunt, as was their custom, and return to the trading posts in summer with furs, this plan was abandoned.

The Indians could not flourish on French diets and possessed virtually no immunity against the insidious contagious diseases of smallpox, typhoid, influenza, and tuberculosis that spread in epidemic proportions throughout the vulnerable native population. It is acknowledged that "Death of the Indians through disease and warfare decimated the aboriginal population in the face of white advance."[9]

In the mid-1700s, French forts on the northern lakes began to succumb to the more forceful British, whose ultimate objective was possession of the land. But the English cared less about successful personal dealings with the Indians and lacked even rudimentary knowledge of the wilderness or the ways of the native people. The friendly relationships previously enjoyed by the Indians with the French were soon replaced by scorn and neglect.

By the early 1760s, the Indian population of the Great Lakes region had become inextricably dependent upon European goods for its existence. The people had largely abandoned traditional tools in favor of more efficient and durable European goods. Their ability to provide for themselves, however, had declined with the increasing elimination of environmental resources, especially game animals which had become necessary in providing furs for the fur trade. Disease, starvation, and the trauma of removal to different environments continued to claim Indian lives – even whole villages. This depopulation and its inexorable effects led to disastrous consequences felt down to the present day.

According to new British policy introduced after 1760, goods could be distributed to the Indians only in exchange for very valuable commodities, namely furs. To further complicate the Indians' way of life, exploitation and fraudulent trade practices arose so that it became more and more evident to the Indian people that the land and its gifts, which they had always considered bequeathed to them and their ancestors by the Great Spirit, truly was being seized by the white race.

Finally, denial of guns and ammunition on which they had grown dependent provoked the Indians to rebellion. Many subsequently joined the French in a military alliance, hoping for their own survival as France and England fought for supremacy in North America. The Indians found themselves entangled in the middle of the embroilment which proved not for their future well-being but for the imperialistic interests of contending European powers.

Known as the French and Indian War (1754-1763), the conflict ended when France finally ceded to Great Britain the Canadian provinces as well as everything east of the Mississippi River. American colonists thus established their own United States government and viewed the "conquered" western lands as open for settlement and development.

Meanwhile, in their frantic search for a livelihood, for food, and for a homeland, the Ojibwe moved constantly. By 1750, they had begun to occupy abandoned Dakota sites on the south side of Red Lake. Around 1755, it is believed that Ponemah, the oldest of the three settlements at Red Lake, had its beginning when some chiefs and their tribes migrated to this northern side near Obashing, or the Narrows.

In 1765, after a bloody battle with their Dakota competitors near Sandy River, the Ojibwe gained a foothold in these northern regions. According to one story handed down, Red Lake inherited its name, Gaamiskwaagamiiwizaaga'igan, "the red water lake," at this encounter.[10] Early French explorers also called the lake "Lac Rouge," or Red Lake.

Wawonjequon, chief of the Red Lake band in 1850 (though not an hereditary chief but one designated by the government), stated that from the time of the expedition of Jean Baptiste Cadotte, explorer and fur trader who was at Red Lake in 1792 or 1793, the settlement at Red Lake by the Ojibwe became permanent.

In 1798, further reports by David Thompson, a British surveyor and trader for the Northwest Company of Montreal who passed through Red Lake, indicated that he had found an old chief, Shesheshepuskut, and six lodges of Indians established here. In 1806, according to an early map, the Northwest Fur Company was operating a trading post at the east end of Red Lake. And in 1823, Count G.C. Beltrami, an Italian explorer with the Major Stephen Long expedition, visited an Indian encampment about one mile south of the outlet on Red Lake. Here he observed about 500 Indians with their chief Kitchiwaboose, or Great Hare.

The authorization of Indian agents as key officers in the relationship between the U.S. and Indian tribes took place in 1818. The first Ojibwe Indian agency in Minnesota was established in 1853. As early as about 1830, white people began to settle permanently at Red Lake, forming one of the oldest villages in northwestern Minnesota.

The lake abounded in fish, and a narrow strip of land along the lake was especially fertile. The Red Lake Indians had successfully raised grain and vegetables here for many years. Reports given by agents indicate that Red Lakers were thrifty farmers and always had enough food, even when Ojibwe of other areas experienced drought or grasshopper plagues. One report, for the winter of 1850-51, however, indicates that the

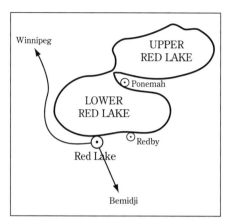

Red Lake Indians suffered from want of food that year. By the first of October they had gathered at the new agency at Sandy Lake to receive their annuities from the government but were kept waiting seven or eight weeks for the arrival of provisions. During this time, measles and dysentery broke out and many died. Being "Indian," it appeared, meant being "second-rate," and starving and degradation increased.

Missionary activity among the Indian people, however, was stepped up in the 1800s following its decline after the French lost territory in America. The first Christian mission at Red Lake was started in 1842 by Reverend and Mrs. Fredrick Ayer, Congregationalist missionaries sent out by the board of Foreign Missions. Their term was short-lived due to ill health and nearby Sioux attacks, but missionary work continued at intervals by other Protestant missioners up to 1857.

As early as 1852, the government system of manual-labor schools was introduced to convert the Indians' ways to white ways. Often the school was entrusted to the church because its well-trained teachers were missionaries. In this way, the government controlled the amount and conditions of the money spent on the school. At Red Lake, a station was formed in 1843, and a school opened that season. The station became the charge of the Congregational American Missionary Association.

Catholic influence at Red Lake began in 1855 with Father Francis Xavier Pierz, who had come to America from the Slovenian (later, Austrian) province of Carniola to work with fellow missioner Father Frederic Baraga. The two priests first met at LaPointe in 1838, where, Pierz wrote, "The Catholic congregation is very numerous, consisting chiefly of Indians and half-breeds. . . . They fill the church daily, conducting themselves devoutly."[11]

When Pierz volunteered for Minnesota missionary work among the Ojibwe, he was placed by Bishop Joseph Cretin of St. Paul in charge of all the mission territory of northern Minnesota with headquarters at Crow Wing, a trading post some 150 miles north of St. Paul.

Pierz was well-versed in agriculture and horticulture. He was well-

Francis Xavier Pierz, Minnesota missioner. Visited Red Lake 1858-1867.

Frederic Baraga, missionary among the Ottawa and Chippewa Indians, 1830-1868.

(Above, left) Catholic Mission at LaPointe, Madeline Island, completed by Baraga in 1841 and dedicated to St. Joseph. (Above, top right) Interior of old Mission Church at LaPointe showing several of the 18 oil paintings acquired by Baraga from Laibach, Austria. (Above, lower right) Old Mission cemetery at LaPointe (ca 1940). [Photos: Lyle M. Lindblad]

Red Lake Ojibwe dress and beadwork (late 1800s). Center: Joseph Strong (Bill and Melvina's father); Right: John Strong (Bill and Melvina's grandfather). [Photo: Bill and Joan Strong, Red Lake]

loved by the Indians wherever he went. They called him Meno-deed, meaning "Good Heart." Through a personal invitation extended by the chief of the village of Red Lake, Pierz was asked to erect a mission in that place. A few Catholic Indians were living at Red Lake at the time. They had been baptized about a quarter century earlier at LaPointe on Madeline Island by Father Baraga. Migrating to the lakes of northern Minnesota, these Catholic Ojibwe – about twenty in number, partly French Canadian through intermarriage – had brought with them the spirit of the early mission, clinging to their faith tenaciously and instructing others.

Pierz, however, was unable to carry out the wish of the chief at Red Lake immediately. Then on June 26, 1858, Father Lawrence Lautischar, a young priest recently engaged in mission work among the Ottawa in Upper Michigan, arrived at Crow Wing as assistant to Pierz. He was, as well, a countryman of Father Pierz. Pierz sent the young man off at once to establish the awaited mission at Red Lake. Lautischar was just thirty-eight years old. His enthusiasm for the missions considerably eclipsed the $82 he held in his thin coat pocket the day he set off.[12]

Pierz joyfully accompanied Lautischar to Red Lake. The journey, an undertaking of twelve days, was faithfully recorded by Lautischar in letters to his friends back home in Austria. His first letter was dated September 22, 1858. He wrote in part:

> We set out from Crow Wing on our way . . . on August 3, the anniversary of my ordination to the priesthood (1845). Fortunately a French blacksmith, a most devout Catholic, happened to be here just then with his wagon and two oxen, and on his way homeward, he carted the most necessary things . . . free of charge while we walked . . . . The road was easy and pleasant excepting the mosquitoes. . . . We cooked our meals twice a day, and in the evening we spread out a specially made mosquito-net under which we slept. . . . Several French Catholics accompanied us and were most kind and obliging.
>
> On the third day we reached . . . Leech Lake. On account of frequent and heavy rains we stayed there in the government storehouse for three days and nights. Here also Father Pierz said Mass on Sunday and preached twice in Indian and French.
>
> On Monday we continued our journey in two canoes accompanied by three young pagan Indians. We traveled through lakes and along small streams; eight times we had to portage our packs and canoes from one lake to another. . . . On Saturday afternoon, August 14th, we arrived at

Red Lake. Pierrish Jourdan, a French-Canadian Catholic, bid us welcome and immediately gave us his house for our dwelling.

Another letter written the following day continued:

. . . This place is situated on the shore of a big lake containing plenty of good fish. The soil is fertile and, if cultivated, it should yield abundant crops. . . . Moreover, there is fishing and hunting. . . .

A considerable number of Indians dwell on the two opposite shores. They have tolerably neat huts, or wigwams, made of cedar or birch bark. Their women are experts in weaving beautiful mats which they spread prettily over their somewhat raised floors. . . . They received us kindly and respectfully in all their wigwams and they converse with us in a friendly manner everywhere else.

On Sunday, the feast of the Assumption of the Blessed Virgin Mary, we celebrated the holy sacrifice of the Mass for the first time in this place. . . .

There are over twenty adult Catholics and some children at this lake. The adults have migrated hither many years ago mostly from LaPointe, where they had been baptized by Father Baraga; the children were born here. Nearly all of them kept their faith and led virtuous lives, but they were very much grieved at having no priest.

There were Protestant teachers and a preacher at this lake for nearly fifteen years; . . . but last year they withdrew. . . .

Here a good Catholic received us into his house which has two rooms, leaving one to ourselves where we also say Mass and teach the children. I shall have to pay ten dollars monthly for everything . . . however, I shall have board, lodging, heating, school, and church in his house. . . . I . . . am satisfied with plain food, such as is raised here: potatoes, corn, wild rice, and fish. . . .[13]

Father Pierz stayed on for six weeks to help Lautischar get started. In letters he, too, sent to his homeland, the same words of hope were echoed:

They [the Indians] . . . filled our spacious Mission house twice a day when they met for instructions and divine services. . . . Thus we established a handsome Christian Congregation and laid the foundation for a mission full of fair hope.[14]

Thus, among these many interwoven circumstances, Catholic activity at Red Lake was underway with the eager anticipation of the mission's first resident priest.

CHAPTER 2

THE EARLY MISSION (1858-1884)

L AWRENCE LAUTISCHAR was an earnest, faithful missionary, as were his counterparts. Nothing seemed too hard or too much for him and for the small congregation he loved nor for the mission "full of fair hope" which he helped found.

Perhaps it was the very impatience of this generous, gentle man's desire for the expansion of God's Kingdom that prompted him to give his life so completely. Called "the holy man" by his friends in Austria, he also was never forgotten by the people of Red Lake. It is noted that out of respect for him, many of the Indians kept track of their own birthdays by this priest's death.[1]

Father Pierz recalled the events that led up to the tragic end of the young missionary's life:

> *I gave my zealous assistant the choice of remaining at Red Lake, or of selecting some other mission to pass the winter . . . . But to do more good he chose . . . to remain at Red Lake. . . . I gave him my benevolent advice to stay in his mission house during the coldest part of winter . . . to gather there . . . but to postpone all trips to outer missions until the coming spring when I would return . . . .*[2]

So Lautischar busied himself serving the needs of the mission, teaching and baptizing. Because of his four years of work previously

among the Ottawa, he was able to communicate well with the Indians of
Red Lake. His sermons in Ojibwe were humble and endearing. He lived
in the lean-to attached to Josens (Joseph) Jordain's shanty, which
served as a church. Jordain was a French/Indian fur trader. It is
believed Lautischar baptized Jordain's daughter Josepha.[3]

On December 3, 1858, it being a pleasant day, he abandoned the
admonitions of Pierz and set off briskly across the frozen lake to
Obashing, "a place where the wind blows through," near the present
Ponemah, a distance of about twelve miles north. He promised to
return by nightfall.

It was the first Friday of Advent, and, according to custom,
Lautischar was fasting. Having arrived at the village, he visited the sick
and spoke at the council, inviting the Indians to accept the Catholic
faith. Meanwhile, an ominous winter storm was developing. The people
begged the priest to stay overnight, but he insisted he had given his
word and must return. It was late afternoon. Father Lautischar was
lightly clad.[4]

A deeply ascetical and zealous man, he also refused the extra food
and warm blanket offered by the Indians for his difficult return trip, and
stumbled homeward through a piercing blizzard now sweeping the lake.

At about seven in the evening, Josens Jordain's dogs in the mission
house kept jumping up at the windows, barking and whining, but no
one took any particular notice. Late that evening, Jordain lit a fire on
top of the bank high above the shore as a guide for the priest in case he
had set out.

The next morning, Lautischar's frozen body was found about a half
mile from shore. Tracks were still visible in the snow indicating he had
dragged himself the last few hundred feet on hands and knees. Perhaps
he had seen the fire. His hands were crossed over his breast as though
in prayer.

The message of Father Lautischar's death was sent immediately to
Pierz at Belle Prairie where he was conducting services. The body was
kept at Red Lake in the little chapel room until December 15, when
Jordain hitched up an Indian sled to an ox and took Lautischar's body
to Crow Wing for burial more than 200 miles away. On December 26,
1858, Pierz laid his friend and hoped-for successor to rest.[5] Lautischar

had served the mission for three and a half months.

Over the next nine years, Father Pierz continued visiting Red Lake from Crow Wing. From 1867 to 1875, Father Joseph F. Buh tended the mission, baptizing small numbers, and staying from two days to a week on his yearly visits.

Father Ignatius Tomazin began visiting Red Lake from his Indian mission at White Earth in March 1875. Both Tomazin and Buh had been recruited by Father Pierz for mission work from their native Carniola (Slovenia). And, like Pierz, both were fluent in the Ojibwe language. Services continued to

Msgr. Joseph Francis Buh

be held in the same mission house used by Pierz and Lautischar on the high bluff overlooking Red Lake.

Meanwhile, white settlers were moving into Minnesota territory and "squatting" on the land of their choice. The Indians could not understand this European pattern of land ownership. They envisaged the land as part of a sacred universe to be held in trust for posterity.

Therefore, the Indians often viewed treaties as a means of preserving themselves as a people and of defending their rights against non-Indian encroachment. Yet most of the land "reserved" for them was ultimately claimed by the U.S. government through treaty or purchase.

The first treaty between the Red Lake and Pembina Ojibwe and the federal government was concluded at the Old Crossing of the Red Lake River on October 2, 1863. A large tract of agricultural land was ceded to the government for homesteaders already in the area; the Indians retained "reserved" land for themselves.

The next year, 1864, a delegation of Ojibwe went to Washington to amend this treaty which included the ceding of about eight million acres of land extending nearly to Devils Lake, North Dakota.

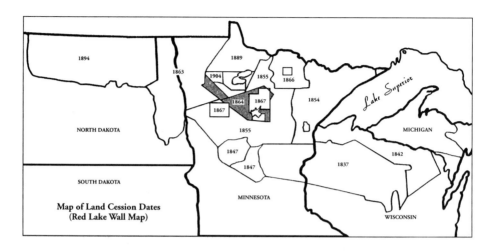

Map of Land Cession Dates
(Red Lake Wall Map)

Originally, the northern Red Lake area was covered with a vast pine forest. In 1871, this stand was estimated at 50 to 75 million feet. In 1872, the Indian agent recommended that the pine be sold. The U.S. Interior Department placed a value of the timber at $2.50 per thousand feet. But it became increasingly difficult to protect the boundaries of this area from pine thievery by whites who threatened occupancy. Red Lakers were finally induced to give up this northern part of the reservation. The money earned from the sale of the land, they were told, would be placed in trust for the Red Lake Indians. In addition, the government pledged schools, farmers, artisans, and physicians, as well as a sawmill, gristmill, oxen, houses, and tools – all with a view of changing the communal Indian into an individualistic, capitalistic farmer working a private plot of cultivated land.

Then in 1888, the Congressional Committee of Indian Affairs proposed a bill disregarding any recommendations for the Indians, stating that they felt the income from a million acres was too much money for the 1100 Ojibwe.

However, on January 11, 1889, Congress passed a law entitled "An Act for the Relief and Civilization of the Chippewa Indians in the State of Minnesota." The bill provided that the President appoint a commission of three to negotiate with the various bands of Ojibwe in Minnesota for the cession of lands, titles, and interests, and for allotment plans.

The Red Lake Indians confronted this proposal at an important series of open council meetings with the commissioners during the summer of 1889. They steadfastly refused to accede to the government's allotment plan, which, in effect, aimed to sever tribal communal bonds and split up the land.

They further reminded the commission of the many unfulfilled treaty promises of the past, the resulting poverty of the people, and the inaction in surveying their boundaries. By drawing an outline of the reservation, they indicated the land they wished to hold in common indefinitely, and insisted on keeping the entire lake, their food "warehouse," intact.

This series of meetings was held at Red Lake from June 29 to July 8, 1889. Assisting the Indians during the negotiations were the three authorized commissioners, Henry M. Rice, Bishop Martin Marty, OSB (Order of St. Benedict), of Dakota territory, and Dr. Joseph B. Whiting of Wisconsin. Two additional appointed aids were Rev. E.S. Peake and Father Aloysius Hermanutz, OSB, pastor of the Catholic mission at Red Lake at the time.

The treaty, known as the Rice Treaty, was signed after much deliberation on July 8, 1889, at the old Red Lake Agency by 247 men, including six of the seven chiefs.[6] By their agreement, the Red Lake Indians consented to a diminished reservation of 2,905,000 acres but they wished to close this remaining land and keep it intact according to the boundaries they had outlined. Further, they would not be subject to allotments or white settlement.[7]

This memorable day is historically considered an "Independence Day" for Red Lakers since they declared their intent to possess the land by right of native title. Lots are not sold on the reservation nor deeds given; the land is held in common. This distinction as a "closed" or autonomous reservation has guaranteed the people the freedom to pursue their own way of life independently.

Meanwhile, Red Lakers had been successfully cultivating the belt of fertile land along the southern and eastern shores of the lake, raising large vegetable crops and corn. Men also found work for wages in the lumber industry. They continued to hunt and fish. In 1880, both Red

Lake and White Earth were reported almost self-sufficient in contrast to Indians of other reservations.

As a result of President Grant's "Peace Policy" in 1870, all reservations in the country had been divided according to religious denomination. White Earth had been given to the Episcopalians, since this denomination had first established a mission there. Catholics were to be removed.

At his resident mission in White Earth, Father Tomazin found himself embroiled in a battle with the government-appointed, non-Catholic agents, whose injustice toward the Catholic Indians at White Earth roused the priest's quick temper and undiplomatic protests.

Attempts on the part of government agents to remove the fiery-tongued Tomazin failed, and he stayed on at White Earth with the support of the Indian people. In 1874, he blessed a small, new log church. However, because of his controversial and temperamental behavior, the new Vicar Apostolic of Northern Minnesota, Bishop Rupert Seidenbusch, OSB, transferred Tomazin to Red Lake in March 1879. Old Chief Little Thunder welcomed Tomazin to Red Lake and pledged the good will of the 200 Catholic Ojibwe there.

Since the Benedictine Order at St. John's Abbey in Collegeville, Minnesota, had decided to take up work among the Indians, Father Aloysius Hermanutz volunteered for Tomazin's place at White Earth along with two Benedictine teaching sisters from St. Joseph. This marked the beginning of Benedictine influence at White Earth.

Upon arrival at Red Lake, Tomazin began immediately to organize the mission. He built a log church (22x30) and lean-to parsonage and a cemetery to the south on five acres of land about two miles west of the Red Lake Agency (site of the present St. Mary's cemetery). The Indians called the place Pikwakwang; that is, "a grove of trees."[8] Tomazin placed the mission under the title of his own patron, St. Ignatius of Antioch.

Services were first held in the little church on Christmas Day, 1879. A year later, on December 14, a new bell arrived and was rung for the first time at the Christmas midnight service.

Tomazin was conscientious about instructing the Indians before baptism. He started a day school for the children and taught them to read their own language and to sing the Ojibwe hymns written by

Father Baraga.[9] But he also encouraged Indian children to leave the reservation for their education.

Tomazin organized a temperance society which flourished for some time, as well as two societies for men and women named St. Joseph's and St. Mary's. Members met in homes for prayer and song, they visited the sick and needy, and held services on Sunday in Tomazin's absence. In October 1882, Bishop Rupert Seidenbusch along with Father Buh visited the mission and confirmed eighty-eight Catholics.

Father Ignatius Tomazin and friends (ca 1880).

But Father Tomazin's imprudent and contentious conduct provoked difficulties, this time with the Indian people themselves and with church and civil authorities. One such difficulty regarded powwow dancing. Tomazin could not tolerate what he considered old superstitions and customs reportedly connected with this ritual. He estranged himself permanently from the people when, on one occasion, very angry at the sight of the dance held at nearby Little Rock, he impulsively drew a knife, cut the drumhead so it could no longer be used, and severely berated the people.[10]

On another occasion, during January 1883, Tomazin, without the permission of the Indian agent, took two sons of an Indian chief off the reservation to cities in the East. Here he lectured, exhibited Indian artifacts, and tried to collect money for the mission and school at Red Lake.[11]

It was the pine thievery on the reservation that led Tomazin into quarrels with interested Indians and government officials at the White Earth Agency. In Washington, Tomazin met the Commissioner of Indian Affairs. He spoke out vehemently about the timber situation, even accusing the commissioner of trespassing and helping loggers steal timber. He said that those in Washington ". . . were under the same blanket with the big lumber men defrauding the Indians." [12]

Tomazin also addressed the injustices regarding the 1863 treaty negotiations for the cession of the eight million Red Lake acres.

However, allegations and sworn statements were being aimed at the personal integrity and lifestyle of Tomazin himself, claiming improper relations with an Indian woman.[13] Church and civil authorities sought to remove Tomazin from the reservation.[14]

Inevitably, Tomazin was denounced as "unworthy" by the Bureau of Catholic Indian Missions and a "rebel" by the Commissioner of Indian Affairs. He was accused of "exciting" the Indians against the government and was "escorted" under much duress from Red Lake to White Earth on June 29, 1883 by the White Earth police force. After this, Tomazin was assigned missions of mostly white settlers around Belle River and as far south as Albany in the St. Cloud diocese.

Aloysius Hermanutz, OSB.

For the next five years, the struggling mission at Red Lake was again without a resident pastor. Father Aloysius Hermanutz came from his station at White Earth once or twice a year to minister to the people, thus initiating the Benedictine connection with the Red Lake community.

Father Aloysius describes his first visit to the Church of St. Ignatius to look after the Blessed Sacrament left there following Tomazin's hasty removal:

On Monday, July 23, [1883] I got ready for the journey feeding my ponies extra portions of oats. . . . I left White Earth with a young Indian as a driver. . . . Our face and necks became swollen from the many bites [of mosquitoes]. . . . At 3 p.m. we reached the home of Simon Roy, a half-breed. He kept a hotel here for woodsmen and their teams who worked in the pineries as it is the only house in which one can find lodging on the road between White Earth and Red Lake. . . .

. . . Just past midnight after three hours rest, I roused my driver to feed the horses and to get ready. Simon Roy served us some warm tea and accurately described the route . . . we pushed deeper and deeper into a mosquito-infested forest. . . . What a lot of pines. No wonder the whites are anxious to get possession of these regions . . . we took a two hour rest. . . . Here a few fierce looking Indians from Red Lake came upon us shouldering their rifles and walking erect as candles. . . . The squaw burdened with her pack and the papoose led the way. . . . The Indians here do not seem to have adopted any of the "palefaces" civilization especially not the ravages of firewater.

At 9:30 we arrived at the mission. It was dark. A half-breed turned over the key to the Church and the house. I lit the sanctuary lamp and said a prayer of thanks for our safe journey. . . .

. . . I had to be up and doing bright and early. At six I rang the Angelus bell and the Indians flocked in from all sides. At 9:00 was Mass and I announced I would be here several days.[15]

Father Aloysius became affectionately known as Wagegyik by the Indians; that is, "Light from Above." But between his visits at the mission, John Baptist Roy carried on caretaking duties and served as deacon. He led church services, visited the sick, baptized sick children, and generally held the mission together. He and his family continued to live in the lean-to parsonage.

With the departure of Father Tomazin from the mission at Red Lake, the day school was abandoned. But the Catholics of the new little church were intent upon procuring both a school and a resident priest. On October 11, 1884, under the leadership of Chief Little Thunder, they addressed the following letter to Abbot Alexius Edelbrock, OSB, St. John's Abbey in Collegeville. The letter contained 112 names or "marks."

Red Lake Indians
Red Lake, Minn.
Oct. 11th, 1884.

Rt. Rev. Habet
        Dear Father
            We are very glad that we heard what the commission Indian affairs told you last winter thus: if you take the Red Lake Mission I will give you the school to runed for me. this is what we heard. If it is true please try to have this Mission that is what we want up here very bad too. and we want Father Aloysius up here to stay with us. because he is well talk Otchibwe. and good nature he is the kind man to preach the new christians and pagans It is over year now since our prist left and we see a prist only three times since that time. Is that enough the new christian to see a prist only three times in sixteen mounths those Missions belong Bishop Seidenbush there is a prist every these Missions round here except here is no prist we dont see why Seidenbush dont tend much of those Indians. Father we would like if you take this Mission and we say again we want Father Aloysius up here we want a prist Right away we want need him Just is well white man dose we want a prist – this is the reason we sign our names here and some of these our Pagans friends they want prist Just is well as christian dose. Father pitty on us and hear us what we in this letter.
        From your childrens R.L. Ind.

(chief)	Little Thunder	his mark	X
(brave)	One ji ke we wi dang	"	X
	Asi ni wi nini	"	X
	Bay Ba ma a mi	"	X

        etc. . . . [16]

Red Lake Indians

Red Lake Minn.
Oct. 7th 1884

Rt. Rev. Habt—
            Dear Father
                        We are very glad that
we heard what the commission Indian affairs
told you last winter thus: if you take the
Red Lake Mission i will give you the school
to runed for me. this is what we heard. If
it is true please try to have this Mission
that is what we want up here very bad
Too. and we want Father Aloysius up here
to stay with us. because he is well Talk
Otchibwe. and good nature he is the kind
Man to preach the new christians and pagans
It is over year now since our priest left
and we see a priest only three times since
that time. so that Enough the new christian
to see a priest only three times in sixteen
Mounths those Missions belong Bishop

Seaden bush there is a priest Every
these Missions round here expet
here is no priest we dont see why
Seaden bush dont tend much of
those Indians. Father we would like if you
take this Mission And we say again we
want Father Aloysius up here we want
a priest Right away we want need
him just is well While man dose
we want a priest this is the reason
we sign our names here And some
of these our Pagans friends they
want priest Just is well as christian
dose. Father pitty on us And hear us
What we in this Letter.

From Your childrens R. J Ind.

(Chief)	Little Thunder	his mark	X
(Brave)	One pi ke me wi daug	"	X
	Asi ni wi nini	"	X
	Bay Ba ma a mi	"	X
	Augustain	"	X
	O mana wi ga bow	"	X
	ga ki ge na na gwad	"	X

We win da ka mi gis skung. ^{his mark} X
A ja mi gi niw   " X
Osmasia wa ji web   " X
Mi ja ki gi niw   " X
Kadog   " X
Mi to gi ji gweb   " X
Jasia go si kung   " X
Paul Kadog   " X
(Brave) Gagi si bush   " X
wi ji madab   " X
wabish ki bi nass   " X
kin ni wanse   " X
Charley Kadog   " X
Mi ja ki gwan ebe   " X
Wa bish Kash   " X
nawa gwe gi shig   , X
kin iw   " X
ne ta mi gi shig   " X
Ba na kins   " X
wa ta ni gwe   " X
na ga nwe wi dang   " X
O ji nawae kash   " X
mas Kodans   " X

Berave, En da wge shig his mark   X
'Pagans) Ke ge ki ma we si kng "   X
"   Ki ni wi gwan   "   X
"   chi gi shig   "   X
Brave) " sha wana ka mi gishkeng " X
B.   " nan da wa wis   "   X
        " wabish wi gwaresh   "   X
        " Ongishinee   "   X
        " Ti tish ko kaning   "   X
chief " Weni ta go shine   "   .X
        " me dwe gan shi   "   X
        " A ki wa jin gi dang   "   X
        " We gi ma a ti taing   "   X
        " Ki chi aive he   "   X
Brave " Basi nass .   "   X
        " wabish ki gwan   "   X
        " We jani mewe dand   "   X
        " naga ni ga bow   "   X
        " Bi dwe we gi shig   "   X
        " Bawawi nind   "   X
        " Ga gi ge ka mi gab   "   X
        " We mi gwa nid   "   X

(Pagans)   "Gagi ge ia bi gi la"   his mark   X

Brave   "   Bay Ba mi gioh ri gwe kaning:X

      "   Ba bi dwe mi daing   "   X

      "   Ge ji gwan eash   "   X

      "   Ze ba se gwan   "   X

      "   Ni gami gwan   "   X

      "   Oded. ga bi ga bow   "   X

      "   We mi ti go sinse   "   X

      "   Ga an Ba   "   X

Brave "   Eia bi' lāng   "   X

       "   wi bin ji   "   X

christine
Brave   O bi mwe gi shig   "   X

          gawi lā bid   "   X

          mes ko gwan   "   X

          E ni wi gwan che   "   X

          Bi chi ga bow   "   X

          a wan ni gi shig   "   X

Mi ja ki ga bow   "   X

Ge be ose   "   X

Ti gwa sense two mark   x
(Brave) Mi ogi shig   "   x
        mi ja ki ki nese "   x
        Kagi ge ti nese   "   x
        Ba mwe ti nese   "   x
Me dwe ka mi gish king "   x
Segate   "   x
Ne sawagiw   "   x
A kin we si   ,,   x
Wa ko wayanae   "   x
Me ni ga Kami gishking "   x
Wa ko way   "   x
   Ka ga Ka da ige   "   x
   Wa wi ie ka mig   "   x
On ti gi shig   "   x
Ko chi chi wi nini "   x
Mi pi we gi niw   "   x
Me mask ka wi ga bau "   x
J. B. Roy   ..   x
F. J. Johnson   ..   x
Henry Defoe   ..   x
Vincent - English   ..   x

Paul Sayers his mark   X
Frank Ginnean   "   X
Lauis star   "   X
Oly Josef Neaddow   ..   X
Peter Garravell   .. X
Benn Neaddow   ..   X
Isaveie Neaddow   ..   X
Baptist - Larence   ..   X
Ze bi gi shig   "   X
ge be ga bou   ..   X
Bay Jie Larence   "   X
J. B. Larn ee   ..   X
Peter Jourdan   ..   X
Paul Smith   X
Frank Rain day   "   X
Simon Praying Day   ..   X
(Pagan) amaiia hi gi shig .. X
Joseph Netaomab   ..   X
J. C. Roy

Abbot Alexius set about seeking ways to fulfill this request. He was eager to expand the work of the Benedictines among the Indian people. But it would be several years before this moving appeal made by Chief Little Thunder and the people of Red Lake would be answered.

CHAPTER 3

THE MISSION CHURCH GROWS (1884-1894)

IN 1886, ABBOT ALEXIUS EDELBROCK of St. John's Abbey wrote a letter to Katharine Drexel, a Philadelphia Catholic heiress, who, with her two sisters, was zealously supporting Indian and Negro missions in the United States:

> . . . I assure you before God that the White Earth Mission is worthy of a helping hand . . . and they have already repeatedly begged me for another priest, for more Sisters, for churches and schools . . . the necessary buildings must first be put up and this requires money. . . . All I can say is the Chippewa Indians of Minnesota have been much abandoned, they cry for bread and there is no one to give it to them.[1]

Katharine Drexel's determination to do all she could for the Indian cause, for their education and preservation of the faith, compelled her to send large amounts of her fortune to the Bureau of Catholic Indian Missions. In 1887, she and her sisters went to Rome and were granted a private interview with Pope Leo XIII. Katharine used this opportunity to plead for the missionary priests so desperately needed in America.

"To my astonishment," she writes, "His Holiness responded, 'Why not, my child, yourself become a missionary?'"[2]

In the fall of 1888, Katharine and her two sisters visited the Indian missions of northern Wisconsin and Minnesota with Bishop James

Very Respectfully, K. M. Drexel

*Mother Katharine Drexel, SBS,
benefactress of St. Mary's Mission.*

O'Connor of Omaha and Father Joseph Stephan, Director of the Bureau of Catholic Indian Missions.

Father Aloysius Hermanutz conducted the little group by horse and lumber wagon from his mission at White Earth to Red Lake, where the Drexels spoke at length with the Red Lake Indian people. Of the 1,124 Red Lake Indians on the southern shore of the lake at this time, one-third were Catholic.

Katharine promised to aid the bleak and struggling mission at once by obtaining a resident priest and teaching sisters. She offered to pay their traveling expenses to Red Lake and the rent for temporary buildings for the missionaries.

Abbot Alexius submitted the project to

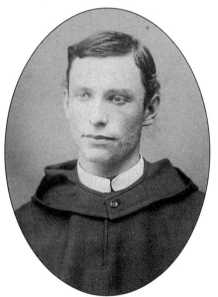

Simon Lampe, OSB

Thomas Borgerding, OSB

the abbey chapter on October 24, 1888. In less than a month, not one but two Benedictine priests, Father Thomas Borgerding and newly ordained Father Simon Lampe, were on their way to Red Lake. Both had volunteered for the mission. Lampe was from Slovenia and had also been recruited by Father Pierz. He spoke Ojibwe fluently, having learned the language from the Indian boys he taught at St. John's Industrial School.

Two Benedictine teaching sisters from St. Joseph also joined this missionary team: Sister Amalia Eich and Sister Evangelista McNulty. The group stopped at White Earth for several days before setting off on the last one hundred or so zigzag miles to Red Lake

Amalia Eich, OSB

by lumberwagon. Sister Amalia recalled, "On these two lumberwagons we had all our belongings and rations: sugar, flour, dried prunes, coffee."[3]

Bouncing through forests and around lakes, streams and swamps, the party reached Red Lake at 5:30 on the eve of the Feast of St. Gertrude, November 15, 1888. Father Thomas remembered their arrival:

> *The Indians rejoiced to have two blackgowns stay with them, and in two councils freely expressed their joy and happiness . . . the council room was packed full of Indians all smoking vigorously. . . .*[4]

At this time, the village sprawled long and narrow beside the lake. It boasted several homes, a store, a government boarding school, agency buildings, post office, sawmill, and an Episcopal Mission church.

The sisters and priests were invited to use some empty agency buildings temporarily. Sister Amalia described the situation:

> *The snow blew in one end and out the other. The Fathers had the front room. We were by ourselves. . . . All we had that winter was pancakes and rice. . . . The Indians brought us no fish. They were suspicious of us. Before we arrived there – some years before, they had the priest who froze*

*to death. That was a holy man. After this priest died, they had a priest
that did not keep his place [Tomazin?]. So it was a mistake now to have
two priests and two sisters come together there – they were suspicious of
us. Jane Horn came there later and told me this. . . . Indian men would
peek in under the shades to see if we were in each other's rooms. The
priests couldn't come into our rooms if they wanted to, it was too cold.
They found out that we never did go to each other's rooms. So the Indians
were always respectful toward us religious.*[5]

The priests soon found lodging with Jacob Detling, the local black-smith and carpenter. The sisters fixed up an old warehouse once used by the Hudson Bay Company for a school. There were a few rough logs to sit on. About twenty-five children appeared the first few days, but there were no books, blackboards, or slates.

During the week, Mass was offered in this warehouse school. At first, the top of a barrel served as an altar. Then an old barn door was scrubbed clean and covered with a bed sheet. Father Thomas built legs for this "altar" and the sisters lined a feed box with coif linen for a tabernacle.

The small log church about a mile away continued to be the site for Sunday services and funerals. These original five acres were said to belong to the mission. An adjoining 2-acre cemetery was nicely kept and "each grave ornamented with a wooden cross."[6]

At the mission, several men who had been Father Tomazin's pupils read and sang the Ojibwe hymns well. One even played the melodies on an old organ. On November 24, 1888, Father Thomas had his first Red Lake baptism.

But by mid-December, food supplies and kerosene were very low. Father Thomas shared potatoes and meat with the Indians, but after paying the bills and buying wood he said they were "bankrupt."

By Christmastime, enrollment at the day school had dwindled to four. Still the missionaries wanted these children to celebrate Christmas. So late on the afternoon of Christmas Day, an evergreen tree was decorated with lights and home-made candy and set up in the blacksmith's house. Father Thomas wrote:

The children were astonished at the lighted tree and the hanging pre-sents. All of the white men and children, numbering seventeen, were gathered around the tree at the blacksmith's.[7]

The little log church had also been trimmed with evergreens. At the Christmas Midnight Mass, Father Thomas reported that not even standing room could be found by latecomers.

Red Lake Reservation, Minn.
From Nov. 9, 1888, to Feb. 13, 1890.   P. Thomas O.S.B.
Day-Book.

1888.

Nov. 9	Nothing on hand. Received cash from Father Abbot,	14.70
" "	Paid fare to Freeport & St. Cloud,	1.40
" "	Rec'd. present at Freeport,	1.
" 10 "	Stipend at St. Cloud,	1.
" "	Pd. fare from St. Cloud to Perham,	3.05
" 12 " "	to Detroit,	.65
" 18	Rec'd cash from F. Abbot,	60.
" 23	Pd. for 18 bu. potatoes,	10.80
" 24 " "	rabbits	.25
" 27 "	N. Fairbanks for oil barrel,	.75
" " "	Pierre Sayers for 2 loads wood,	.75
" 29	Rec'd from P. Simon O.S.B.	16.
" " "	" Sr. Evangelista O.S.B	20.
" "	Pd. N. Fairbanks in full for freight bro't. by him from De-troit to Red Lake up to date (in all 5574 lbs. at $1.50 per cwt)	83.61
" 30	Pd. Jos. C. Roy for 150 ft. boards,	3.
" " "	Jas. B. Roy for 50 lbs. pork,	3.

Enrollment in the school rose to about sixty after Christmas. In February 1889, Father Thomas tried out a kind of boarding school venture by having some children stay over. But by April, the sap had risen in the sugar maples and school was forgotten as children joined adults in the sugar bush.

There was great concern about regular school attendance, and the thinking of the time was that the best way to insure this was to establish a boarding school. So the sisters did. A contract was made with the federal government to cover pupil costs, and several buildings were rented: a store from G.A. Morrison at $5 a month for a chapel and girls' dorm; an old trading post from Allen Jourdain and another building from Clem Beaulieu for a boys' dorm and classroom.

The boarding school opened April 16, 1889. Only twenty-seven children appeared because of work in the sugar bush. But the first boarder to be enrolled was the daughter of Ombigijig (later, Mrs. Charles Prentice), whose grandfather, Bassinans, had been a great medicine man.

By May, there were thirty-five students in residence, which, together with the day students, brought attendance up to sixty. Some children had already been to school and some were just beginning.

Because the government insisted that the children speak only English, they spoke very little in class and then as though reading the language. Father Thomas said that " . . . teaching the English language undoubtedly slowed up their learning."[8]

In addition to the supplies and money provided by the Drexels (more than $7000 in two years), the government contract with the Catholic Indian Bureau allowed $108 per pupil (the first thirty-five) per year, or nine dollars a month.

The sisters continued living in the agency building. Sister Amalia was twenty-seven years old at the time of her arrival. Since she was a nurse, she

Evangelista McNulty, OSB

went regularly to the Indians' homes to care for the sick. She says in her memoirs that the floors of these homes were of dirt, and that is where she knelt to care for the Indian women. Most homes had only one room. Life was quite simple, but according to Father Thomas, "Women were without doubt the hardest workers and they raised crops, picked berries, and made sugar."[9]

Sister Evangelista was the appointed superior in the convent. She was forty-three years old and would spend the next ten years teaching at St. Mary's.

That same spring, Sister Augustine Terhaar and Sister Euphrasia Hirtenberger arrived from St. Joseph. With them was the young candidate and Ojibwe girl from White Earth, Jane Horn. Jane proved an invaluable assistant and interpreter for Sister Amalia in visiting the people. She also helped round up the school children playing truant. Jane later became Sister Marciana, OSB.

Three sisters cooked and served meals for the priests and students. Food and supplies first came by oxcart from Detroit Lakes, but much was also provided by the farmers from their gardens and herds.

The priests were also very busy. Father Thomas quickly endeared

Father Thomas visiting an Indian wigwam (ca 1900).

himself to the people. He was deeply prayerful, kind and generous. He was hardly able to refuse anyone anything though he said he usually asked the people to repay in work whatever he gave them. Only twenty-seven years old when he arrived at Red Lake, Father Thomas became proficient in the Ojibwe language as he studied with Father Simon, using the Baraga dictionary and speaking with the people. In this way, he learned the language and the Ojibwe history and culture at the same time.

Dedicated to the Rule of St. Benedict, Father Thomas conscientiously submitted to the abbot at St. John's his "orde diurnus" (order of the day) which he followed all his missionary life:

> 5:00 rise
> 5:30 pray the minor hours
> 6:00 meditation
> 6:30 Mass
> After dinner – Vespers and Compline
> Just before supper – spiritual reading
> Evening – Matins and Lauds[10]

In an article published by T.J. Welsh who met Father Thomas in 1895, ". . . the form, the qualities of godliness radiating in and from the personality of Father Thomas lifts him above all the rest. He stands out as the richest man, the most humble, the most admirable, the most courageous man I have ever known."[11]

Managerial and business skills, however, were not among Father Thomas' stronger assets, and the little mission always struggled financially. Yet after spending forty-one years there, his invaluable memoirs have provided a rich historical legacy for the people of St. Mary's.

Father Simon, too, was young, only twenty-two. His sermons, whether in English or Ojibwe, were forceful and fluent. He was tall and had a fine singing voice. The people called him Gaminotagosid, or, "The man pleasant to listen to" and "The man with the big voice."

As assistant, Father Simon did much of the outlying mission work all over northern Minnesota, including Cass Lake, Leech Lake, Cloquet, Kettle River, and Rutlege, traveling by canoe, horse, or on foot. His service to St. Mary's Mission spread over twenty-five years.

First sisters' house with girls and dog! Built in 1889. Benedictine Sisters, left to right: Amalia Eich, Evangelista McNulty, Alphonsa O'Donnell, Augustine Terhaar, and Euphrasia Hirtenberger.

In the fall of 1889, construction began on the first permanent mission buildings on 245 acres set aside in 1887 by the Department of the Interior for mission use, both educational and religious. This land was located about one half mile east of the original log church and cemetery site. In 1908, Congress passed an act, signed by President Theodore Roosevelt, which gave the title for this land to the Catholic Indian Bureau in Washington, D.C.[12]

A number of Indians had been living on this land and farming it, raising corn and potatoes and even keeping herds of cows which were not milked but allowed to wander with their calves over the summer months.

With a gift of $6000 from Katharine Drexel, an L-shaped log structure, 25x52, was erected on the land.[13] It stood about fifty feet west of the present convent. The downstairs contained a kitchen, recreation room, and refectory for serving meals. Upstairs were sleeping quarters for the sisters and the girls. It was very crowded. Another house about a quarter of a mile away was purchased from Mark Hart and used as a boys' dormitory.

Nearer the road, about where the present church stands, a small 16x22 log dwelling for the priests was built for about $625. Downstairs presented a front room open to everyone, anytime, and a private sleeping room in back for the priests. A chapel upstairs was used for daily Mass. Sunday services continued to be held in the old log church a mile away.

Both new buildings were constructed by Mr. Petersen (nicknamed "Silver Hairs" because of his white hair) of Fosston, sixty miles southwest. Here the green lumber was picked up by Indians at the railroad terminus and transported by oxen to Red Lake. It was a long, expensive process and roads were often muddy and difficult to travel.

A third building was begun (with a church in mind) but left unfinished due to lack of funds.

On October 3, 1889, the Red Lake Mission became part of the rapidly expanding Diocese of Duluth and remained so until the Diocese of Crookston was formed on December 31, 1909, to serve the spiritual interests of northwestern Minnesota, including the Red Lake Indian Reservation.

Life at the Mission continued busy and full. Gardens were made, and a barn was built in 1890 for the horses and cows. Father Thomas bought the Mission's first cow from a man near Fosston. This cow is said to have parented the whole herd of Jerseys which later made up a successful dairy farm benefitting the Mission for years to come.

The sisters taught, superintended housekeeping and meals, and kept the children in clean clothing. Among Sister Amalia's duties were prefecting, helping in the kitchen, teaching sewing and mending to the girls, and taking charge of the chapel and the cows. "And that was enough!" she exclaimed. "We went to bed at 10:30 and got up at 4:45. . . ."[14]

Sister Euphrasia made the breakfast. She also taught the little girls (the refectory was her classroom) and seems to have had a tender heart. Sister Ambrosia Rettenmaier, who was at St. Mary's with Sister Euphrasia, recalls that she even spoiled the calves by letting them come to the kitchen to be fed.[15]

Sister Ambrosia was a seamstress. She had come from St. Benedict's in July 1890, along with Sister Nepomucene Chalupsky, a teacher. These two planted a large garden of melons, cucumbers, and corn the next spring. They reported the garden was a lot of work, however, and the mosquitoes very bad.

The old church of St. Ignatius was definitely too small by now, too dilapidated, and too far away from the "colony." So on August 5, 1890, the cornerstone was laid for a new temporary church, 25x41. It was a little west of the present school. On August 13, Father Thomas wrote to the Abbot:

> *The Indians claim that Miss Drexel promised to build a new church and we are still using the old . . . this makes the Indians discontented and suspicious. . . . Miss Drexel has now spent more than $7000 for this mission. . . .*[16]

Old logs stored on Mission land were used, some cut into boards at the saw mill, and some sold to buy windows for the structure. Work commenced slowly and was not completed for over a year. John Roy's son helped, but volunteers among the Indians were hard to find.

Katharine Drexel, meanwhile, had entered the religious community of the Sisters of Mercy at Pittsburgh, Pennsylvania. She was still intensely interested and able to aid St. Mary's financially, but she also believed the Indian people themselves should help in building their own church.

Workmen finally had to be hired to finish the new temporary church. It was blessed on December 8, 1891 "sub titulo" (under the title of) the Immaculate Conception, a name suggested earlier by Father Aloysius Hermanutz.

But conditions continued to grow more crowded and resources more scarce. About sixty students packed into the little school while government grants covered the education of only forty. It finally became impossible to keep all the children, and many stayed home rather than attend the government school on the reservation because people were more pleased with the way in which the sisters cared for and trained the children.

Earlier, in January 1891, J.C. Roy had addressed a petition signed by many members of the reservation to the Secretary of the Interior, John W. Noble, in Washington, D.C., on behalf of the school, its children, and the parents who wanted them there. An accompanying letter to Rev. J.A. Stephan, Director of the Bureau of Catholic Missions, stated in part:

It was . . . distinctly understood that in case the commission were success-
ful, a Catholic school would be built and maintained in such a manner
as to accommodate all the children whom their parents might choose to
send there, a portion of the money reserved by the act (1/4 of the inter-
est) approved Jan. 14, 1889, for educational purposes should go to the
support of this school.[17]

Although the Mission boarding school continued to have at least
fifty students in attendance each year, government funds diminished
year by year until 1900, when they were entirely discontinued. After
this, "the school had to run on fresh air and water" along with the generosity of Mother Katharine Drexel, St. John's Abbey, the Sisters of St.
Benedict, and a small amount from the Catholic Indian Bureau.[18]

In 1892, Father Simon took up a census and found 135 Catholic families on the reservation. (See Appendix A for 1892 Church Circular.)
Father Thomas then began contemplating a new church. He wrote:

My little old log church is overcrowded each Sunday. The altar consists of
boards put together by myself, a tiny crucifix, four pictures and two stat-
uettes. This with some homely pews are the only ornaments that decorate
our church.[19]

He also attempted to explain the situation to Mother Katharine in a
letter dated February 14, 1892:

Your favors of Jan. 9 and Jan. 25 are at hand. The buildings at this
mission are, as far as my knowledge goes, not insured. . . . The school
building contains about $2000 worth of furniture, bedding, clothing, etc.
There are no chimneys in any of the buildings, but the stove pipes are
everywhere provided with safes, so that there is little more danger than
with chimneys.

In the line of vestments the Sisters much desire the following: alb, sur-
plice, red, violet, and black chasubles, antependium, cinctures, mon-
strance, holy water pot with sprinkler, bread iron with cutter, sanctuary
lamp, 3 prs. candlesticks, altar card, stations of the Cross, crucifix for altar.

Last fall, while completing a building to be used temporarily as a
church, we asked them [the Indian people] to help, as the funds on hand
would not suffice. Nearly all showed themselves willing and promised to
help, but only two or three really came. At that time, however, the people
were unusually busy. . . . Should you conclude to help us once more we
would certainly be very glad.[20]

With the assurance of both Father Thomas and Bishop James McGolrick of Duluth that the Indian people would be encouraged to do all they could themselves by way of hauling lumber and bringing logs to the mill for the building of a new frame church, Mother Katharine sent a new financial gift which spurred the Mission forward toward construction.

Building got underway in the spring of 1893. James Brady of Red Lake Falls was given the contract for the job. He received $3.50 a day for his work, but it seems he was not entirely dependable and slipped out of town for a drink every now and then. Brady's assistant and two Indian men, Amos Bigbird, a carpenter, and Alex Gorneau, a blacksmith, each received $2.50 a day for their work on the new church.

Immaculate Conception Church, 1893.

The logs used in construction may have been among those purchased by Mother Katharine four years earlier and stored in the old mill pond. At any rate, they were sawed into suitable lumber and shingles at the sawmill at Shell Lake about seven miles away.[21]

The main part of the church and its bell tower were built. Then the old bell from Tomazin's original church was installed. (In 1950, this same bell was still in use.) But sanctuary and sacristies as we know them today were only added twenty years later.

By June, the church was almost complete, and Father Thomas wrote to Mother Katharine describing the situation:

> *The building is now nearly finished, with the exception of gallery, windows, doors, spire, cedar shingles, to be heated by a furnace in the cellar. Everything is made strong and handsome, and we expect to make it as warm as any church in the country.*
>
> *It appears that the church, when complete, will cost about $2500 besides the work the Indians contributed gratis, which will be worth some $300.*
>
> *Could you again send us some help?*[22]

According to Father Thomas, the Indian people "were not at home or otherwise occupied" when much of the work had to be done.[23] It was maple sugar time. So again, more of the work had to be done by hired laborers than first anticipated. Mother Katharine furnished a total of $2500 for the completion of the church.

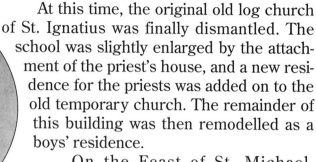

At this time, the original old log church of St. Ignatius was finally dismantled. The school was slightly enlarged by the attachment of the priest's house, and a new residence for the priests was added on to the old temporary church. The remainder of this building was then remodelled as a boys' residence.

On the Feast of St. Michael, September 29, 1893, all was ready to welcome Bishop James McGolrick of Duluth for the dedication and blessing of the new church. Father Thomas described the prelate's eventful trip:

Bishop McGolrick started from Duluth at the beginning of the week. . . . At that time, there was a railroad from Duluth to Crookston. When he arrived at Crookston he hired a team to take him to Thief River Falls. From there, he intended to go on by boat. But the Red Lake River was so shallow at the time that the boat had to remain back about 20 miles up the river. So, they had to go on to High Landing where the boat was waiting. This meant a delay of a day or two. Then they arrived at Red Lake on Friday morning, September 29 after being on the road for four days. Besides dedicating the church, he gave Confirmation [to thirty-eight, mostly adults; the second Confirmation class to be held at the Mission] and stayed around for awhile. The captain of the steamboat wanted to leave that evening about five o'clock. I tried to urge the Bishop to stay, but he was anxious to be on his way. He had a speech scheduled at Superior, Wisconsin, and had promised to be there on Monday.[24]

It is interesting to note that Mother Aloysius Bath from St. Benedict's was also present for this occasion but was unable to stay overnight because there were no beds.

In another letter to Abbot Bernard Locnikar at St. John's, Father Thomas reported that ". . . all were present in order to see the 'great blackrobe' and to hear him . . . the Bishop was happy about the enthusiasm of the Indians."[25]

An article in the *Thief River Falls News* announced:

> *The addition of the new Catholic Church at Red Lake is an auspicious event. Four years ago Miss Kate Drexel in company with her sister . . . came to Red Lake in order to personally see after the spiritual wants of the Indians. Through munificent gifts the . . . Catholic School [has] been built . . . and the church which just has been dedicated shall ever stand as a monument to her generosity.*
>
> *Miss Drexel, shortly after founding this school and the one at White Earth . . . abandoned the world and sought seclusion behind convent walls, but the good she has done remains to the world after her departure.*[26]

There were five sisters at the Mission during this school year along with the near-usual sixty boarding students. The children received food and clothing in addition to their education, but several still had to be refused due to lack of space and resources. The children's ages ranged from six to eighteen.

The new school year also brought, through the intervention of Abbot Locnikar, the arrival of a boys' prefect, Peter Aloysius Schloer, who served faithfully at the Mission for the next twenty years. This position had been held by John Baptist Roy and other local men.

Prior to his work at St. Mary's, Schloer had helped out at the Jesuit Indian mission at St. Peter, Montana. He had also worked for a time at a Catholic hospital in Minneapolis. But his heart was with the Indians, and he soon endeared himself to all and came to be known as the "Grand Old Man." He had charge of the farm and gardens. He stayed with the boys, even tending them when they were sick. He trained them to serve at the altar. He himself led an exemplary life, and was often called upon by the people for his knowledge of medicine. He worked without pay for his board and room.

As 1893 drew to a close, Father Thomas had another cause for rejoic-ing. November 15 marked his fifth year as pastor at Red Lake. With pride, he drew up a personal inventory of all that had been accomplished, includ-ing the building of the school and church. He acknowledged that his mis-sionary work was no light task but that the people "were becoming more acquainted with the truth and spirit of Christianity." [27]

The work of Fathers Thomas and Simon also included ministry to four other small Indian missions within a hundred-mile radius of Red Lake, a total of some 600 Catholics. The priests never found themselves without work. As yet, neither they nor the sisters received a salary for their labors. It was a labor of generous commitment from them and their respective monasteries.

Even the village of Red Lake found itself caught up in bustling activity and growth. Settlers and traders passing through stopped at hotels overnight and stocked up on supplies at the stores; steamboats plied the Red Lake River and the lake hauling freight and towing logs; a physician was on hand; and, of course, the U.S. post office was always a busy hub. The census in 1892 indicated 1,259 Red Lake Ojibwe.

Thus, after thirty-five years of challenging existence, St. Mary's at Red Lake was in a celebratory mood yet fully aware that the future would continue to require of them the faith and good will of their dedi-cated lives.

CHAPTER 4
STEPS INTO THE TWENTIETH CENTURY
(1894-1911)

OLLOWING ABBOT BERNARD LOCNIKAR'S sudden death in November 1894, Peter Engel was elected the new abbot of St. John's Abbey and quietly ushered the Benedictine tradition into a progressive 20th century.

Over the next twenty-seven years, Abbot Peter often visited the Mission at Red Lake and offered suggestions and encouragement to the people. One area of his expertise concerned good farming practices. However, attempting to create large-scale farmers among the Indian people did not succeed. As early as 1850, Indian missionary Bishop Baraga addressed this issue in the introduction to his *Otchipwe Grammar:*

> *Moreover, the idea that the Indian must first be induced to become a farmer in order to make him a civilized man is absurd. All his Indian instincts revolt against it. He is quite willing to cultivate a small patch of land to raise some potatoes, cabbage, onions, etc., but to farm on a large scale, as his white brother does, is disagreeable to him.*[1]

Yet, until 1940, it was the theory of the boarding school to remove Indian children as far as possible from their home environment and teach them how to farm and perform domestic tasks (mostly for the

benefit of white society); to forbid them to speak their language; to cut
their hair and change their dress – thus "civilizing" them by altering
their behavior and destroying their own Indian ways, culture, and
traditions.[2]

In 1893, Congress made it compulsory to speak only English in
school. Indian children were punished if they did not comply, and parents were even denied rations and subsistence. According to a government statement, ". . . the instruction of the Indians in the vernacular
(Chippewa) is not only of no use to them, but detrimental to the cause
of their education and civilization."[3]

In mission schools, too, these laws and regulations were upheld
because it was the government that paid pupil costs while the repre-
senting religious group built and supplied the school. At St. Mary's,
however, Father Thomas reported, "We ran the mission school largely
according to our own ideas and no outside force set the educational
standards for us."[4] Even though English was taught in compliance with
the government, Father Thomas taught Ojibwe whenever he could.

Enrollment climbed to eighty by 1900. In order to collect the government funds per student, the children were required to attend the
full school year which, at St. Mary's, lasted ten months. Boarders could
go home once a month from Friday evening until Sunday morning.
Along with "reading, writing, and arithmetic," domestic or industrial
work was part of the school curriculum and included:

sewing	painting	dairying
shoemaking	laundry	cooking
tailoring	housekeeping	carpentry
upholstery	harness making	canning
gardening	blacksmithing	

It seemed, however, that the mission schools were not "civilizing"
the Indians well and fast enough; consequently, the Indian Bureau in
Washington decided to remove the children from the reservations alto-
gether and bring them to "industrial schools." For several years, the
government contracted with private institutions for the care and education of a certain number of these young students per year.

In 1884, with a government contract, the St. John's Industrial School for Indian boys had been established at Collegeville, as well as an industrial school for Indian girls at nearby St. Joseph, conducted by the Sisters of St. Benedict. Tours were made by the sisters and priests, during which Indian parents were interviewed and encouraged to let their children go to these schools to be educated, to study some trade, and be part of a religious program, thus fulfilling the government desires and rules for boarding schools designed to acculturate the young.

But most children, ages nine to fifteen, could not endure the loneliness of being separated from their parents' homes, nor the humiliation, the dehumanization, of having been "shipped off," and they often ran away. This method of education by removal from native culture was short-lived among the Benedictines. In fact, by 1896, even the government dropped this contract system of Indian education.

Father Thomas and Father Simon, meanwhile, were ministering to some 300 Catholic families scattered across the northern reservation land at this time. This activity, along with the operation of the Mission school and church, kept everyone busy.

Then, in 1895, the government contract for the boarding school was cut. With only the funds supplied by St. John's and St. Benedict's and the Catholic Bureau of Indian Missions, Father Thomas anxiously wrote another letter to Mother Katharine begging for a temporary loan of $1000 to help defray Mission expenses.

Even amid this financial worry and the over-crowded conditions at the Mission, this idealistic missionary decided to start a hospital. Perhaps the fact that a resident physician was stationed the year before at Red Lake to give medical care to the Indians, prompted Father Thomas to extend the Catholic Mission's service as well.

There were many illnesses among the Indian people, particularly tuberculosis. People had no place to go, and whole households were exposed during times of epidemic. According to Father Thomas, the disease mortality rate was fifty per one thousand people. More than a third of newborns died before they were a few years old. Many of the people's traditional ways of using roots and berries to fend off illnesses were no longer effective in a world of white people's diseases.

On December 22, 1897, many sick were received at the Mission and cared for by the sisters and the boys' prefect, Peter Schloer, who was skilled in homeopathic remedies and medicinal herbs. But after just a few weeks, the new Red Lake physician informed Father Thomas that no one could just start practicing medicine on the reservation without having graduated with a medical degree and without a state or federal license. Father Thomas was further told that he needed permission from the Indian Office before establishing a hospital.

Thus, on January 29, 1898, Father Thomas wrote to the Commissioner of Indian Affairs in Washington, D.C., seeking an application for the Benedictines to build and operate a St. Mary's hospital at the Mission. In February, he was informed by Washington that neither the erection nor operation of such a hospital was approved, and the last sick person of Father Thomas' newest dreamchild was discharged on April 16, 1898.

But life went on at the Mission. Since Father Simon had been transferred to White Earth in 1896, Father Thomas was without an assistant until September 1898, when Father Felix Nelles arrived from St. John's. With him came two sisters from St. Benedict's: Sister Basilia Cosgrove, to teach fourth and fifth grades, and Sister Euphrasia Hirtenberger for a second term on the Mission.

Felix Nelles, OSB

Sister Basilia noted that the trip to Red Lake was very round-about and frustrating. Once in St. Cloud from St. Joseph, she said, the party took a train to Thief River Falls, then a river boat up the Thief River to an outlet at Red Lake. One morning when they awoke, their boat had even been grounded.[5]

Father Felix was supposed to take care of the outlying missions. The Indian people gave him the name Babamadisid, meaning "Traveler." However, he observed that during his first year at Red Lake he couldn't do much at all except work in school until he learned the

Ojibwe language.[6]

As the turn of the century approached, Father Felix moved temporarily to White Earth, and Father Corbinian Hermanutz, OSB, arrived at St. Mary's not only to serve but to recover from an illness. Because he spent much time outdoors in the woods, the Indians called him Giosseweinni; that is, "The huntsman."

Around 1897, St. Mary's boasted 600 church members and five Mission buildings: a girls' and sisters' house which also served as the school, a boys' residence, priests' house, church, and a barn. Fifty acres of land were under cultivation and the rest lay in woodland and pasture.

Corbinian Hermanutz, OSB

But the year 1900 marked the end of the government contract with St. Mary's School, and a new policy was initiated by the Commission of Indian Affairs, which stated that it was the duty first of all to build up the government school and that Indian parents had ". . . no right to designate which school their children shall attend."[7]

This "Browning Ruling," as it was called, was short-lived, being abolished in 1902. Still, the Mission was not given any government school contract and had to depend on donations from the Catholic Indian Bureau, Mother Katharine Drexel, St. John's, and money collected by the sisters at the neighboring lumber camps.

About this time, Father Thomas tried out another idea to help the Mission. He started a cattle ranch on some meadow land loaned the Mission between the Red Lake and Clearwater rivers. He built a house here for an Indian caretaker and a shed for one hundred head of cattle. But heavy rains that summer destroyed much of the hay stored along the river, and an extremely cold winter claimed the lives of some thirty cows. One more brave undertaking appeared washed away before it had barely begun.

Next, an epidemic of smallpox broke out on the reservation. Thirty students at the Mission School were quarantined and an Indian woman had to come to care for them. The Indians were opposed to vaccination because, in some cases, individuals had become sick and died. Though many deaths were reported on the reservation, mostly adults, Father Thomas claimed there were none at the Mission related to the disease.

In 1903, with new plans afoot to repair and improve Mission buildings, Father Thomas began collecting money. Since gleanings were small, he again sought the help of Mother Katharine. This time he asked for $2000 to $2500, or even any part of that amount, in order to have logs and lumber hauled during the upcoming winter. But well-laid plans went askew once more.

There had been heavy winds and rain, damaging timber around the south side of the lake, and on May 11, 1904, a very windy day, Father Thomas was on his way to the sisters' and students' refectory for dinner when he saw flames shooting into the boys' building from the shingle roof. Because of the intense wind, nothing could be done except watch this building burn and try to keep the fire from spreading. Father Thomas was crestfallen.

The fire was believed to have started from sparks falling from the stove pipe onto the roof. Losses amounted to about $4000. Some fifty boys were displaced: some being dismissed and others crowded into existing buildings until school was out at the end of June.

Nevertheless, Father Thomas would not give up. Although he wanted to rebuild, there were only thirty dollars left in the building fund.

One asset the Mission did have on hand, however, was about 30,000 feet of lumber – all paid for. Difficult as it was, Father Thomas entreated Mother Katharine again. He wrote her about the fire and about his dreams for a new two-story frame house, 48x64, with full basement. The upper floor he planned for a dorm, and the lower floor would have two or three rooms, all to accommodate about seventy boys.

The cost for this new building? About $2200. But he hastened to remind Mother Katharine that though their enrollment had grown, the government school nearby was "anxious for more pupils" and had modern improvements and conveniences.[8]

In September 1904, Father Thomas wrote dejectedly to Mother Katharine regarding his fund raising efforts, saying, "All that I have obtained amounts to less than two hundred dollars." Mother Katharine responded with $800 ". . . to meet some bills entailed by the school building and to continue your work."[9]

Life regained its rosy hue then, as a grateful, determined Father Thomas began construction immediately.

Meanwhile, the process by the government to reduce the Indians' land base, especially if an area was suspected of containing minerals or was valuable for its towering pines, continued. In 1902, a treaty to cede 256,152 acres was signed by the seven chiefs and 213 other male adults. This land, known as the eleven western townships, was offered for sale to homesteaders at a public auction in 1904. It sold for $1,265,000, which was credited to the tribal fund.

Logging trains were already running into Red Lake during this time and dumping logs for floating downriver. But in 1905, with some reorganization, passenger train services for the Minneapolis, Red Lake, and Manitoba Railroad Co. were extended from Nebish to Bemidji through Redby on 320 acres selected from the reservation as right-of-way by an act of Congress. White people – railroad men and their families – settled on some of this land in Redby.

The prospect of any kind of train coming to Red Lake excited Father Thomas, and he wrote glowingly of the possibility:

And so our modest school, who knows, may yet develop into a college as an important town will spring up here and through trains will run from here to St. Paul, so that we may leave here after Mass and come to St. John's in time for Vespers. . . .[10]

Such a railway, of course, never materialized. But even coming as close as Redby, five miles away, did help everyone feel more in touch with the rest of the world.

Then Father Thomas became very ill. His spirits fell so low that even to carry on his work at the Mission was a great effort. The poverty of the place, his financial woes, and shattered dreams all seemed to get the best of him.

To make matters worse, just as he was recuperating, other disasters fell. On the night of November 11, 1905, an alarm sounded from the

(Left) Temporary church of the Immaculate Conception, 1891. Later, the building served as a boys' residence until 1904.

(Right) 1905. Fire destroys the first sisters' and girls' house.

St. Mary's Mission (ca 1908). Left to right: sisters' and girls' house, barns, school,

(Left) St. John's Industrial School for Indian boys (ca 1887). First Communion.

(Right) Indian Industrial School for girls, St. Joseph, MN – 1886.

church, boys' residence, and priests' house.

sisters' and girls' building. Fire had started in the basement where a lantern was always kept burning to keep the vegetables from freezing. The fire was quickly extinguished. But a month later, on December 8, while everyone was celebrating the Feast of the Immaculate Conception in church, the same building caught fire again. This time, it burned to the ground despite efforts to save it. Father Thomas had to watch the whole thing from the window as he was still confined to his room.

Only a few pieces of furniture could be saved, along with some clothing, dry goods, and groceries. Father Thomas blamed himself over and over because he had not installed brick chimneys (he felt they were too expensive) as the abbot had suggested. Therefore, the building could not be insured. His grief overflowed in a letter to Abbot Peter dated December 12, 1905:

> As I ruminate over the trouble of recent years, I sometimes think of applying to myself the words of the prophet Jonah: "Take me and cast me into the sea – for I know that on account of me this great tempest is come upon you!"[11]

But life again took a turn for the better. By 1906, Father Thomas was involved in rebuilding the sisters' and girls' house – a venture that would take many summers to fully complete.

For a time, the sisters and girls lived in the lower level of the boys' building – completed around 1905 – until the front part of their new house was hastily put under cover. In mid-summer, Father Julius Locnikar, OSB, arrived to serve as Father Thomas' assistant for several months.

The basement of the new house contained a bathroom and vegetable cellar; the first floor had a kitchen, laundry, dining room, parlor, and recreation room; second floor had a chapel and the sisters' rooms; and the third floor was devoted to the girls' dorm and wardrobe.

Mother Katharine carefully regarded the building expenses she incurred as Father Thomas laid out itemized statements:

> mason's wages $112, cistern $30,
> well and pump $40, hauling $25,
> completed excavation $75, lime $30, laths $24.

In August of 1908, Father Thomas reported to Mother Katharine

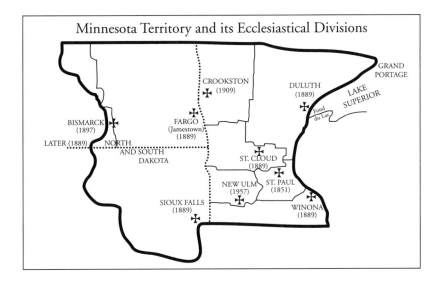

Minnesota Territory and its Ecclesiastical Divisions

GRAND PORTAGE

CROOKSTON (1909)

DULUTH (1889)

LAKE SUPERIOR

Fond du Lac

BISMARCK (1897)

LATER (1889)

FARGO (Jamestown) (1889)

NORTH AND SOUTH DAKOTA

ST. CLOUD (1889)

NEW ULM (1957)

ST. PAUL (1851)

SIOUX FALLS (1889)

WINONA (1889)

that work was progressing fast and he hoped to have the plastering finished for the opening of school on September 1. He boasted in a letter to Abbot Peter, ". . . it will be guaranteed to be the warmest house of its size in this part of the state."[12]

However, Father Thomas' financial woes were ongoing, and his dislike for bookkeeping and report-making became a great trial to him as well as to his anxious, upset donors. There were complaints that he spent too much money just helping people out. But the generous-hearted missionary, who couldn't turn his back on the poor, tried to secure money wherever he could: from friends, relatives, the bishop, Mother Katharine; by begging and touring; and from the small collections of the Indian people themselves.

Enthusiasm waxed strong again as Bishop McGolrick of Duluth visited the Mission at the end of February 1908, and confirmed 120 persons. A man motivated by social justice, McGolrick had particular solicitude for the Indians within his diocese and raised his voice many times on their behalf. Named Indian Commissioner to succeed Bishop Marty, McGolrick would visit all eleven reservations in his diocese. Being a lover of the great out-of-doors, he visited Red Lake by canoe.

But McGolrick's diocese was becoming so great that he could not continue to meet all its needs. Therefore, a fifth diocese (Crookston) in Minnesota, previously the western half of the Diocese of Duluth, was formed in 1909, and Red Lake was placed under its jurisdiction.

By 1909, the Red Lake Indian population had risen to 1,366. But alcohol consumption was becoming an ever-graver problem, affecting even the women and children. Over the years, to the present, the Tribal Council enforced a policy prohibiting the sale of liquor on the reservation, although there was no restriction on bringing it in. As the Indian people found themselves caught in increasing poverty, alcohol afforded a kind of temporary relief from a life of "quiet desperation." Drinking became a social activity in which even adolescents engaged.

More employment was offered Red Lakers at the sawmill, which was improved and enlarged. It boasted a yearly output of about one million feet of lumber which, when sold, increased the benefits of the people. However, bad winds and natural fires continued to damage forests yearly so that "dead and down" timber brought many losses. The Indian police service at Red Lake could offer only minimal protection. In 1912, the first forest ranger was appointed. He was instrumental in developing a forestry telephone system and constructing a number of ranger stations and lookout towers.

In the summer of 1909, Sister Hyacinthe Simmer arrived at St. Mary's Mission from St. Benedict's. As the new principal of the boarding school, she started a busy, exciting life that fall for eighty-nine youngsters. She also proved to be a strong and enthusiastic support for Father Thomas and his successors over the next twenty-two years.

George Head, a ninety-year-old resident of Red Lake (in 1992), was a little boy at the Mission School during these years and remembered the days well:

> . . . The girls lived in the convent building. Sister Hyacinthe was a cook. . . . She also taught music. . . . We used to have plays. . . . I hoed potatoes, milked cows – I had to learn how. We milked morning and night. There were fields all along the lake, and south of here was good land. I was a server and served at chapel in the convent. . . . I served for Father Florian. Now he was a teacher! "You don't forget what you know," he said. He taught us a lot. . . . Father Thomas taught math to my father. My father became a forester. He also helped bust up the rocks for the back end of the church where they're all fitted in the foundation. [13]

As 1910 drew to a close, a significant event occurred. The Mission was visited by two Sioux laymen from Fort Totten, North Dakota, who talked to the people about the annual Indian Congress. This Congress had been held since 1891 for the purpose of encouraging and enhancing the faith among Catholic Indians of Montana and the Dakotas.

The people of St. Mary's were interested. With an invitation to attend the next gathering in 1911 near Fort Totten, a small delegation agreed to participate. Indeed, another part of the foundation of faith for this young church was being fitted together.

Spear fishing – John Strong [Bill Strong's and Melvina Johnson's grandfather] (late 1800s). [Photo: Bill and Joan Strong]

CHAPTER 5

EMPTY PURSES – FULL HEARTS (1911-1923)

AT THE INDIAN CONGRESS in the summer of 1911 at Fort Totten, St. Mary's Mission Church, Red Lake, was admitted into the official St. Mary's and St. Joseph's Societies, a "first step" toward full participation in the Congress. The next year, from July 13-15, the International Indian Congress was held at Red Lake for the first time. All the Indian missions in Minnesota where new branch societies had been organized received invitations. A large delegation of Sioux and Ojibwe Indians also arrived by boat from North and South Dakota and camped on the shores of Red Lake at Pike Creek. Bishop Timothy Corbett (first bishop of Crookston) and Abbot Peter Engel, OSB, offered the Masses. Many religious activities, hymn fests, and feasts filled the days. Sermons were given in Sioux, Ojibwe, and English. Despite the good will of the people, however, much frustration and time were spent translating

Chief Wanetam of the Totten Tribe, Fort Totten, ND

the languages. It was finally agreed that both the Sioux and the Ojibwe would hold independent Congresses in the future.

Modelled on the North Dakota Congress, Red Lake wrote its own constitution, effective June 19, 1914. St. Mary's has continued to participate in the International Indian Congress to the present day. The Congress, attended by Catholic Indian people from around Minnesota, was hosted in the early days by the societies of several districts – including Bena, Ballclub, Cass Lake, Cloquet, Naytahwaush, Onigum (Leech Lake), Ponsford, White Earth and, of course, Red Lake. Father Thomas served as general director for many years, even when he was no longer pastor at St. Mary's.

The Congress was often a four-day event. At St. Mary's, it was held under large bowers especially constructed for the occasion, or in large tents seating five or six hundred. This center was surrounded by camp-sites where the people stayed. Talks and presentations were made in both Ojibwe and English. As part of the spiritual renewal of these days, hymn singing, prayer, catechetical instruction, the celebration of Mass and the sacraments, discussions, traditional meals, and games all took place. The presence of bishops and/or an abbot lent the occasion special pageantry.

Meanwhile, St. Mary's Mission Church was in need of some remodeling. In the summer of 1911, construction began on the present sanctuary and sacristies. With the help of Theodore Duhr, who lived at the Mission, and other local carpenters, work was completed in 1913.

An electric light plant and waterworks were also installed in the basement of the sisters' house and operated by Duhr. But this house (the north part of the present convent), begun in 1906, still stood unfinished. Father Thomas, writing to Mother Katharine Drexel in 1911, lamented the situation:

The whole basement must yet have partitions and be plastered. There is no sewerage whatever. The house, though built nearly five years ago, has thus far received only one coat of paint. The stairways are only temporary ones. The kitchen and dining room serve also as laundry and drying rooms. The ventilating system has never been finished or put in working order. The classrooms, a separate building, have no ventilation

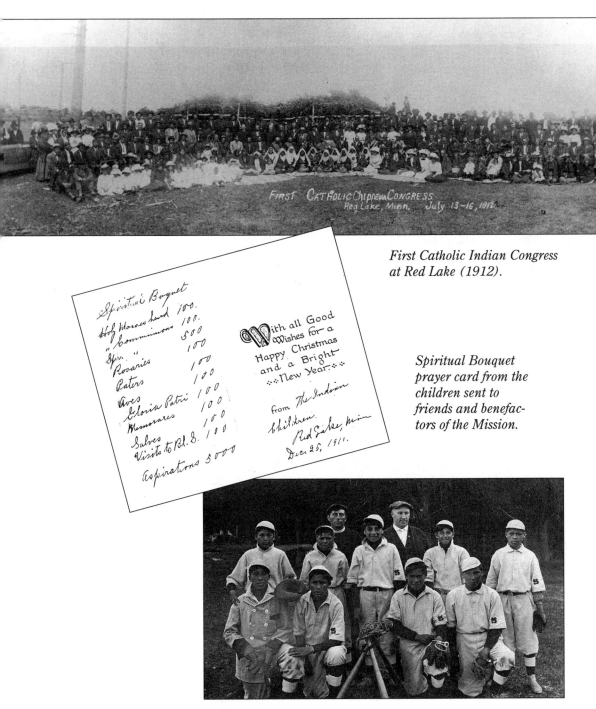

First Catholic Indian Congress
at Red Lake (1912).

Spiritual Bouquet
prayer card from the
children sent to
friends and benefac-
tors of the Mission.

Florian Locnikar, OSB, (top left), and St. Mary's baseball team
(1916).

Church of the Immaculate Conception, 1916. Members of the St. Joseph and St. Mary Societies.

*whatever except by opening doors and windows, which is rather unpleas-
ant in winter. . . .* [1]

The financial responsibility of these buildings had become a bur-
den. Though the people tried to help themselves, Father explained to
Mother Katharine that a series of "much bad luck, fires, failure of
crops, etc." had set them back. The parish had collected $800 for the
church addition, but now there was nothing left. Father hoped that
Mother Katharine could again help them out financially.

The next year, men from St. John's came to put up walls in the sisters' house and to enclose the open stairway. But it would still be several years before the building was completed.

A kind of inertia or weariness had caught up with Father Thomas.
Despite his twenty-five years of service at St. Mary's Mission, it was
still poor. He wrote sadly to the Abbot, ". . . the time is gone and the
work not done. I indeed daily remember that my remaining days are
becoming fewer and fewer." [2]

However, the staunch fifty-two-year-old missionary was considered
a great and holy man by the people. He always had time for them. And
he loved his priestly vocation. It is said that he wore his religious habit
even while working around the farm machinery. One day, he set off in a
car instead of a buggy and without wearing his usual religious garb.
The children observed this and cried, "Oh, Father Thomas has his
pants on!" [3]

Sister Hyacinthe, the superior and principal during these years, was
also a good manager. In her regular correspondence with Abbot Peter
at St. John's, she noted that the revered missionary priest desperately
needed a helper to put the Mission on sound and sure footing. She herself skimped and "made do," even saving the paper from business letters for the children to write on in school. But she was very concerned
about the dispirited pastor. She wrote to Abbot Peter:

> *Father Thomas' habit is getting very poor so that it cannot be mended.
> He looked up an old one but there is no scapular to that and the scapular
> is worse than the habit. We told him to ask for a new one when at retreat
> but probably he did not since it did not come yet.* [4]

Sister Claudina Locnikar, OSB, who had come from St. Benedict's in

August 1910 to do general housework at the Mission, also voiced concern for Father Thomas in a letter to her seminarian brother, Florian, at St. John's:

> *If poor Father Thomas only could have an assistant, he has so much to look after. The Sisters are helping him today to do some writing. That would be your job next summer when you come. You can help me in the gardens, turn the churn, and the washmachine and help me feed the chickens. I'll help you along so as not to get lonesome.*[5]

Florian Locnikar did come to Red Lake for several summers to help out. In 1915 he came to stay as a new assistant priest with Father Thomas. The younger man's energies and talents over the next twenty-five years helped the struggling Mission expand its resources and vision.

According to Sister Ortrude Nester, OSB, who also served at the Mission during these years, Sister Hyacinthe was a well chosen superior; in fact, Sister Ortrude observed, ". . . we had a saint, what I considered a saint, for a superior."[6] Sister Hyacinthe seemed gifted at perceiving the difficulties of the Mission and taking them in hand. Among her many responsibilities, from bookkeeper to storekeeper to principal, was her initiation of a "kitchen garden" (continued and modified over the years to the present) to help supply the needs of a demanding food service.

Sister Ortrude taught grades two, three, and four. She was also students' prefect and had charge of the church and sacristy. She said, ". . . [W]e all did the work of two, three people!" This was true. Sister Heliodora Wensmann, OSB, for example, stoked two furnaces downstairs each night in winter, served in the kitchen daily, and conscientiously recycled the bread crumbs from the bread cutter, ground them up, baked them, and served these creative "grape nuts" with hot milk for the children's breakfasts. Sister Octavia Roth, OSB, started the fire each morning in the school building, sewed, washed, sorted, and mended the children's clothing. Sister Aegidia Braegelmann, OSB, was in charge of the laundry. She also conducted "darning classes" for about an hour a day with girls "too old to be playing all the time but too young to do hard work!"[7]

The sisters carried out their heroic daily schedule amid circumstances of poverty, loneliness, cold, and hard work. They rose at 5 a.m. for prayer, then prepared and served breakfast at 6:30 for students and staff, and began school at 8:30. At noon they paused for dinner and a visit to the Blessed Sacrament. Supper was at 6 p.m. and night prayers at 8:30. Often seasonal work such as harvesting or canning kept them up later than their regular 9 p.m. retiring time. They served as nurses when sickness struck among the children, often suffering themselves from sheer exhaustion.

St. Mary's Mission Boarding School, 1916. Sisters Octavia Roth, Aegidia Braegelmann, Hyacinthe Simmer, Claudina Locnikar, Tharsilla Weinans, Sylvina Ettel and Father Thomas Borgerding, OSB.

Contagious diseases were prevalent at the boarding school. Ervin "Tippie" Branchaud, recalled getting pneumonia when he was eleven. His bed was beside a very drafty window. "Tippie" had to be hospitalized and was never well enough to return to the Mission School.[8] Leo Desjarlait also talks about the wind-swept boys' building. "It was a cold place in winter," he agrees. "There was a big old furnace downstairs, and we boys were squeezed together on cots upstairs."[9]

Often there were as many as thirty or forty boys together in the two dorms of the boys' building. Some of these "boys" were as old as twenty. A prefect lived with them and saw to it that the boys made their own beds and kept the building in order. The older boys helped care for the younger ones.

The girls slept on the third floor of the sisters' house, the older girls in a big dorm at the front of the house and the younger ones in a smaller, open room. The bathroom had a tub and a toilet with a pull chain. The older girls carried hot water up from the basement to the third floor for bathing.

Not all the boarding school children were from Red Lake. An increasing number of children from other reservations were being assigned by the Indian agent and social worker to attend the Mission School. Some came from as far away as Minneapolis, Duluth, Cloquet, White Earth or Cass Lake. Some, closer to home, attended as day students only. White children, too, were occasionally enrolled.

The schedule of the children was also arduous. According to eighty-two-year-old Frank Lajeunesse, who attended the Mission School, they were up at 6 a.m. "I split wood," he said. "The boys had to milk cows, too. We helped on the farm and dug potatoes over in the field where the hospital is now. We had men who were working at the Mission as our bosses."[10] Eighty-year-old Ed Lussier, also a boarder, recalled, "I hauled wood and split it, too. The farm had hogs, cattle, and chickens, and we boys helped with the chores. Our clothes really smelled sometimes!"[11]

Leo Desjarlait was six years old when he came to the boarding school in 1921. He stayed until he was in the fifth grade. "I worked in the dairy," he reports. "I cleaned out the barn and I milked. I got the horses out for water, but I never worked in the fields." Mary Ann Aitken remembered her job at the Mission School around this same time. "I worked in the laundry on the mangle. I did the men's and boys' clothes. It was fun. I also learned to embroider."[12]

But life wasn't all work, and efforts were made to create fun whenever and wherever possible to ease the harshness of the times. Sister Octavia recalled taking the girls swimming in Red Lake sometimes, at the edge of Mission property. They would wade out in their slips, she said. One time, returning home across the field, they picked up some potatoes, made a little fire, baked the potatoes, and had a picnic on the spot. The girls required no baths that day but simply hung up their slips to dry.

The sisters played ball with the children, told them stories, took them on walks, and even went sliding with them in the winter down the hill by the pond behind the house. They slid on paper boxes until the school got a toboggan. The sisters learned Ojibwe from the children even though they were not supposed to speak it and taught only English in school.

Some children, like Leo Desjarlait, knew English before they came to school. "But," he said, "Father Thomas spoke the Ojibwe language. He was real nice. We called him the 'old man.'" Some of Leo's other favorite people included Sister Arleen Jundt, OSB, his lower grade teacher, and Sister Ortrude, who was "very kind and good" to him and for whom he cheerfully cleaned the blackboards. "During my last year at school I was an altar boy, and I served in the sisters' chapel."

Ed Lussier recalled playing ball in the playroom of the boys' building. "It had hanging kerosene lamps at first," he said. "We put bushel baskets over them so they wouldn't break. Then when I was about twelve, we got electric lights. Later on, we played basketball with Father Florian in the new gym." Among Ed's classmates were Roger Jourdain, who later became Tribal Chairman, and George Fairbanks, who became a Benedictine priest.

Lussier summed up his stay at the boarding school with these words: "I appreciated the school. We had good care and good food but I didn't like spinach or rutabagas!"

Food did indeed play an important role in daily life. It had to be procured and prepared, and in most cases it was enjoyed. The active, growing children were hungry and liked most foods, but fresh, warm cornbread was one of their favorites. Some were not used to drinking milk, but they loved ice cream and gladly helped make it. There were plenty of wild blueberries, strawberries, chokecherries and plums in the woods to be gathered and made into jams and pies. There were wild game and fish. There were eggs and butter and meat from the farm. Thanksgiving and Christmas dinners were special with cranberries, turkey, mashed potatoes, and pie.

Some of the children's parents kept small gardens of their own and preserved many foods. Some helped supply the Mission with meat and berries. Leo Desjarlait remembers that his dad sold cordwood to the Mission School. For the most part, people lived simple lives, as Father Thomas explained:

The Indians . . . raise[d] a lot of corn and plenty of potatoes. . . . They didn't do any canning in those days. They would dry fish and deer and wolf meat by putting it up somewhere. . . . About the fifteenth of July they would begin to pick blueberries. They would eat most of them in season but dry some of them for winter use. In the spring they gathered strawberries. They would grind their corn with a pestle . . . and then they cooked the meal into mush. . . . In the fall they moved out to Rice Lake in all different directions for ricing. . . . There was always a big herd of Indian cows ranging around the country all summer long. In the spring, when the Indians started to make sugar, they turned their cattle loose . . . until the snow fell. They didn't milk the cows but let the calves go with them . . . these calves were beauties. . . . They raised quite a bit of beef that way. [13]

The Mission farm, operated by Father Thomas and Peter Schloer, would not have been the success it was without the help of the children, the sisters (who also tended the chickens), and the clerics and brothers of St. John's who came in the summer to work. In October 1912, eighteen hundred bushels of potatoes and six hundred bushels of corn were harvested. The Jersey herd had increased to forty cows and heifers, and the farm boasted a span of horses.

But with only charitable contributions to depend on for their operation, the financial picture of the Mission was shaky until the spring of 1914, when a delegation of people went to Washington to present a petition requesting that some of their tribal funds be available to defray the expenses of the Mission boarding school. A new contract was subsequently drawn up, but in order to receive the funds, detailed reports had to be submitted regularly. This became an increasingly difficult task for Father Thomas.

The Mission School continued to teach all the regular subjects with special emphasis on the domestic arts: cooking, sewing, laundering, gardening and farming. Father Thomas wrote:

We were supposed to advance our pupils to the eighth grade if possible and, if not, hold them to the age of eighteen. . . . Only a few went on to Flandreau [high school]. . . . We generally let the pupils go home once a month – from Friday evening to Sunday morning. . . .

We had to run our school as economically as possible. . . . Food for the boarding school came from various places. We bought a good deal

*from farmers who came through. . . . We got beef and pork for our school
from these farmers. They would supply us with meat for the whole
winter.*[14]

Christmas continued to be a particularly happy and memorable time
for everyone. Despite the poverty, parish and community were committed to making this feast as joyful as possible for the children. Many
elders today, who, as children, took part in these celebrations, still
cherish fond memories of the beauty and excitement of the feast.

"I remember Christmas Midnight Mass with the church all decorated and a big Christmas tree in the boys' building where I lived," reminisced Frank Lajeunesse. According to Ed Lussier and others, that
Christmas tree was a "community" tree and towered to the ceiling.
Albert Drouillard remembers it having real candles but with sand buck-
ets nearby in case of fire.[15]

The boys and girls all came together around the tree along with
their parents to receive the gifts that had been hung there. Gifts for the
children, provided by their parents and the Mission, included toys and
candy. Useful articles like colorful bandanas, snuff, and tobacco were
exchanged by the adults. According to Betty Beaulieu and others who
remember the tradition, **real rabbits** were also sometimes hung on the
tree as practical jokes! At any rate, it was a time of much joy.

The sisters prepared Christmas treats for the children, often working late into the night after their other work was done: popcorn balls,
frosted cookies, bags of candy, nuts, and apples. Betty remembers
being too excited to go back to bed after Midnight Mass to wait for
Christmas morning. Ed Lussier recalled that the boys often went to bed
"chewing on candy." The other wonderful thing was that the children
had five whole days "off" and didn't need to be back to school until New
Year's.

The "community" Christmas tree remained a custom at St. Mary's
for many years, and when the new gym was built, the Christmas celebration was held there, followed by Midnight Mass.

As a little girl, Mary Ann Aitken remembered coming to Midnight
Mass on Christmas Eve with her family: "We'd come in sleighs pulled
by horses with bells on their harnesses. There'd be a whole string of

1. Pisindawig genawenimadjig
       Manishtanishan wadjiwing
    Ga-bi-niginidjin Jesusan
       Eji-nagamotawawad.
       Gloria in excelsis Deo.
2. Jaigwa kid odissigonan
       Aw ge-wi-nodjimoinang,
    Gigangwan o gi-nigiigon,
       Win igo Kije-Manito.
       Gloria in excelsis Deo.
3. Mamakadendagwad iw **geget:**
       Pijikiwigamigong sa
    Kitchi kitimagisiwining
       Gi-bi-ondadisi Jesus.
       Gloria in excelsis Deo.
4. Ambessa onanigwendanda,
       Ki wi-agwashimigonan
    Kagige ishkoteng kakina,
       Win igo Debeniminang.
       Gloria in excelsis Deo.
5. Nagamoda, enamiaieg,
       Pasweweshinda mamawi,
    Tchi wi-mamoiawamang **Jesus,**
       Gi-kitchi-jaweniminang.
       Gloria in excelsis Deo.

"Angels We Have Heard on High" from Baraga's *Katolik Anamie Masinaigan.*

other sleighs coming to church. The snow was so deep. The old people sang Chippewa. We sang carols and the 'Gloria in Excelsis' in Chippewa. It was really nice."

Life for the boys changed on November 5, 1913, when prefect Peter Schloer died. He was only fifty-eight years old. Schloer had served the Mission for twenty years not only as the boys' prefect but as a friend and teacher and farm foreman. He was laid to rest in the Mission cemetery. A monument was later erected in his memory with money collected by his former students. Many short-term successors attempted to fill Schloer's place over the next ten years, but it was not until 1924, when Leo Schwartz was hired, that this position was permanently filled.

On August 15, 1915, Father Florian Locnikar arrived from St. John's as assistant to Father Thomas and as caretaker of the farm. He was a quiet, generally reserved man but lively and talkative with the children. He did not know Ojibwe at first, but this did not prevent him from getting involved. He eventually learned enough of the language to hear confessions. He taught the boys farming and gardening, baseball and basketball. In fact, the priest's reputation as an excellent coach grew with each succeeding win of the season. He often took the boys' team on a tour of several games at the end of a season, playing schools at Bemidji, Brainerd, Duluth, or Minneapolis.

Leo Desjarlait recalls, "We had no building to play basketball in at first so we played outside. Father Florian played with us. He was easygoing, always laughing. When he wasn't playing he'd be puffing on his

5-act drama staged by the Mission School in 1917: "The Shepherdess of Lourdes." Mary Pierre, 13, played Bernadette.

St. Mary's Cemetery (ca 1924).

Thomas Borgerding, OSB (ca 1923) and the "flivver."

Sisters' and girls' house, with St. Mary's students (ca 1916).

Remodelled sisters' house (ca 1940).

Corpus Christi Procession, St. Mary's Mission, Redlake (1916).

cigar. When you got close to him he smelled like an old cigar factory!"

The people loved Father Florian and named him Gapasikawadang, "He who hits the ball out of sight."

Meanwhile, Father Thomas was having great difficulty submitting his detailed reports to the government on time despite reminders. This delay, as well as leaving payments unacknowledged, impeded coveted funds and upset his superiors. Furthermore, a U.S. inspector said, unless improvements were made on the school buildings, the contract with the government would not be renewed.

Buildings were definitely in need of attention. The boys' building still had no bathing or plumbing facilities; space was lacking for the girls, whose dorms were full to overflowing; the laundry was "very primitive," making work there by the sisters and girls a drudgery.[16]

Slowly, an addition began to rise on the southern end of the sisters' house. Father Florian reported in 1916, "Our new addition to the Sisters' building is coming along. Its capacity will equal the original building."[17]

School started that September with forty-four boys and thirty-six girls. But, as had become the custom, more students continued to arrive long after opening day. The government contract allowed $125 each for the first ninety-six students. Any additional children assigned to the school had to be simply taken in "on charity."

Activity broadened at the Mission. A telephone was installed in the parish house in 1916. In the spring of 1918, Father Florian reported: ". . . a large marble altar was obtained to enhance the church. Corpus Christi . . . always a gala day at Red Lake, was carried on with our usual pomp . . . . In the procession of the Blessed Sacrament members of the societies preceded with their large banners. And the Indian ladies vied with one another in splendidly decorating two temporary altars outside."[18]

Then hard times fell again with the onset of World War I. Food became scarce and expensive. Three of the school's prefects were called to serve in the war. Livestock on the Mission farm suffered from lack of proper food and care. To make matters worse, government inspectors threatened to withhold the school contract unless steam heat and water works were installed and maintained in the kitchen. Never had the Mission financial statement appeared so RED. It was over $10,000 short.

In 1918, hoping to allay some of these mounting difficulties, Abbot Peter appointed Father Florian in full charge of the farm. The Abbot also requested Father Thomas to relinquish his financial authority over both farm and school. This was "easier said than done" for Father Thomas, who had always managed both. Meanwhile, Father Florian developed a dairy herd of registered Jersey cows. He built a root cellar to keep the potatoes in, rather than in the church basement. In 1921 he became operator of a Model-T Ford allowed the Mission with permission from Abbot Peter. When school was in session, Father Florian always kept this "flivver" cranked up to dash off at a moment's notice to retrieve youngsters fleeing the rigors of the classroom. Their "flight" was the cause of considerable worry, especially when the weather turned cold.

Other developments were also taking place on the reservation. On April 13, 1918, a General Council of the Red Lake Band of Chippewa Indians was formed and a Constitution adopted. Traditionally, governmental structure was based on adherence to an hereditary clan chieftainship system among the people, and the right to participate in clan decisions was an inherited right. The Constitution of 1918 provided for a General Council consisting of seven recognized chiefs and five appointees by each chief. This governing body of forty-two also appointed a chairman and a secretary-treasurer to help manage tribal property and transact business affairs. Peter Graves, who was instrumental in the organization of the Council and was its first treasurer, said, "We want this reservation protected for our children and our grandchildren."[19]

This continues to be the hallmark that identifies Red Lake. Its hereditary chiefs have chosen down through the years to hold the reservation in common for the people. Red Lake claims this distinction as one of only two such "closed" reservations in the United States (the other is Warm Springs, Oregon). The land is held in trust by the United States, and the Tribal Council (so called after a revision of the

Constitution in 1958) continues to be recognized by the U.S. Department of the Interior as the representative governing body of the Red Lake people.

An election at St. John's Abbey in Collegeville in December 1921, created a change in leadership here, and placed Abbot Alcuin Deutsch, OSB, in office. The new abbot soon requested a detailed financial statement from Father Thomas regarding St. Mary's Mission at Red Lake. When the report did not arrive and the situation grew more grave (some $17,000 in debt), Abbot Alcuin decided to move Father Thomas to Cloquet on the Fond du Lac Reservation and bring Father Simon Lampe back to Red Lake – the two priests thus exchanging mission territory – in hopes of filling the "empty purses" of St. Mary's.

But "full hearts" were suddenly empty, too, and it was with great sadness that Father Thomas finally bid farewell to his beloved Indian friends of thirty-five years. He reluctantly departed in July 1923. The people were saddened and troubled by the event. Several years later, a group of women from Red Lake wrote to Monsignor William Hughes of the Bureau of Catholic Indian Missions, still grieving their loss of Father Thomas:

> *Rev. Father Thomas Borgerding . . . a real true friend and missionary. It was a painful sense of guilt when he was taken away from us. He came here for a visit once during an Indian Catholic Congress. The truth of it was when he was ready to leave why it was not surprising to see one another cry. We hated to see him leave, even the non-Catholic Indians hold respect for him. As he was and is a real and God-sent true friend to us Red Lake Indians.* [20]

Red Lake children on school steps (early 1920s).

CHAPTER 6

DEMISE OF THE BOARDING SCHOOL
(1923-1940)

A "TRUE FRIEND" HAD INDEED LEFT ST. MARY'S, and Father Simon Lampe, now aged fifty-seven, moved in to carry on the work of his predecessor. Father Simon had barely escaped the ravaging forest fire of 1918 at his mission in Cloquet, Minnesota. Both his church and home had been destroyed, and, quite probably, with them, his valuable Chippewa Grammar and Dictionary manuscript which he had spent many years working on.

Father Simon was gifted and proficient in languages. He knew French, Algonquian, Ottawa and Ojibwe. His first sermon preached at Red Lake in 1888 had been in Ojibwe. Now, assigned here a second time, his expertise in the language proved a real boon for the older people. "They thought it was especially nice," recounted Mary Ann Aitken, who was a youngster at the time in the boarding school and who still continued to speak Ojibwe with her friends in her later years.

A division of labor was arranged with Father Simon's pastorate: he assumed the spiritual leadership of the parish while his assistant, Father Florian, carried out the duties of farm and school. Sermons delivered by the big man with the booming voice were fiery and often severe. The people missed the more gentle ways of Father Thomas, who, it was said, respected and knew each person's entire family tree in detail. Father Simon, on the other hand, tended not to visit the people or even break his schedule to look after their needs.

Leo Desjarlait was a boy at the boarding school during this time. He recalls: "Father Simon preached in the Indian language, but he was hot-tempered and was that way in church. He misunderstood me on some things. I remember making a mistake once as an altar boy. I was carrying the censer and ran right into my partner. Father was very angry. Afterwards, Sister Ortrude practiced with me. We couldn't make a single mistake for Father Simon."

One of the first things the new pastor did was to plan a parish mission for the spring of 1924. By this event, he hoped to renew what he considered a "lukewarm" condition of faith among the parishioners.

Father Florian, in addition to his charge of the farm, was named superintendent of the school, given the maintenance of all the mission buildings, and saddled with the task of reducing the huge parish debt. Thus he continued to upgrade the dairy herd and other income-producing resources of the farm. Charles Barrett, from nearby Clearwater, worked on the farm with Father Florian. He lived with his family in a log house east of the sisters' house on Mission land.

Lourdes Grotto Park (1930). Note new barn through right arch.

Restaurant-Confectionery

H. F. HOPKINS, PROP.

MEALS, LUNCHES
FRUITS, CANDIES
SOFT DRINKS
CIGARS, TOBACCO

REDBY, MINN., *Sept. 5, 1924*

I, Susan Schenborn, being of sound mind,
do hereby turn over to Rev. Simon Lampe Catholic
Priest at Red Lake, Minn., the following of my children:
Ervin, aged 14, Bernice, aged 12, Elmer, aged 10, and
Paul, aged 8, to care for and educate in the mission
school at Red Lake, Minn., and to have full and sole
control of them up to and until such time as the
said named children are able and competent
to care for themselves.

Edward P. Garrigan   Susan Schenborn

Witnesses: J. Morrison

Subscribed and sworn to before me, a Notary Public
this 5th day of September, 1924

J. H. Morrison Jr.
Notary Public Beltrami Co. Minn.
My commission expires Apr 30, 1931

A needy mother gives the care of her children over to the Mission School.

Mr. Leo Schwartz, hired in 1924 as the boys' prefect and teacher, cared for the boys and organized and directed their work activities. Though considered exemplary in his position by some, many former "boys" recall Mr. Schwartz' severity and intolerance, his inability, as they say, to "have fun." He served as boys' prefect through 1940, as long as the boarding school lasted. During his time at St. Mary's, Mr. Schwartz built the stone grotto of Our Lady of Lourdes near the convent, and donated the statue of Mary.

Classes were underway in September 1924 with ninety students enrolled and with a renewed government contract for aid, bearing the repeated injunction to provide and repair the necessary facilities, particularly waterworks for bathing.

Meanwhile, the government boarding school at Red Lake, first established in 1877 and rebuilt in 1900, was gradually giving way to a public day school system which provided elementary education for both Indian and non-Indian students. As a result, St. Mary's made greater efforts to attract Catholic students from Red Lake – and Father Florian was very helpful.

Everyone liked the priest. The boys' basketball team, under his expert coaching, played very well, and boys were proud to be on his team. Father spent time with the other children, too. According to Albert Drouillard, a boarder during these years, "Whether it was tag, marbles, or kick-the-can, he [Father Florian] was there. He was fun, and told us tall tales, swearing they were all true!" The children, in turn, were grateful to Father Florian for his shorter Masses and English sermons, since most of them no longer understood the Ojibwe preached by Father Simon.

Sister Hyacinthe remained principal of the school. Delphine "Duffy" Fuller, who attended from first through eighth grade during these years, reported on life as a boarder in the sisters' house:

> *We prayed and prayed and prayed – every time we turned around we prayed! My first night there I was so lonesome I crawled in bed with my sister in the big girls' dorm. I was able to do this until Christmas.*
>
> *We got up early for Mass and breakfast and then school. Recess was my favorite. We played ball, soft ball, and "scrub." We had "charges." A*

group cleaned the dorms. We had to keep everything clean. At noon we helped with dishes. Some girls baked in the baking room. But the youngest girls peeled spuds; the next oldest darned socks; and the oldest patched and sewed on machines in the sewing room. I thought that was the greatest.

But those potatoes! We had peelers and scraped the potatoes against ourselves so that all our dresses had dark spots in the middle where we held the potatoes. We couldn't talk during work time. That was no fun, so we used to dump the potatoes down the basement steps just so we could laugh and laugh picking them up!

The boys helped with laundry one day a week. We had a big fenced-in clothesline so the cows couldn't get in. [1]

My first grade teacher was Sister Leo (Boller). We gave plays in the gym and watched one another perform. I liked reading and writing but hated arithmetic. We had art twice a week. The older girls got to sing in the choir. We had black missals with green letters on – I can still see them – and we had to sit an hour to study the Latin.

Bedtime was at seven for the youngest and eight or nine for the older ones. We older girls would keep singing "Goodnight, Ladies" to linger longer. We had a lot of energy left. I have good memories and wonder what happened to all those kids. [2]

Betty Beaulieu is one of "those kids." She was one of the "potato peelers" (peeling about three washtubs full a day, she says), and one of the "sock darners."

"Sister Valois' [Barthel] class was responsible for the darning and mending," Betty reports. "I remember she had a contest once to see who was the best darner. I got first prize. She said my darning was like weaving . . . but I haven't darned a sock since!"[3]

Betty also remembers how cold it was in the classroom of the boys' building during the winter and how the children had to sit on one foot and keep their coats on to stay warm. She was in many plays and recalls practicing until everything was perfect. She was small for her age so was allowed to go to the dining room or playroom after school for bread and milk. "And if we were undernourished, we had to take cod-liver-oil. Then in the spring, we were all given a spoonful of sulfur and molasses. The sisters also cleaned our heads regularly with kerosene and vinegar. We'd all line up by the tables and they'd comb

Sept. 7 1930,   Red lake

Minn,

Dear mother Just a ~~few~~ lines
to you. I am lonesome here and I
cry every day, How are you are
you the same. Say ma will
you send me some money and
rice ~~Please~~ How is ~~ugean~~ and
rita, say ma I am going home
Christmas vacation with
Henry. If they let me ride as far
as bonsford. they fight us ma
I am crying now when I am
writing my letter. Dear ma
I am lonesome, will you send
me some money and rice,
Please, me and ~~Peter~~ are
Having fun. I am Josch Peray
your son, I get candy from
francis. good By mother Please
write back,

A letter home from a lonely boy at the Mission School. Note the teardrop smudges!

through our hair with fine combs."

Ervin "Tippie" Branchaud's home was at White Earth, and for the two years he was a boarder at St. Mary's, he was very lonesome. Many of the boys and girls were, he said, especially those from farther away. Tippie played on the swings and merry-go-round and went sliding in the winter which helped dispel his lonesomeness.

Adolf "Punce" Barrett felt luckier. He started boarding school at seven, but when his family moved into a log house on the Mission, he became a day scholar. Boarders, he recalls, came from as far away as Minneapolis, Brainerd, and Duluth. They were both Indian and non-Indian children.

"I helped my dad [Charles Barrett] on the Mission farm," Punce explains. "We were up at 4 a.m. to milk thirty-two cows. The Jersey milk was like cream. I also cut and carried cordwood for the furnaces. I served in the convent chapel. After eighth grade, my brothers and I continued to work on the Mission farm for a few years."[4]

Albert Drouillard, a boy boarder from 1929 to 1932, retains a keen memory of the layout of the Mission at this time and the floor plan of the boys' building where he lived. "Except for the smaller children," he says, "we all had chores to do. Some saw to it that all the buildings had firewood stacked outside and piled next to the furnaces (mostly cord-wood except for the kitchen). Most of the work was done after school or on Saturday mornings, except for the cows which were milked twice a day: early morning before breakfast and again in the evening."[5]

Albert remembers the beautiful northern lights in the sky on frosty mornings on his way to the barn. He remembers making ice cream out on the steps of the convent, churning the rich cream very slowly; picking wild grapes with his friends in the fall near Big Thunder and Little Thunder lakes; gathering corn from the fields in gunny sacks; making hay; catching and riding wild ponies; learning to play the mandolin from Sister Seraphica Kennedy; and staying one whole summer with his brother and sister on the Mission.

Frank Donnell, born at White Earth, where his family had a large farm, attended the boarding school after moving with his family to Farm Station. Father Florian named the boy "Farmer," a name that "stuck" for life. At the Mission farm, Farmer washed and milked the

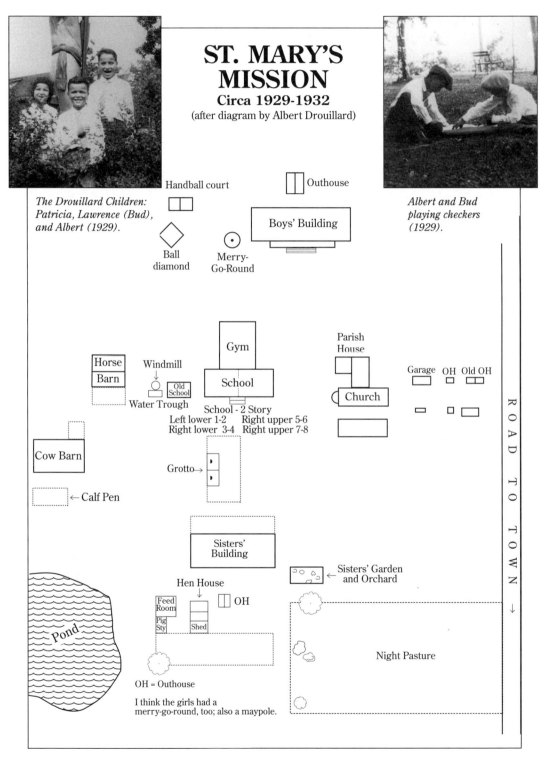

ST. MARY'S MISSION
Circa 1929-1932
(after diagram by Albert Drouillard)

*The Drouillard Children:
Patricia, Lawrence (Bud),
and Albert (1929).*

*Albert and Bud
playing checkers
(1929).*

Handball court

Outhouse

Boys' Building

Ball
diamond

Merry-
Go-Round

Gym

Parish
House

School

Garage   OH   Old OH

Horse
Barn

Windmill

Old
School

Church

Water Trough

School - 2 Story
Left lower 1-2   Right upper 5-6
Right lower 3-4   Right upper 7-8

Cow Barn

Grotto →

← Calf Pen

Sisters'
Building

Sisters' Garden
and Orchard

Hen House

Feed
Room

OH

Pig
Sty

Shed

Pond

Night Pasture

ROAD TO TOWN

OH = Outhouse

I think the girls had a
merry-go-round, too; also a maypole.

BOYS' BUILDING

2 Story • Circa 1929-32 (after diagram by Albert Drouillard)

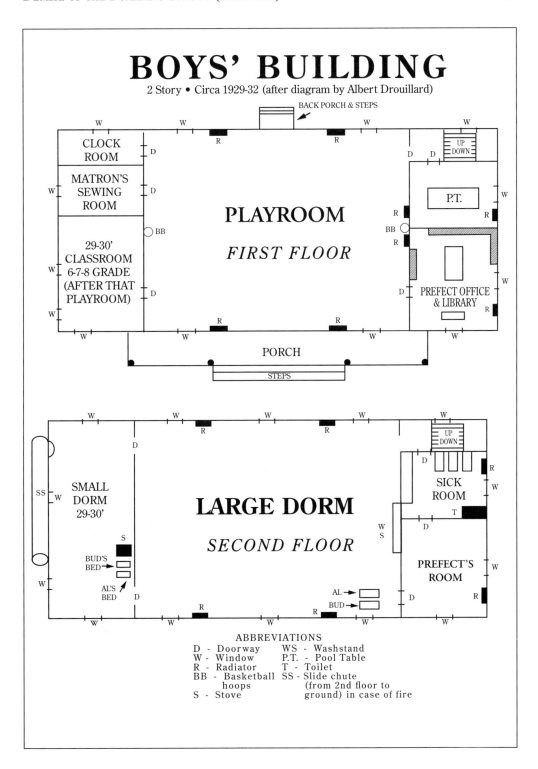

ABBREVIATIONS

D - Doorway   WS - Washstand
W - Window   P.T. - Pool Table
R - Radiator   T - Toilet
BB - Basketball   SS - Slide chute
     hoops   (from 2nd floor to
S - Stove   ground) in case of fire

cows and carried the milk to the convent to be hand-separated. "Here," he says, "we boys would get extra milk and bread from the sisters."[6]

At the end of 1924, the annual report for the Church of the Immaculate Conception at Red Lake indicated a total of 215 Catholic families or 900 Ojibwe parishioners. There were 13 marriages recorded for the year, 46 infant baptisms, 9 adult baptisms, 50 burials, and 20 First Communions.

It was time to do some building.

In the summer of 1926, a large new dairy barn (34x120) began to rise south of the convent and school with lumber cut from Mission land. It housed all the cattle previously scattered over various pastures, and served as a teaching model for the boys' training in farming. Abbot Alcuin Deutsch also suggested cutting enough lumber at the same time for building a new parish house.

The boys' building was in a sorry state. Little, if anything, had been done by way of repair or improvements. The bathroom had never been completed, and outdoor toilets were still used. Leonard Donnell reports that during his school days, as late as the 1930s, the boys "couldn't use any indoor facilities."[7]

During the later part of 1927, work on a new parish house just west of the church was begun with funds collected by Father Simon.

When Sister Celestia Lauerman, OSB, arrived the next year to replace Sister Hyacinthe as superior, she was appalled, however, at the condition of the girls' building and school. She wrote in the St. Mary's Mission edition of *The Indian Sentinel*:

> *. . . The heating plant does not function, the plumbing does not work, the plaster is off the ceilings, the floors of the porches are falling in and there is a general air of dilapidation all over the place. The building is a veritable fire trap. . . . Our school rooms are scattered. Two rooms are in an old (house), a third in the girls' house, and a fourth in the boys' house. The building housing the [12] Sisters and [60] girls is about two blocks from the buildings the [98] boys are in so is all very inconvenient as it is necessary to go back and forth for meals, sometimes in a temperature of forty below zero. A new building is the only remedy of the present condition. . . .*[8]

The new barn under construction (1926); church in background.

New parish house, built in 1927.

New Mission School - Lautischar Memorial Hall - *1929. Combination classrooms, gymnasium and auditorium. Old school behind.*

Father Florian and the St. Mary's girls' basketball team – 1930.

Sisters Eucharia Koltes and Laura Hesch with school children (mid-1930s).

Perhaps these concerns as well as the fact that two years earlier a new four-room public elementary day school with auditorium had been built at Red Lake, hastened St. Mary's on to repair and building.

In 1929, a new school building rose beside the old, midway between the boys' and the girls' buildings. It contained four classrooms – two upstairs and two down – and a large gymnasium, all for a cost of four thousand dollars. The structure was dedicated on November 28, 1929, and called *Lautischar Memorial Hall* after the beloved missionary priest who had given his life for the mission in 1858. The building opened its doors for the first time on December 3, 1929.

Abbot Alcuin Deutsch, however, was not satisfied with the name of the structure. He felt that since a memorial tablet had just been erected to Lautischar, the memory of Mother Katharine Drexel, the Mission's great benefactress, ought to be kept alive.[9] However, it wasn't until St. Mary's Centennial in 1958 that the name of the building was finally changed to *Drexel Hall*.

Lautischar Memorial Tablet at St. Mary's Mission.

Through the 1920s and 1930s, the Indian people of Red Lake continued to observe some traditional ways of life. This was difficult in light of the "culture clash" in which they were immersed. They gathered maple sugar and wild rice. They hunted and fished, made wood for the winter, and tended small gardens. A few had cows. Many lived in good log houses built by hand. Some were employed in the lumber business, some in the newly organized fishing industry.

Indian agents were allowing school policies to disintegrate, however. Many teenagers roamed irresponsibly about the reservation engaging in delinquent and immoral conduct – much to the disapproval of parents. In April 1929 a group of concerned women from St. Mary's wrote a letter to Monsignor Hughes of the Bureau of Catholic Indian Missions in Washington, D.C., regarding the situation. In the same letter, they also addressed the hurt they were feeling from Father Simon's severe treatment: ". . . many times we come out of church crying because he calls us down to the lowest," they wrote, adding that this severity was driving the young people away from church.[10]

Father Simon was a strict enforcer of church rules. Agnes and Jim Roberts attest to their frustration at the time with a particular policy: "We were married in the Church by Father Simon. He was very strict. But one of our children died and was not baptized so had to be buried outside the cemetery."[11] Though this practice was common in the Church at the time, the experience was particularly distressing for people suffering the loss of many long-established customs surrounding death and burial.

The spiritual expression of the Red Lake people had long been connected to a particular way of life. This expression (Midewiwin) was significantly developed at the time of the Ojibwe migration to Lake Superior's southern shore in the 1300s. With the advent of Christianity, elements of Mide expression were often renounced or were blended with Christian beliefs. As more cultural clashes were encountered, the early spiritual bonds faded among those embracing Christianity, and the Catholic element was sustained. Yet some customs and ceremonies surrounding life and death continue to be passed down from community to community, teacher to student, parent to child.

The people of St. Mary's have remained faithful to the Catholic faith they received as well as to Ojibwe traditions passed on to them. Ageless values of community living, sharing, respect for life, harmony with nature, simplicity, resourcefulness, and hospitality are blended, forming the foundation for growth and grace.

Julius Beckermann, OSB, stands at the site of the last remaining spirit houses on St. Mary's Cemetery. "We see in this mode of burial much that shows their [Indian] belief in the immortality of the soul and their tender love and regard for the dead." Life and Labors of Rt. Rev. Frederic Baraga *by Chrysostomus P. Verwyst. [Photo: Placid Stuckenschneider, OSB.]*

Some religious practices that Betty Beaulieu recalls from St. Mary's in the early 1930s demonstrate the meaning and blending of these values. "We'd walk all the way to the cemetery for All Soul's Day," she says. "People gathered there and put food – including candy and popcorn – and flowers or crosses on the graves of loved ones. They'd ask us children to pray at the graves and partake of the food."

"Yes," adds Vi Donnell, smiling at the memory. "And we kids were eager to pray for the dead so we could eat the goodies!"[12]

Today, the graves of the dead continue to be visited and decorated. Three spirit houses remain on the edge of St. Mary's west cemetery. Often the traditional offering of food or tobacco is left at the graves as a sign of honor. Catholics and non-Catholics alike gather at wakes and funerals to remember the deceased, to tell stories, to drum and sing the old Ojibwe songs, to burn sage, tobacco, or incense, and to share a meal.

"Also, on Corpus Christi," Betty continues, "we used to have a procession all around the Mission grounds. There were little altars prepared and decorated by the women, where we'd stop to pray."

These and other recollections of faith-sharing form a keen and colorful history to be cherished and preserved as signs of God's loving presence.

The Mission in the 1930s extended its spiritual arms around its children. But providing the physical means to continue its service in education required constant effort and vigilance. The Commissioner of Indian Affairs reported that instruction and care of the girls was "quite satisfactory" – this, despite limited resources. But since the Mission was taking no steps toward repairs on the convent and girls' building or for necessary equipment for school, the sisters themselves made a new plea directly to Bishop Timothy Corbett of Crookston.[13]

Little improvement had been done on the boys' building as well. Along with the lack of usable indoor toilets and showers, a shop building was desperately needed for the boys to work in. The Commissioner urgently recommended that a matron be placed on duty to create greater order among the boys. In 1931, Nellie Micklewright was hired and remained in this position until June 1939, when the status of the school changed. She was respected but often remembered as "strict" by the boys.

As many as fourteen sisters a year staffed the Mission in the 1930s, each receiving a stipend of $100 per year. Though very busy, they reported they were happy. After all, the Mission was "home" – sometimes for many years. For instance, Sister Valois Barthel, OSB, stayed from 1932 to 1960 teaching sewing and working in the kitchen, among her many duties. Sister Adelma Roers, OSB, spent thirty-seven years teaching home economics, managing the Mission store, visiting the sick and homebound, and performing a variety of other tasks.

The school was crowded in the 1930s. In the little girls' dorms, Sister Adelma attests, beds were packed "tight, tight, tight," and pupils and teachers alike were very poor.[14] Betty Beaulieu recalls carrying water up to a big sink on third floor. Each girl had her own basin to fill for washing and brushing her teeth and for a "sponge bath" on Saturday night. Once a month, the girls took baths in the basement in big round tubs with curtains around them.

Ruth Jourdain-Fevig remembers trying to sneak into bed with her older sisters, but the sister in charge, who slept midway between the younger girls on the south end and the older ones on the north, usually discovered this and escorted her back.[15]

Agatha Starkey, who attended the Mission School from 1929 to 1937 and whose seven-year-old brother died there of pneumonia, remembers a little girl on third floor who also died. Her name was Eliza DeFoe. Afterwards, the girls felt the place was haunted because they heard whistling. When a Sister came to stand at the spot, the whistling moved. This continued, Agatha says, until Father blessed the place.[16]

The year 1932 brought a large influx of some two hundred students. Leonard Donnell was one of them. He worked with Charlie Barrett and his sons, Robert and Adolf, with the cows. "On Wednesdays," Leonard says, "we were off school in order to bring cordwood around. On Saturday mornings, we scrubbed the boys' building." Leonard remembers the two big furnaces in the convent basement. Here, he confides, he and his pals secretly roasted potatoes they'd helped themselves to from the potato bin.

Many were the escapades of these boarders. With the addition of the root house built above the pond behind the convent, an expanded winter playground was opened for the children, who used the roof of the root house for a toboggan slide.

Sister Laura Hesch, OSB, on a picnic with the 8th grade, 1936.

But the financial burdens of the school and farm became still more complicated as the country entered the years of the Great Depression. Funds stretched in 1934 for the construction of cement sidewalks to replace the board ones between the church, school, and convent. But most other projects were put on hold.

This was the same year St. Mary's hosted a golden jubilee celebration honoring Father Thomas Borgerding. The revered former pastor returned for the festivities from Cloquet, where he was engaged in ministry to the Indian people of that area. The occasion coincided with the fifty-year Benedictine presence at St. Mary's Church.

The summer of 1934 was indeed a busy one. It was at this time that Joseph Kapsner came to work on the Mission farm. According to Father Alban, it happened this way:

> *Joe was courting a lady and he thought he was doing alright and planned to get married. One Sunday morning he came to church and listened to the announcements and heard that the same lady he was courting was going to marry someone else! That almost broke his heart. So Joe's brother, Father Roland, told him, 'You have to get away from here,' and took him to Red Lake where Father Florian, who was a very sympathetic man, told him to stay for a couple of weeks and forget about the woman. Joe stayed two weeks and liked it.* [17]

Thus, Joseph Kapsner moved into the former priests' house near the church. He became a familiar figure around the Mission for the next thirty-five years as he quietly plowed and harvested, milked, and tended his responsibilities faithfully. He lived simply and frugally. His savings helped build the new parish center in 1993; it was named the *Kapsner Center* in his honor.

Other workmen helped out on the Mission over these years. They included Martin Schwab, Johnny Pitzel, who subbed for Leo Schwartz when he broke a leg jumping out of the car to chase runaway boys, and Harry Rolf, who lived with his family on Mission land behind the boys' building and did shoe repair, carpentry, and maintenance.

In May 1937, St. Mary's was the scene of a parish mission, and in June, it hosted the Catholic Indian Congress. June was also the month the parish celebrated the first Solemn High Mass of Father Aldrich (Andrew) Huhne, OSB, a non-Indian and an orphan who had been

First Communion class, 1936.
Father Simon Lampe, OSB.

First Solemn High Mass of
Aldrich Huhne, OSB, June
1937.

Florian Fairbanks, OSB (ca
1955), Assumption Abbey,
Richardton, ND.

Picking carrots (ca 1940). [Double exposure] Left: Florian Locnikar, OSB, Joe Kapsner; right: Charlie Barrett, Florian Locnikar, OSB.

School and Boys' Building (ca 1938).

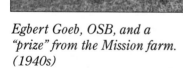

Egbert Goeb, OSB, and a "prize" from the Mission farm. (1940s)

Joe Kapsner – faithful employee.

raised by St. Mary's Mission boarding school and later attended St. John's for college and seminary training. Following his ordination, Father Aldrich taught chemistry, math, and woodworking at St. John's. He also served as a chaplain in the army during WWII. He was the recipient of two bronze stars and held the rank of captain. He later served as pastor in Beaulieu, Minnesota, and as chaplain of the Memorial Hospital in Cando, North Dakota. Father Aldrich died in 1987.

On October 4, 1938, the parish observed the golden jubilee of Father Simon Lampe. This occasion also marked the priest's fifty years of missionary activity among the Indian people. It was truly a "golden year" for the Mission School as well, celebrating its own fiftieth birthday. Among the many invited guests was Sister Amalia Eich, OSB, who, along with Fathers Simon and Thomas, had pioneered the Benedictine school in 1888 and served as its first teacher.

As she reminisced, Sister Veronette Schramel, who arrived at the Mission during this time of jubilee, described Father Simon as ". . . just like I saw him in pictures. He wore a little black beanie. He came to the convent for meals and I waited on him. He once told me to speak more distinctly,"[18] – aptly put for a man attuned to a lifetime of language study.

More parish events crowded into the decade of the '30s. On May 21, 1939, Florian (George) Fairbanks of Red Lake celebrated his first Solemn High Mass. He, too, had attended St. John's from 1924 to 1930 and then transferred to Assumption Abbey in Richardton, North Dakota. Out of respect for his mentor, Father Florian Locnikar, the younger priest took the older man's name. Today, Father Florian Fairbanks continues his active parish ministry near Mandan, North Dakota.

On November 4, 1939, Father Florian Locnikar observed the twenty-fifth anniversary of his ordination to the priesthood. All but one of these years had been spent at Red Lake. Sister Veronette again shared her remembrances of this priest: "Father Florian was so happy-go-lucky. He would come in for dinner laughing and whistling. But it was during this time that be became sick." Father Florian had cancer.

Father Simon's health also broke down, but he was allowed to retire at the Mission while Father Florian shouldered the responsibility as pastor. In June 1940, Father Egbert Goeb, OSB, former procurator of St. John's, arrived to take charge of the school and farm.

A few months later, on November 9, Father Simon, "The man with the big voice," died, wracked by pneumonia and diabetes. He was seventy-four years old. Father Simon is remembered for his preservation of the language and history of the people through his Ojibwe dictionary, well-kept diaries, and Mission records.

Father Florian, appointed pastor that same year, barely saw the year out. He underwent serious surgery and was transferred to the mission at Ponsford. His condition here grew worse until finally "He who hits the ball out of sight" returned to St. John's, where he died Janaury 9, 1944, at age fifty-six.

Father Egbert, meanwhile, was intent upon raising the financial status of the Mission. Sister Veronette remembered his zeal for the cause: "He told us right off not to eat so much cream, to save it to sell for the Mission. So we ate raspberries and things with blue milk on instead." In time, a reputable sixty percent of the Mission's income would come from the farm.

Times were changing at the boarding school, too. In 1938, the General Council of the Red Lake Band of Indians sent a resolution to the Bureau of Catholic Indian Missions objecting "strenuously" to the use of tribal funds in the care of Indian children at St. Mary's.[19] Father J.B. Tennelly, Director of the Bureau, cited overcrowding as a major weakness of the boarding school.

Those at the Mission rallied their forces in defense. Father Florian, prior to his illness, Leo Schwartz, and Sister Ethelbert Krenik, OSB, principal, all wrote letters and reports to refute the citations and to enhance the achievements, goals, and importance of the school. Parents, too, expressed their desire to continue the school at St. Mary's, even if it meant operating as a day school only.

So it was that by 1939, only some sixty of the more needy children were allowed to attend as boarders. Father Florian flew into action. He announced that in the fall of 1940, St. Mary's Mission School would continue on as a day school and without the assistance of the federal government. In addition, he said, free bussing for the children would be provided (the Buick was traded in on an International station wagon which served as a school bus, packing in twenty children at a time, six times a day), and the children would receive a free hot lunch daily. They would make it somehow.

But before school started in September 1940, the Mission had an unwelcome visitor.

According to the U.S. Department of Education, the amount of state aid granted the operation of public schools depended upon the number of students attending. Fewer students meant less aid. It was pointed out to Father Egbert that because compulsory school attendance was in effect at Red Lake, the principal of the Catholic school must make reports to the superintendent of the public school of all children enrolled who were not attending school regularly so that the law could be enforced.

Now eleven dependent children from the reservation were to be sent to the Indian boarding school at Pipestone, Minnesota, but St. Mary's happened to be boarding some of these youngsters at the request of their parents. This posed a problem for the state, and one day, Mrs. Kirkland, the social worker, arrived at the Mission with a big truck to claim these children.

Young Ephraim Sayers refused to go. He and his sister, Carrie, had been brought to the Mission in 1936. Their mother had died and their father had abandoned the children. Father Florian had promised to care for them. Ephraim decided to run away rather than be packed off to another home.

Father Egbert found out about the boy's plan and hid Ephraim's clothing to prevent his leaving. The boy was thus forced to stay in bed, and Mrs. Kirkland later marched Ephraim off along with six other protesting, crying orphans to the public institution at Pipestone.

St. Mary Mission Church interior (1940).

CHAPTER 7

RUMORS AND REALITIES (1940-1957)

R UMORS THAT THE MISSION SCHOOL would close with the loss of its status as a boarding school completely dissipated that September 1940, as some 142 students trooped back through the hallways of the day school. According to Wilfred McGraw, who was a day student at St. Mary's at the time, a few orphan children also remained boarding at the Mission. Among them were Valerian and Francis Blake and Baptiste Thunder.[1]

To prepare for the opening of the day school, much hard work and donated time and money were invested in the boys' building, converting the main floor into classrooms and the basement into a shop and playroom. The convent and girls' building (begun in 1906) was also completed and remodelled, including the long awaited plumbing and heating.

But with government assistance no longer available for student and operating costs, improvements, maintenance, and subsistence continued to be a serious matter. New rumors circulated that the school could not financially endure beyond Christmas. The

Baptiste Thunder and Francis Blake (1940)

reality was, however, that it did – and beyond.

Father Egbert showed great affection for the school children and helped pick them up by bus each morning. He even went so far as to part with a proven herd-sire bull from the farm in order to have money for a new school bus. He "bussed" some of the children directly to Sister Adelma in the morning for breakfast and some "sprucing up" for school. He later wrote about this experience:

Sister Ethelbert Krenik, OSB, and pupils Marilyn Brun, Ida Sayers, Mary May B., Ramona N. (1940s)

How often did I see an Indian boy or girl meet the bus in the morning munching on a cracker. It was all they had. They were poor; so were we but nobody knew it.

One would not like to pass over the fact that the children came dressed neatly though they had little to wear . . . . It happened that a certain girl was absent quite regularly. In checking into the matter we found that the mother washed the dress on that day while the child remained in bed until the dress had dried.

All in all there was a spirit of sacrifice deeply embedded in the lives of the Indian people and their children . . . . The teachers had nothing to work with. There were few books, the classrooms were not warm, the chalk was short, water in the gallon jugs froze. . . . Many and great were the sacrifices, noble was the spirit in those early days of the teachers and pupils alike . . . it gave birth to a new life of cheerfulness and happiness that pervaded the school.[2]

The eleven Benedictine sisters staffing the Mission that year gave witness to this new spirit referred to by Father Egbert in their lives of generous service and multiplicity of works. They were Sisters:

> Ethelbert Krenik, principal and superior
> Eucharia Koltes   Rhabana Scheuren
> Almeda Schroeder   Aniceta Drontle
> Valois Barthel   Annina Zierden
> Adelma Roers   Rosabel Schweitzer
> Sidonia Zeug   Alonzo Winkleman

The teachers in this group could as easily be found in the milk house washing separators and milk pails as in the classroom teaching spelling. Together they gardened, harvested, and canned. They cleaned the men's house, parish house, the school, and the church. The diocesan stipend which they received was sent directly to St. Benedict's Convent in St. Joseph which, at the time, sent no further financial assistance to the Mission.

This "hard row to hoe" might dissuade less intent missioners, but not this group. Gradually, the old rumors of closing gave way to new realities and challenges. A basement was excavated beneath the school building for shower rooms and a furnace room. At the same time, the gym was lengthened and three small music rooms added.

When Sister Mary Ida Klehr, OSB, arrived in 1942 as upper grade teacher and later principal, she ignited a spark of creative energy among the students. Prior to her arrival, in the early 1930s, world-renowned Father Virgil Michel, OSB, of St. John's Abbey, inspirer of the American Liturgical Movement, had visited the Mission School. He felt the children needed music to motivate them, to "catch their hearts and minds."[3] So Sister Mary Ida took this recommendation to heart. She was joined in her efforts in 1946 by Sister Roman (Genevieve) Leuer, OSB, teacher of music.

Together, these two initiated a decade and more of outstanding musical and dramatic development at the Mission School. Their first small harmonica band soon mushroomed into a full-fledged orchestra, including accordion, piano, violin, saxophone, and trumpet (instruments donated by the Paul Schmitt Music Company of Minneapolis). Sister Genevieve wrote music around this medley of instruments so that the group could play harmoniously together. A children's choir was added, and liturgical and church music became part of the repertoire. The children played and sang for Masses, for special events in the parish, for benefactors and other visitors, and for the school's big Annual Achievement and Appreciation Days. The fifty-six member orchestra performed works by Strauss, Sousa, Mozart, Sibelius and Schubert. Particular charm was added in 1951 by three very young and capable conductors: third-graders Leon Cook and twins Audrey and Beverly Lussier.

"Our uniforms were donated by a school in Minneapolis," Sister Genevieve reports. "Chief Peter Graves was so impressed with the children that he encouraged us to perform state-wide."[4] So the musical ensemble took to the road. Select members also played on the radio. Stage productions at home took on the pageantry and artistry of professionals, enhancing even end-of-the-year programs demonstrating accomplishments in sewing, needle art, and baking.

As these youngsters grew older, many wished to stay on at St. Mary's to form a ninth grade. This was a dream come true as Father Egbert eagerly rustled up eighty unused desks and transformed the two upstairs rooms into 7th, 8th, and, 9th grade classrooms offering departmentalized education.

During the school year of 1948-49, St. Mary's reached a high of 224 students. Throughout the 1950s, the school continued to grow and to enjoy what was called its "golden age."[5] Enthusiastic school spirit led its basketball team, under Father Egbert's skillful coaching, to fame by winning the state tournament two years in a row, 1949-1951. Father Egbert was instrumental in getting uniforms for the boys: a red set, which the boys preferred, and a white set. When the boys stepped out on the basketball floor, they created quite a stir. Though small in size, they were excellent players and soon had the spectators cheering for them. Their consistent display of good sportsmanship was accompanied by the girls' cheering section playing rousing tunes on the accordion.

Another kind of "golden age" was under way in the convent kitchen. Here, Sister Gudilia Duclos, OSB, set the pace. Sister recalls her first meeting with Father Egbert when he picked her up at Bemidji. "What are you going to do [at the Mission]?" he queried. She replied that she really didn't know except that the Reverend Mother had sent her there to work, to cook, or do whatever. She describes the moment:

After we were on the road awhile, he [Father Egbert] said, "Pretty soon we'll be at St. Mary's." Then we stopped at an old shack beside the road. "Here's your new mission," he chuckled. I took one look and burst into tears. Of course, he was teasing. When we did get to the Mission, he took me into the kitchen and announced, "Here's the new cook!" Then I knew what I was to do.[6]

Virgil Michel, OSB, and Florian Locnikar, OSB, visit a sweat lodge (ca 1934).

Left to right: Sisters Adelma Roers, Alonzo Winkelman, Almeda Schroeder, Ethelbert Krenik, and Valois Barthel.

St. Mary's Mission Church, gate and workman's house (later removed) – 1940s.

1941 Christmas pageant.

Schoolbus brings children from Redby (1947).

Lunchtime!

Laurentia Colhoff, age 11, accompanies congregational singing (1947).

St. Mary's School accordion band performs – 1950s.

1950s St. Mary's basketball team. Top row (l to r): Simon Beaulieu, Arnold Brun, Douglas ("Pug") Needham; Front Row (l to r): Hubert Roy, Billy King, Henry Sumner.

Sister Aniceta Drontle, OSB, with the graduating class of 1942.

A thriving endeavor (1945).

Leon Cook, student conductor of St. Mary's School orchestra (1951).

The kitchen became a community hub for work, fun, and laughter. Sister Gudilia, descriptively dubbed "Goodie," contributed a flair of good humor, enthusiasm, and creativity to each event. She expanded coffee breaks to include dainties and delectables from her expert culinary coffers as well as homey conversation. After just one month at Red Lake she was able to exclaim, "Not even Reverend Mother could pull me away now!"

Sister Gudilia Duclos, OSB (ca 1950).

Over the next twelve years, Sister continued to season life on the Mission, which could be lonely and very difficult at times, with her generous community-building preservatives of good cheer, compassion, and understanding.

The work of providing and preparing food for the Mission had become quite a feat. "We thought nothing of canning two or three hundred quarts of peas and thirty or thirty-five gallons of sauerkraut a year," Sister recalls. "We did our own meat processing. We had the largest cooler on the reservation. We smoked our own hams, bacon, and sausage. Mr. Peter Graves brought us big wash tubs full of walleye and white fish. Sometimes we cleaned fish till all hours of the night. We dug carrots and potatoes and put away 150-200 bushels of carrots in the root house."

Sister Aaronette Herzog, OSB, who worked with Sister Gudilia, says, "Red Lake was my first assignment and it became my favorite. We did work hard. We had to be up at 4:30 a.m. to get breakfast. In those days, we fed over two hundred people a day, and there were always guests. We never knew exactly how many would be there at mealtime."[7]

The lived realities of extraordinary simplicity, hospitality and unflagging energy at the Mission appear ordinary and commonplace as Sister Gudilia sums up the experience: "We had nothing, really, but we were happy. We worked hard and everyone helped together. We never needed a parlor. Everyone was always in the kitchen!"

Stories abound of other "realities" on the Mission. Sister Debora Herda, OSB, recalls that the winters were sometimes so cold that nails

Sisters off for a harvesting adventure (1950s).

actually popped out of the roof. "It's true," she claims. "They sounded like guns going off. The brothers investigated, and they discovered that when the hot smoke from the chimneys traveled along the freezing roof, it pulled out the nails!"[8]

Caring for a flock of chickens and selling eggs to make money for the Mission provided not only work but also good stories to tell. One day, it is said, Sister Karen Nordick, OSB, whose wholehearted, simple nature could always add a comical twist to a situation, unwittingly tossed out the eggs she had just collected in her bucket in place of chicken feed to a whole party of astonished hens and roosters.

The sisters remember berry-picking adventures. Outfitted in the monks' hip boots to get into the wetlands, they'd gather green marsh cranberries, arrange them in flat boxes, and place them in the sun to ripen for Thanksgiving Day. Usually, an Indian guide accompanied the sisters in this quest. Once, while blueberry picking, young Billy Brun (about twelve years old) went along to guide the group to a perfect patch. Sister Genevieve tells what happened:

> We drove and drove – as far as the outlet. But Billy would always say, "Just over the next hill." Finally he jumped up and screamed, "There it is!" And sure enough, just as his dad had told him, there ahead lay a wonderful patch of berries that no one had yet touched. We felt so lucky, and filled our buckets to overflowing.

Sister Eulalia Siebels, OSB, who worked as laundress and in the children's dining room, says that most of the children liked rutabagas, fresh tomatoes, soups and stews. "But they didn't like everything," she adds. "Sometimes they'd say, 'Can't eat it,' or they'd hide the food under the table to take home to 'mama.'"[9]

Several Mission enterprises began to taste "golden success," also, starting with the farm. Father Egbert was a knowledgeable farmer as well as a good coach and financier, and he initiated improvements for better farming methods. Since the farm owned no machinery to speak of (in the past, it was rented from the government), he purchased a new tractor and brought other farm equipment from St. John's. He built a silo. He put aluminum siding on the barn. Although sixty-five acres were already under cultivation, he opened up more to farming and grazing. He hired Charlie Barrett as the new herdsman. And, in time, the quality (bloodlines) and quantity of the Jersey stock increased.

The Mission store also prospered, netting as much as $12,000 per year. Its proprietor, Sister Adelma, whose many years at St. Mary's provided her with a variety of jobs, fell heir to its bags and bundles in 1939 after Sister Laura Hesch, OSB, left. The store had been started in 1932 as another way to support the Mission. It depended upon the generosity of individual and group donors for its constant stock of household items, clothing, bedding, toys, and even candy – all of which were sold at reasonable prices. It was here that Sister Adelma earned her reputation as a good steward, and helped the store succeed.

Affectionately referred to by the people as Zazaagis, "The stingy one," Sister kept a watchful eye on the things that came and went in the store. Nevertheless, her greatest gift was a remarkable ability to touch the lives of the people she met daily with kindness and compassion. Sister Elaine Schindler, OSB, who was with Sister Adelma at Red Lake for several years, observes that if an Indian remarked, "I want to go to the store," that usually meant he or she wanted to talk to Sister Adelma – not necessarily to buy anything."[10]

Zazaagis listened; and she understood and spoke Ojibwe. By the time she left the Mission in 1974, she was considered a "permanent fixture" by the people. Wilfred McGraw, who knew Sister Adelma from childhood, adds: "I used to think she was born and raised here!"

It was the common service done with care that meant so much to the people, Sister Elmer (Marie) Reisinger observes. She remembers how the sisters treated the cuts and bruises of the children. Supplies were sent over from the hospital. "This expressed love meant the most to them," she says. "And in return, I saw such wonderful qualities in the people: their deep appreciation of beauty, their sense of God. They were very perceptive, intuitive, and faithful."[11]

Sister Thea Grieman, OSB, an organist for eighteen years at Redlake, Redby, and Nebish, was likewise touched by the people's sensitivity and faith. These were qualities, she says, that the Indian people "express differently than we do" but which are very meaningful and intense. For instance, at powwows, she explains, "You could feel the rhythm through the ground as the dancers passed by."[12] The people also had great love and respect for the bishop, Bishop Francis Schenk of Crookston, who came for confirmations in those days. They inducted him into the Tribe by giving him a beautiful headdress to wear and an Indian name which meant "Red-golden Eagle."

Efforts were begun at the Mission School to revive some of the traditional ways and values of the people which had been suppressed earlier. Although the Ojibwe language and arts (with the exception of beading) were not taught specifically, greater awareness and appreciation were encouraged. At home, some children learned traditional ways from their parents or grandparents, as did Mary Rose Skinaway, who attended St. Mary's day school in 1941:

> *I set nets and ran boats as a child. I hunted and helped skin muskrat and dry the skins on stretchers. My mother and grandmother showed me how to prepare meat for the winter and how to make birch bark baskets to keep food in. I learned how to make cherry patties and dry them for the winter. I made my own jingle dress and danced in the powwows. I learned Ojibwe from my grandparents.*[13]

Several generations had, by now, grown up with little knowledge of their native language or customs as these continued to be suppressed by the government up through the boarding school days. With the advent of the welfare system in the 1930s, even gardening and farming declined, affecting the self- sufficiency of the people.

Meanwhile, pastors and assistant pastors came and went, leaving their imprint on St. Mary's Church, but none more lovingly than Father Thomas Borgerding, who returned from St. John's in 1944 to celebrate his diamond jubilee. The old missionary was still "hale and hearty" at

Sister Adelma Roers, OSB, serves a young patron in the Mission store.

Sister Thea Grieman, OSB, leads a group of songsters (1956).

Sister Valois Barthel, OSB, supervises a baking project (1956).

Father Thomas Borgerding, OSB, celebrates his Diamond Jubilee, February 13, 1944, with Bishop Francis Schenk. Top row (far right): Father Egbert Goeb, OSB; (next to Bishop): Father Aldrich Huhne, OSB; (behind Father Thomas): Brother William Borgerding, OSB; (cross bearer): Quentin Fairbanks.

Leo Hoppe, OSB, celebrating his Silver Jubilee with members of Christ the King Church, Redby, June 9, 1943.

age eighty-three and claimed the honor of being the oldest active priest in the United States. He used no cane, wore no glasses, and took no medicine. He was known to the Indian people as the "Great Healer" because he always carried a bag of natural healing herbs with him to administer to the sick. He had continued to visit St. Mary's in the summer to offer Mass and to hear confessions in Ojibwe. In the 1940s and again in 1954, he dictated his memoirs. In these colorful reminiscences, much of the history of St. Mary's is revealed.[14]

The Benedictine brothers began coming from St. John's in 1948 to serve year-around in various capacities of mission life. One, Brother Placid Stuckenschneider, happened to be at St. Mary's in 1954 when Dr. Charles Vandersluis was conducting interviews with Father Thomas for his memoirs. Brother Placid relates the following humorous situation:

> *Father Thomas' room was next to mine. He was very hard of hearing. Dr. Vandersluis came right to his room to record his memoirs. Now Dr. Vandersluis also had a problem. He stuttered badly. One day, after many efforts to speak, I heard him finally manage to complete a sentence: 'I would like to put to you a question,' to which Thomas, probably leaning in close to hear, responded, 'Eh?' And Dr. Vandersluis had to begin all over again. I can't imagine how those two ever completed the interviews!* [15]

Interior of Christ the King Church, Redby (1957). Crucifix by Placid Stuckenschneider, OSB, presently hangs in the sisters' house at Redlake.

In 1940, a church for the people in nearby Redby became a reality. Prior to 1930, Catholics gathered about once a month in an old store in Redby to celebrate Mass with a priest from St. Mary's. Around 1930, a monetary gift was given them to build their own church, but the pastor of St. Mary's at the time was not encouraging, and a church was never built. Some time later, a member of the Red Lake Railway Company donated three lots for a church at Redby. This time, the people bought an old school house and moved it onto the lots. The building was repaired and a sanctuary and sacristy added on. On August 15, 1940, this "new" church was blessed and dedicated to Christ the King. Some fourteen families – including the Maxwells, Taylors, Donnells and Morrisons – supported the Redby church. Later, a hall was added to host dinners and social events.

Another significant event at St. Mary's Mission occurred in June 1945, when Red Lake hosted the 34th Chippewa Indian Congress. Eleven participating societies set up tents outside the church for overnight accommodations, and the usual opportunities for spiritual renewal and camaraderie were available. Father Thomas Borgerding led the prayers in Ojibwe. Main speakers for the event were Jane T. Beaulieu (who became the next president of the Congress) and Simon Spears, who later became a deacon of the Catholic Church.

The "church societies" of St. Joseph and Mary remained active throughout the 1940s. "Jane T." and Ida Blue were good organizers who also involved the children in celebrations of the church, such as making crepe paper flowers to honor the dead on All Souls' Day.

Father Florian left the Mission in 1941, and Father Leo Hoppe, OSB, became the new pastor. Father Leo was a well-liked man, zealous and kind-hearted. In July 1947 he was planning a two-car garage for the parish house and had just hired two men to tear down the old rectory north of the church for lumber. On the evening of the first day's work, Father went out to check on some disturbance near the gym. He was suddenly attacked by the two workmen, who were very intoxicated. Father was found unconscious a while later by Father Egbert. He never fully recovered from this serious injury and had to leave Red Lake that same year.

Father Benno Watrin, OSB, replaced Father Leo in October. Father

Benno was the last pastor able to understand and converse fluently with the people in Ojibwe. He has left valuable memoirs of the early days of the White Earth and Red Lake Missions, of Father Pierz, and of Ojibwe life. Father Benno had to resign due to ill health after only five years at the Mission. Father Columban Kremer, OSB, served as the next pastor until 1955.

An associate pastor change occurred in 1951, when Father Omer Maus, OSB, replaced Father Egbert. Since Father Omer's brother Celestine had a degree in animal husbandry from the University of Minnesota, he was hired to work as farm manager on the Mission farm. He joined the "crew" of Joe Kapsner, Charlie Barrett, Ivan "Happy" Andre, carpenter and handyman, Earl Downfeather, Brothers Felix Neussendorfer and Placid Stuckenschneider, OSB, and Ed Lussier, mechanic.

During this time, the dairy barn was modernized and stanchions and drinking cups added. The seventeen milk cows "increased and multiplied" to about thirty. Besides providing milk and meat for the Mission, more equipment helped produce a Grade A milk which was delivered daily to the creamery in Bemidji. Father Omer reports that the farm earned $40,000 per year from 1952 to 1954. Much of the credit for this success went to the dedicated work of the Benedictine brothers. However, not all were farmers.

Brother Placid tells about his assignment to the Mission right after art school. He was supposed to help with the farming, but, he admits, "I didn't know much about farming or about machinery. Father Egbert just told me to 'go ahead anyway!' So one day when I was supposed to cultivate the garden and didn't know what to do, he said to me, 'Just go ahead, go ahead anyway!' So I did, and the cultivator nearly dropped on his toes. I could hear the sisters in the garden laughing."

Brother Placid adds, "I was really so hungry for art that one day when I was working in the silo I started drawing on the walls covered with hoarfrost."

Luckily for Brother Placid (and the Mission), he was joined over the next few years by three brothers who did have an affinity for farming. Brother Placid was then able to "cultivate" his artistic talents, and for the next five years, between bus driving, maintenance, and some farm

Brother Placid driving the school bus (1950s).

work, he plied brush, chisel, and saw in carpentry projects. He also designed Christmas cards and newsletters, took photos, and painted. He began carving using whatever materials were at hand. For example, from the back of a discarded pew, he carved a statue of St. Joseph, the carpenter; from pieces of white oak, he carved Mary and Joseph for the sisters' chapel. He carved a cross depicting Christ the King for the church at Redby. In the 1950s, he painted the Stations of the Cross (all Indian figures) for St. Mary's Church. All of these art pieces remain in use on the Mission today.

Station of the Cross by Placid Stucken- schneider, OSB.

In 1954, Benedictine Brothers Elmer Cichy and Michael Laux teamed up with the Mission staff. They worked on the farm, did the milking, taught shop, and coached boys' athletics. Brother Elmer stayed only two years; he was supposed to get over his hay fever at Red Lake, and that didn't happen. Brother Michael, on the other hand, stayed nineteen years. He also drove the school bus and operated a ham radio as a hobby which helped him stay in touch with brother monks stationed in Puerto Rico.

In 1955, Brother William Borgerding, OSB, a nephew to Father Thomas, arrived to take over the farm, since by this time Celestine Maus was working primarily for the Red Lake Tribal government. Brother "Willy" was an experienced herdsman from St. John's. He took to the Mission's fast-growing prize Jersey herd with gusto. He also learned a lesson he would not easily forget about bulls. "One day," he relates, "this Jersey bull wouldn't move for me. I had a pitchfork so I jabbed him and he took off after me. I happened to be all taped up from an appendicitis operation. That bull hooked me under the ribs and tossed me up and down in front of a fence post. I yelled for Mike, and the bull let go. I learned NEVER to turn my eyes away from a bull for even a second!"[16]

But sometimes Brother Willy's eyes DID close for more than a second (not around bulls, of course). The men worked long hours. They were up at 4:30 a.m. for milking, Mass, breakfast, and finally for driving the school bus. "I was always sleepy," Brother Willy says. "I slept in church once during Father Alban's sermon on the Trinity. When I heard 'Father, Son and Holy Spirit,' I leaped to my feet – right there in front of everybody!"

It was a race for the brothers to get all their work done on time and to change their barn clothes for chapel ones. The abrupt switch had its side effects, Brother Placid recalls. "Once I turned around in my pew to look for my missal and saw an AIRWICK can tucked in the corner – an attempt to dispel the clinging odor that was not of sanctity," he laughs. "But it was a poor life we lived partly because the Indian people themselves lived poorly. Yet everywhere there was a sense of hospitality."

Brother Willy agrees. "The important thing we at the Mission tried to do was live the Christian life. To witness to that, not necessarily to teach people how to build or bake or make money. That's not the Indian way. The people are not attached to property or money. We learned from them, for example, how to be quiet and just sit and wait before speaking right away. They don't even believe in interfering when someone is doing something even if it's a mistake because they're great respecters of persons."

Though time was measured differently at Red Lake, and life did flow together – monks, priests, sisters, people, companionably almost like a family – there were surprises to interrupt the ordinary. "Like the time," Brother Placid notes, "that a famous skating pair came to visit. Well, we showed them around like we would anybody and gave them lunch. But they were so shocked to see our poor kitchen stove and how we had to carry coal and ashes so they gave us $300 right on the spot. Then at Christmas, a big box came from them. It was a new gas stove!"

From 1954 to 1959, the Mission published a newsletter. It was started by Brothers Placid and Elmer and was called the *Red Lake*

Herring. When the new associate, Father Alban Fruth, OSB, took over as editor the next year, the name was changed to *Red Lake Benedictine*. Brother Placid continued to contribute photos and to do the humorous cover drawings. This newsletter came out four times a year and was mailed to all friends and benefactors of the Mission.

During Father Omer's three years at St. Mary's, he enlisted the help of the Tribal Council to cover food and clothing expenses for St. Mary's School. Other agencies helped, too. The Catholic Indian Bureau and the Diocese of Crookston donated monies to help pay school bus transportation, school supplies, and teachers' salaries.

Father Omer reflects on these years at the Mission:

> *Being in Red Lake gave me a new perspective for which I am grateful. The people considered the earth sacred and I think we need to incorporate more of that thinking into Christianity. The people had always lived communally. They didn't own or sell land. Their Chief, Peter Graves, helped to keep the reservation closed. "This is Indian country," he always said.*
>
> *But the people have sadly been influenced by non-Indian ways. I remember "culture clashes" such as "bobbing" the children's hair. We did it for cleanliness' sake, but the people didn't see it that way. "Bobbed" hair was a sign of prostitution.*[17]

Father Alban took Father Omer's place in 1954. One of his first tasks was to prepare the parish history for the centennial celebration in 1958. He also ministered to both the Redby and Nebish missions and, finally, helped build a new church at Nebish, a community located just outside the reservation.

Father Alban deplored many undesirable behaviors cropping up among Red Lakers at this time, involving the use and abuse of alcohol, a lack of recreational programs for youth, and a kind of general malaise. He made this comment in 1956:

> *The most important source of income for many families is work in the lumber mill at Redby; the average pay is $1.50 an hour or $300 per month. Commercial fishing affords seasonal employment to others; when conditions are right, the top pay is $100 a week. Old age pension and*

(Above) One of Brother Placid Stucken-schneider's humorous cover cartoons appearing on the Red Lake Benedictine for March 1958. Food preparation, even canning bear meat, was not an unusual task for students at St. Mary's as shown here (left) in a 1941 demonstration at the Annual Achievement Program. Students are Vivian and Marian Beaulieu.

Legion of Mary meeting (1956) with Brother
Michael Laux, OSB (top left) and Brother Elmer
Cichy, OSB (far right)

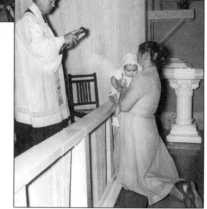

Father Alban Fruth, OSB,
administers a baptism (ca
1957).

Mission School girls picking up potatoes (1952).

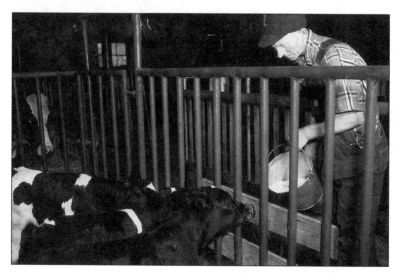

Brother Willy Borgerding, OSB, feeding the calves (1949).

Father Omer Maus, OSB.

Ed Lussier, Mission mechanic (1959).

Celestine "Celly" Maus with a big catch!

Joseph Kapsner and school children picking up potatoes (1956).

ST✦MARY'S✦IN

1955 View of the Mission by Placid Stuckenschneider, OSB.

veterans' benefits help some. Mothers with dependent children get ADC from the government. Most families are large (5-10) and don't raise their own vegetables so must resort to the local welfare agency and other charitable institutions.

The local hospital, Indian Agency, public school, police and road maintenance departments employ a limited number of Indians . . . .

. . . The few professional people such as nurses, teachers and office workers have to go elsewhere for work. There are seventy-eight men and women in the U.S. armed forces.

Much remains to be done to develop the natural resources, to establish industries, to improve law enforcement, to develop civic-minded leaders before the Indian people will enjoy the amenities of life to which they have a right. [18]

Sometimes those who chose to leave the reservation in search of better work or educational opportunities, returned, unprepared to meet the predominating non-Indian lifestyle of urban America; or they remained in the big cities and accepted substandard housing. Leon Cook, having attended St. Mary's School, St. John's University, and the University of Minnesota, chose to remain in the Cities (Minneapolis/St. Paul) to help Indian people there adjust and find work. He observed that for people used to living communal lives (Indian tradition), working in a competitive system was very difficult.

At St. Mary's Mission School, the "golden age" of the 1950s happily continued to bear fruit. Enrollment topped 254 during the 1955-56 school year. Stephanie Cobenais, a student at the time, describes the atmosphere:

Along with academics, we girls had sewing and cooking classes. The boys had shop (carpentry). All grades attended daily Mass and we sat by grades. If you were in the chorus, you got to go upstairs and sing Latin like crazy! There were a lot of us in the chorus from all grades, boys and girls.

During gym classes we square danced together. The big orchestra was declining but we still did elaborate Christmas plays.

The hot noon meal was still the main meal of the day for most of us.

We really had fun picking potatoes all day. Girls got to bring pants to school to wear in the fields (see photo on p. 126). We'd have cold sand-

wiches for lunch. A real treat and break in the routine.

We all knew Sister Adelma. She knew all of us, who we were related to, who our family members were . . . . I remember how displeased and disappointed she was to hear of a family in Red Lake who had a baby shower for a child born to a single mother. Sister thought this was encouraging the breakdown of the family.[19]

During this decade, the Mission farm and dairy reached an all-time high in production. One hundred eighty acres of arable land were in use. And the church received a face-lifting: its wood burning heating system was overhauled and a ventilating system installed; interior remodeling and painting were completed with Brother Placid's creative brush; and a new electric organ was purchased to enhance congregational singing. The steadfast adult choir, including Joe Kapsner, Sister Valois, Jane T. Beaulieu and Simon Spears, continued song leadership under the direction of Sisters Genevieve and Thea.

Other improvements took place. Celestine Maus maintained his interest in the Mission even after he was appointed Credit Officer for the Red Lake Indian Agency. He worked cooperatively with Peter Graves to support the school. He was instrumental in connecting the Mission to the public water system and in having the road tarred near the church and school at the same time the reservation roads were done.

Then, on the evening of June 16, 1956, catastrophe struck. Someone broke into the granary and set off a gasoline explosion, igniting a turbulent fire. Strong winds fanned the flames toward a nearby, newly constructed machine shed. Everyone worked together to drag out machinery. The Red Lake fire department finally gained control of the shed fire, but by midnight the granary lay in ashes along with nearly all the grain and corn and feed-grinding equipment. The buildings were not covered by insurance, and the total loss was estimated near $7000.

The end of this school year also marked the termination of ninth grade, due to insufficient finances and personnel. As smoke from the smoldering grain continued to rise over the summer, painting was done and repairs were made on the school, church, and convent with funds donated by parishioners, and another granary was hastily erected to contain the fall harvest.

Francis J. Schenk, Bishop of Crookston, with Thomas Borgerding, OSB (ca 1954).

In August a new pastor, Father Cassian Osendorf, OSB, arrived to help lift the spirits of the disheartened people with a spark of fresh energy for building, renovating, and community bonding. Two hundred thirty students enrolled for the 1956-57 school year, and the church census revealed a Catholic population of 1,587 on the reservation .

But before the year ended, another sad event took place. On November 27, 1956, the beloved old missionary priest, Father Thomas, died at St. John's Abbey in Collegeville. He was ninety-five years old. Word spread among the people: Kitchi Akiwensi, "Great Old Man," is dead!

Just three months earlier, Father Thomas had written to Father Alban lamenting the fact that he would probably not be able to get to Red Lake as usual that summer "without bothering anybody"; that is, without having to ask someone for help. But he carefully pointed out that there were still "several dozen Catholic Indians [at Red Lake] who understood very little English," and he assured Father Alban that even though he could not hear well or "preach loud," he could still speak well and he hoped that the "holy angels would arrange this affair" as they usually did![20]

The angels did – but with a bit different itinerary. Perhaps this time, they accompanied the venerable priest over Red Lake and heavenward, leaving blessings behind: blessings of devoted love and an indefatigable spirit.

CHAPTER 8

COMMUNITY AND COMMITMENT
(1957-1974)

A S WINTER TURNED TO SPRING, 1957, another loss in the Red Lake community affected many, including members of St. Mary's. "Chief" Peter Graves died on March 14th. He had always been a faithful friend and supporter of the Mission.

Born at Red Lake, Peter Graves held a long record of service to his people. He had served as secretary-treasurer of the General Council of the Red Lake Band of Chippewa Indians until his death. Mr. Graves' reputation for affirming justice and for preserving Ojibwe heritage was admirable.

After his death, Peter's son Joseph succeeded him in office and served as chairman

Chief Peter Graves (right) confers the honorary name of "Bishigandagogishig," (Beautiful Day) upon Bishop Francis Schenk of Crookston (1950s).

of the General Council. But a few months later, Joseph died, and the succession of leadership passed on to his son, Byron Graves.

For some Red Lakers, opposition arose regarding this form of leadership by succession. Concern for what might be considered family dominance and/or some illegal dismissals spurred an investigation by the U.S. Department of the Interior and a call for a reform of the original 1918 Constitution.

The reservation was subsequently divided into four electoral districts. On May 22, 1958, a seven-member constitutional committee was chosen and a new constitution drawn up. On January 6, 1959, an election was held for members of a new Tribal Council. Roger Jourdain (Gwanannish, "Eagle Flying in the Wind") was elected chairman.

This new form of Tribal Council by popular election gave all enrolled members of the Red Lake Band greater opportunities as well as responsibilities for involvement while reaffirming the undivided status of tribal property. In 1957, the Red Lake Band resided on 407,668 acres of reservation land along with 156,698 acres of restored ceded land in the northern part of the state.

At St. Mary's Mission, some changes were also underway. A growing problem with the older east section of the parish cemetery prompted some action. Brush and trees and weeds had overrun the area with years of neglect. Mounds of dirt and tumbled tombstones made the ground uneven and difficult to mow. Father Cassian, as pastor, felt a need to clean the cemetery up and make it easier to maintain. He explained:

> I wanted to level [the cemetery] with the mower and chopper to make it easier for cutting and taking care of. We had several meetings about it and good turnouts among the people – like forty-five or fifty adults. At first they didn't like the idea. Then I said, "What should we do, Bill?" [McGraw]. So they voted for it.
>
> First we began brush cutting and took out the trees. A few came to help but when no one else came, I was irritated. Then we took the old fence down. We took the top stones off so we could level the earth. We measured and marked everything so we'd know right where to put the stones again. We took the base stones out and loaded them in the woods.

*Steve Cobenais from the highway department wanted to put them along
the road by the lake where it was washing out. This made some people
angry. But there was no desecration since these were only the base stones.
The stones with the names on are there in the ground. We laid them flat
for cutting and maintaining the cemetery. They are probably buried
under now with ground and grass.*[1]

Unrest regarding what may have happened at the cemetery lingered for several years. Then, in 1993, a critical article against Father Cassian and the cemetery issue appeared in *The Native American Press.*[2] Questions were raised again. At this time, Brother Placid Stuckenschneider, who had worked at the Mission in the early 1950s, wrote the following response:

*... What happened shouldn't have happened, but ... let me try to clear
up a few points. ... Father Cassian, with the help of a few of the Native
Americans from the parish who showed up such as the Fullers and Bill
McGraw, cleaned up the weeds and brush so that one man on a tractor
and mower could keep the grounds clean. I am sure some of the graves
lost name tags and location in the process. This was not good, but it
wasn't desecration. ... There were no graves "plowed up". ...*[3]

Encouraged by Father Cassian's explanation of events, a search for the long-buried grave stones commenced in the summer of 1993. Leonard Donnell and Mike Branchaud prodded the earth with an iron rod and uncovered several stone markers. Then, with the help of volunteers from three parishes in South Bend, Indiana, about fifty markers were unearthed and repositioned. The volunteers prepared a stone memorial in the center of this part of the cemetery where all the names of those known to be buried at the site were listed. More markers will probably still be found.

On October 3, 1993, Bishop Victor Balke from Crookston, Abbot Timothy Kelly, OSB, from St. John's, representatives from the Sisters of the Order of St. Benedict at St. Joseph, the pastor, Msgr. William Mehrkens, and parishioners held a reconciliation and rededication service for this part of the cemetery. Abbot Timothy addressed the group:

*Some years ago an astronaut flew high above the earth, looked back
at the "beautiful planet," and had the conversion experience of his life*

when he suddenly knew that the earth and all creation is one. Many centuries ago, men and women stood on this continent, looked at the earth around them, at the people living with them, at the hills, the clouds, the blue sky, and the night sky, and came to the same conclusion: the earth and all creation is one.

Today, many people look upon the same reality of earth, sea, hills, mountains, clouds, stars, sky – but fail to see creation in its oneness, or men and women as their brothers and sisters, or interdependence as the ground of peace.

An astronaut in the silence of space finally listened deeply enough to hear the Spirit speaking through creation. Centuries ago the Anishinabe of this continent listened deeply and heard together the Spirit speaking through creation. Today, because you have been patient with us we are learning to listen deeply with you to the Spirit speaking through creation telling us we are all one. And if we would continue to hear the Spirit making known to us all that God has taught, then we will do it with you or not hear at all!

My Benedictine heritage tells me in the very first word of The Rule of St. Benedict *to "Listen." Today I come to confess that we have heard only partially, and because of our arrogance and pride we have not listened to the Spirit speaking through your experience, your suffering, your silence. Those of you who remember men like Fathers Thomas Borgerding, Egbert*

Abbot Timothy Kelly, OSB, blesses the newly dedicated East cemetery – 1993.

Goeb, Leo Hoppe, Benno Watrin, and Brother Julius Beckermann know
we have not been entirely deaf. But you, and now we, also know that par-
tial hearing has been responsible for deep hurts and even painful insults.

The forgiveness the gospel proclaims in Jesus Christ also demands of
me and those I represent here today that in their name I ask of you for-
giveness for past wrongs, prayer that our reconciliation will be real, and
hope that one day together we will live in peace in the reign of God when
our oneness is made evident by the sharing of the one Great Spirit. May
the one event of a past wrong against you committed by us that brings
us together today now symbolize our sorrow for all acts of unlistening that
we have been guilty of. May we all be one as indeed is the call of God, so
that the world might know their hope, too, in Jesus Christ our Lord.

Refurbishing the cemetery was not the only
project begun that summer of 1957. Father
Cassian also began excavation of the church
basement in order to provide more secure
footing for the building. Until then, fieldstone
footing had held up the church. This basement never became much more than a stor-
age area and was often wet and damp. Father
described the process:

Bill McGraw and I did the work. We used a
scraper and old tractor to haul out the gravel (a
donated dump-truck deposited the ground on the
pasture where a skating rink was being built). We

Cassian Osendorf, OSB.

put in new walls. We used a wooden form to pour the cement. Mrs.
McGraw (and others) helped mix the cement. We had a good time work-
ing together but it took several years. The south end was the last to do. We
cut down the red clay and pulled dirt out from inside with a cable.

By August 1957, another project at Red Lake was completed. Erwin F.
Mittleholtz, president of the Beltrami County Historical Society, published his book, *Historical Review of the Red Lake Indian Reservation*. The
book commemorated one hundred years of Ojibwe history at Red Lake.

At St. Joseph, Minnesota, the Benedictine Sisters were also observing their 100-year history of ministry to the people of Minnesota,

including seventy years to the people of Red Lake. A delegation of parishioners from St. Mary's attended the celebration along with Fathers Cassian and Alban.

Father Alban, meanwhile, was deeply engrossed in writing the history of St. Mary's for its own upcoming centennial. His ability to read nine languages was a great boon to his work. Research took him to Michigan to the grave of early missionary Bishop Frederic Baraga and to an examination of the first Ojibwe hymn book compiled by Baraga; to original historical sources of Monsignor John L. Zaplotnik; to first-hand encounters with Father Thomas Borgerding, Peter Graves, Ed Lussier, Jane T. Beaulieu, Joe Kapsner, Father J.B. Tennelly of the Bureau of Catholic Indian Missions, Roger Jourdain and other significant contemporaries.

A good harvest in the fall of 1957 from the 325-acre farm along with "favorable publicity" awarded the Jersey herd buoyed up the spirits of the Mission.[4] A fire-proof shed was also under construction to house newly purchased fire fighting equipment in case of an emergency such as experienced the year before.

The future looked promising as some 260 students filed into St. Mary's School that September, committed to another year of studies. A new school bus was purchased with generous donated monies, spelling "comfort" to Father Alban and Brother Mike who had been driving buses destined, they said, to "break down any time on account of old age!"[5] Regarding bus service, Brother Michael reminisces: "You know, we never missed a day of school because of weather. It could be 50° below zero but those little kids would be standing out there waiting for the bus!"

In 1958, Brother Dunstan Nordick, OSB, joined the Mission staff for one year. He brought with him his expertise as a ham radio operator, joining forces with Brother Mike.

The big event of 1958 was, of course, the Centennial set for August 15th, the Feast of the Assumption of the Blessed Virgin Mary, the day on which Father Lawrence Lautischar had arrived at Red Lake in 1858: the official establishment of St. Mary's Mission Church.

As Father Alban's manuscript, 147 typed, double-spaced pages, neared completion, it was scrutinized by Bishop Francis J. Schenk of

Bishop Francis Schenk offers the Pontifical High Mass at the Mission's Centennial celebration , August 15, 1958.

1858   1958

CENTENNIAL

Crookston, who made several suggestions for change. These changes involved casting a softer light on controversial figures who "had much clay on their feet," such as Father Tomazin, Father Thomas Borgerding, and Father Simon Lampe. The bishop suggested the "shortcomings" of these men be simply referred to in footnotes which could be researched further by anyone who cared to.[6]

Father Alban said that he felt "neutral about the whole thing" and added in retrospect that "history should be truthful and there are always two sides."[7] In addition, he prepared a 16 mm. colored movie of the people and the activities on the Mission, accompanied by Ojibwe music.[8]

Other preparations for the 1958 Centennial included an abundance of food, which, Father Alban attested, "we were eating for weeks" afterwards. Roger Head was the main speaker of the day. But after all the visitors had gathered, the crowd was small, and both Fathers Cassian and Alban expressed disappointment.

At 6 p.m., a festive Mass was celebrated outdoors in front of the old boys' building. Bishop Francis J. Schenk of Crookston was the presider, with Abbot Baldwin Dworschak, OSB, of St. John's Abbey as homilist. It was a day to give thanks and renew commitments.

Because he was school superintendent, Father Alban's interests lay with the education of the children and the ongoing education of the teachers. He took them to observe other Indian schools, including those at Pipestone, Yankton, Watertown, Bismarck and even into Canada. At the close of each school year, he also liked to take the children with perfect attendance on a trip.

Sister Herbert Dehler, OSB, superior, principal, and upper grade teacher at this time, voices regret, however, regarding the lack of teacher preparedness for Indian culture: "We didn't teach Indian ways in school. We didn't know any. And we didn't have parent-teacher meetings nor did we visit the homes. But I felt a need for that. I found people eating from one big kettle and living in one room. They were very poor and slept on the floor. They carried their water to their homes from far away. Other homes, on the other hand, were different. But I think we failed the Indians by insisting on our way of life instead of seeing how they lived."[9]

Father Alban, who picked the children up by bus and knew where families lived, agreed: "It takes special training to minister to the Indian people and we never got any training in mission work. That definitely was a mistake. On the other hand, Father Thomas was an extraordinary missionary."[10]

Sister Louise Koltes, OSB, taught the primary grades during the late 1950s. She explains:

> *I was not prepared to meet the Indian culture either. I actually never thought about the people as being different. But I was told to "keep the children in line; don't let them get out of hand!" That scared me and colored my way of thinking about the people. But I soon learned that these were the kind of people who didn't need "control" like that. The children were very quiet until you became more acquainted. They loved to play ball at recess and always had a good time. Many, I hoped, would go on to Catholic high schools.*[11]

Some of the children did, often through the instrumentality of their teachers and principals. At this time these included:

Leon Cook, Roger Head, and Duane Lussier to St. John's;
Gladys Hill, Stephanie Cobenais, Georgia Fairbanks, Judy Lawrence, Sandy DeFoe, and Maryilyn Head to St. Benedict's;
Sharon Donnell and Lorena Hansen to Little Falls;
Ruth Strong, Gerald Beaulieu, Gerald Sayers, Bruce Sayers, Bernadine Beaulieu, Leo Downwind, Mitchel Gurno, Cheryl Stately, and Harold Cobenais to Marty, SD.

In 1962, Sister Aniceta Drontl, OSB, returned to the Mission as superior, principal, and upper grade teacher for the next six years. From her "Faculty Handbook," one learns that attending Mass was still a daily expectation of pupils; modern math was "in" as well as Junior Great Books. Emphasis was placed on cooperative effort in forming a Christian atmosphere ". . . wherein pupils may learn by example, by guidance, and by practice, the intellectual and moral values"; and any kind of physical discipline, ridicule, sarcasm or other types of personal indignities were to be avoided.[12]

But parents and home remained the primary educators. Here children learned the way of their people and expressed this in their relationships with one another and with their teachers.

Sister Catherine (Loretta) Ludwig, OSB, who taught fifth and sixth grades in the late 1950s notes that her students possessed a non-competitive quality and wouldn't "show a classmate up" by raising their hands even if they knew the right answer. Qualities of communal living were evident in the classroom, she says: "The children were not trained to be capitalists; they enjoyed a simple lifestyle among themselves."[13]

Brother Willy also relates, "Children weren't spanked at home. Instead, they were given a stare by their parents which hurt more because it meant a breach of love. Children were sent off for awhile in those days to find out who they were."[14]

Brother Gregory Eibensteiner, OSB, who spent several months at the Mission in 1957, recalls that hospitality was also a basic element of the people's lives. "Even if families were poor," he says, "they shared. Many a cold bean sandwich I ate when I'd bring a sick child home on the bus."[15]

As the years progressed, teachers became more attuned to Indian ways and culture. Native arts and music, especially beadwork and dance, were incorporated into the curriculum.

Meanwhile, some physical improvements were being made around the Mission. In the summer of 1959, the church foundation and vestibule were completed; only the basement floor needed finishing. In the convent, a walk-in freezer was added (in place of one of the men's dining rooms) through the instrumentality of Sister Mary John Sweeney, OSB, who came to help out for a year. This new freezer was an important addition as food service continued to be a major commitment. In addition to the 200 plus children at noon, there were the regular meals for monks, sisters, hired men, and guests.

The bunk house offered overnight accommodations for visitors. Sister Louise Koltes will never forget the time two of her newly-married sisters stopped by to see her on their honeymoon. "When it came time to go to bed," she laughs, "they went to the 'guest rooms' in the bunk house next to the chickens. In the morning they had no trouble waking up by the chickens and always remembered their honeymoon at Red Lake!"

At this time, the Mission gardens extended from the church to the present convent garage and out toward Highway 1. Beyond the tall pine trees, potato and corn fields covered what is now the site of the hospital and nursing home complex. The Mission still butchered its own beef, hogs, and chickens, and people often contributed venison and fish. The new walk-in freezer was a great blessing for food preservation. The community of Red Lake also benefited when hunters got moose in the hot weather and were able to store their meat here temporarily.

Government commodities for the children's meals included butter and cheese but not many vegetables; thus, the "kitchen garden" was very important. Sister Loretta (DePorres) Rothstein, OSB, recalls how careful she had to be with the food served the children, making sure they got their proper vitamins and minerals. "Inspectors popped in anytime during the year to check on things," she says.[16]

While Sister Mary John was at St. Mary's, she was "chauffeur" for the sisters since most of them weren't driving yet and depended upon the priests or brothers for transportation. But in the early 1960s, other sisters became involved. Sister Louise remembers her driving lessons from Father Alban, who had received permission from the Reverend Mother at St. Joseph for three sisters to learn to drive in 1962: "I learned to back up on the playground by making figure eights around the bushes. Then Father had me go through a plowed field so I'd know what it would be like in winter on slippery roads!"

In order to smooth out other bumps in mission living and help the work run more easily, Abbot Baldwin Dworschak, OSB, of St. John's wrote to Father Cassian suggesting that ". . . one person be responsible for all the work at Red Lake whether it is the work of the parish or the work of the mission."[17] The previous custom of dividing the work of the church and the school/farm between pastor and associate was thus abolished. With this new arrangement, everything was brought "under one umbrella," so to speak, with Father Cassian ultimately responsible – even for the assignment of work to the new associate, Father Adrian Foxxe, OSB.

Father Adrian had come to St. John's from Iowa and was of Cherokee lineage. A quiet, gentle person, he served the Mission from 1960 to 1965, ministering to the church at Nebish, making trips to the Twin Cities and St. John's to pick up clothing for the Mission store, carrying on correspondence with donors, and extending Mission communication via his ham radio.

During Father Cassian's time at St. Mary's, much was done to unite the spirit of the Mission. "We did things together," Brother Michael explains. "For example, when we butchered, everyone helped but Sister Johnette was in charge. Sister Gudilia was great in making things homey. Father Cassian didn't tell us what to do. He pitched in and so did we all. This was his accomplishment. It was a good feeling to be 'one'."[18]

Father Cassian's language could be rough and gruff yet "his bark was worse than his bite." He was an independent, wholehearted, and supportive man. He was later to say of himself, "I'm going to express myself. I have lots of opinions. I have lots of ideas – but I don't have all the answers."[19] He enjoyed teasing. He loved to hunt and fish, and his quarry, unplucked and often uncleaned, was usually dropped on the convent porch for the next meal!

Sister Madonna Niebolte, OSB, who taught sixth and seventh grades, recalls a time in the late 1960s when several sisters went with Father Cassian and an Indian guide to pick blueberries. "We left the car," she relates, "and got on a hay rack until it had a flat tire. Then we wandered off picking berries and Sister Aniceta got lost. Father Cassian shot off the gun to help her locate us. It worked but she said to the sisters afterwards, 'See that you hang on to a rope when you go berry picking because you'll either get lost or meet a bear!'"[20]

In 1965, the Jersey dairy herd, the financial mainstay of the Mission for almost seventy-five years, came to an end. The herd was sold, "piece by piece," Brother Willy laments. "It just didn't pay anymore and it was a lot of work." Over the next ten years, the Mission tried to substitute raising chickens and selling eggs, but this endeavor never measured up to the financial support the herd had once been.

Brother Willy departed, too, in 1966, for St. John's, where he started work as night watchman with the University campus security while continuing woodworking. Brother Dunstan Nordick returned to the Mission in 1967 for a second time.

Other changes at St. Mary's included a new associate pastor, Father

Sister Louise Koltes, OSB, playing ball with her students (ca 1958). [Photo: Sister Louise Koltes, OSB]

Four-room addition to the Mission School, 1966.

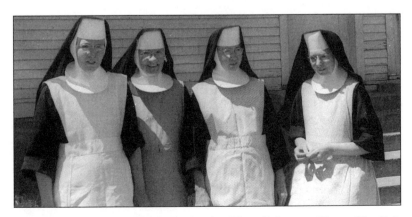

Sisters Loretta (De Porres) Rothstein, Thea Grieman, Karen Nordick and Frances Lorraine Eisenschenk, OSB (1959).

Brother Julius Beckermann,
OSB, collecting eggs, 1973.
[Photo: Julius Beckermann,
OSB]

(Right) Brother Michael
Laux, OSB, with St. Mary's
basketball team (ca. 1970).

Benedictine Sisters Benet Frandrup
and Lynette Primus try out the new
snowmobile, 1970. [Photo: Michael
Laux, OSB]

Fathers Adrian Foxxe, Cassian Osendorf,
and Brother "Willy" Borgerding, OSB, with
"Princess Kay of the Milky Way" during a
visit at the 4th of July Powwow (ca 1962).

(Right) Sister Johnette
Kohorst, OSB.

Maurice Hurrle, OSB, in 1965; the departure of Joe Kapsner for a nursing home after more than thirty years of service; and the death of Bill
McGraw at age fifty-eight. These would be missed. Bill had sung in the
parish choir. He had helped raise money for the parish by putting on
music shows; the pews in church were purchased this way.

In the early 1960s, Father Cassian was busy with building plans for
a four-room addition to the school. Money from the sale of the dairy
herd along with a $1000 donation from the Tribal Council gave this pro-
ject a "quick start."

The addition would replace the old boys' building to the west which
had served the school well for over a half century. It would cost about
$45,000. According to Celestine Maus, much of the labor on the new
addition was donated by Sister Valois' relatives (Sister Valois had spent
a total of twenty-eight years at the Mission). Sister Thea reports that
religious medals were laid in the northwest corner of the foundation by
Sister Edna Rader, OSB, who was serving the Mission as housekeeper
and kitchen assistant at the time.

In November 1965, the fireproof, cement block addition was completed and ready for classes. At an open house held January 23, 1966,
Father Cassian expressed his thanks to the Tribal Council for their
monetary gift toward the new building, saying, "The thing that pleases
me most about this contribution is the fact that it was made as a memorial to the former Father Borgerding, OSB, who worked here so long
and who had such a deep, lasting affection for the
Indian people."[21]

Another renovation was soon under way in the
convent. The dorm on third floor at the south end
was transformed into individual bedrooms for the
sisters – a welcome improvement.

In 1968, Father Ignatius Candrian, OSB,
arrived at St. Mary's as associate pastor to replace
Father Maurice.[22] He served as bookkeeper, ministered to Nebish, and helped with Masses at
Christ the King in Redby. He also worked hard on
the farm and took great pride in the corn he
raised. "Iggie," as he was affectionately called,

Ignatius Candrian, OSB

dearly loved the children and was, in turn, loved by all.

Brothers Mike and Dunstan were busy caring for the 2000 hens housed in the renovated horse barn and selling the eggs at stores in Redlake and Redby. Potatoes remained an important crop which the children still helped harvest. Sister Johnette Kohorst, OSB, in charge of the kitchen, said, "Everyone helped at harvest time. We froze corn and had a big raspberry patch. We were a community. Only the two dogs didn't get along: our German Shepherd DUKE and the barn dog JAKE. But that changed, too, when DUKE was hit by a car one day and JAKE brought him to our back door, barked and walked off!"[23]

Changes in mission and school life impacted the lives of the people, but none perhaps as keenly as the changes in Church worship after Vatican Council II in 1965. The Liturgical Movement in America had already helped deepen among many Catholics the importance of Christian living and of liturgical ideals in the celebration of the Mass and feastdays. Now, as the Church called the laity to greater participation in liturgical events and a return to the roots of religious custom and tradition, a new spiritual renewal was also begun at St. Mary's. The Mass was celebrated in English; lay lectors were prepared to do the readings (Judy Roy was the first lay lector, a service she continues today along with several other parishioners); congregational singing was furthered; the old altar was removed and a new one installed (designed by Brother Placid) to face the people.

In their everyday lives, Red Lakers continued to observe the traditional ways of fishing, hunting, powwows, berry picking, and making maple sugar. But earning an adequate living was still difficult. Leon Cook, who had spent several years in tribal development, suggests that it was the paternalistic efforts of the federal and tribal governments to create and control jobs that kept the people from creating their own, motivated by profit. "People should go into business to make money," he challenged.[24]

The Red Lake Fisheries Association had developed as a cooperative enterprise which returned its profits to the members of the Fishery Coop. It did offer a job alternative. Here, everyone worked hard, some in

walleye and white fish spawning operations, others in lake maintenance, setting
nets, or in the processing and shipping of
fish. Today, the Fishery continues to be a
sustainable asset of the people; however,
overfishing the lake has posed new problems, and commercial fishing was temporarily curtailed in 1997.

Forestry also helped play an important
part in the benefits and economy of the
reservation, offering jobs in planting, in
harvesting and marketing of Norway pine,
white pine, white spruce; in controlling forest diseases; in providing fire control; in
wildlife reporting; and in the operation of

Fish nets drying.

the Red Lake dam regulating lake levels. Truckers hauled logs to the
Redby mill, which expanded its facilities for the production of lumber.

The Red Lake Indian Hospital (built in 1914) and a Health Clinic
(1956) near the BIA headquarters employed some forty people who
ministered to the health needs of Red Lakers. After the hospital was
razed in the mid-1970s, the Tribe requested approximately sixty acres
of shoreline property no longer needed by the Mission for agriculture
purposes, to be returned to them for a new hospital and related facilities. Groundbreaking took place in 1977, and the hospital was completed in the spring of 1981. Homes for employees were built in the
same area. In 1989, the Jourdain/Perpich Extended Care Facility was
added to the hospital.

Ongoing concern for youth of the reservation precipitated the establishment of Project Headstart for pre-schoolers in the early 1960s and
provided necessary jobs for many women including Veronica "Thern"
Donnell (Hegstrom), who became a teacher with Headstart and has
remained with the program for twenty-eight years. Since 1994, Thern has
also worked as Disability and Health Coordinator at the Red Lake Center.

Judy Lawrence (Roy) returned from the College of Saint Benedict
with a major in communication and theatre and also began teaching at
Headstart. She held this position for two years and was the program's

director for twenty years. Judy also served on the parish and public school boards during these years. In 1990 she became Executive Director of Administration for the Tribal Government and served in this capacity until 1994, when she was elected Tribal Secretary.

In the 1960s and 1970s, many people of the reservation were concerned about the increase in violence and began antiviolence meetings to see what could be done. They organized various activities for youth, including alternative recreational opportunities.

Some residents of Red Lake were involved in leadership positions with the Substance-Abuse Prevention Program, the Juvenile Program, and, at Redby, the Indian Action Program, which helps train young people in vocational skills such as carpentry, electrical and heavy equipment work, and in nursing.

Leon Cook continued his work in the Twin City area helping people locate jobs and deal with alcohol problems. He supported AIM (American Indian Movement), which spoke out in the '60s and '70s against the poverty and oppression among people choosing to live off the reservation in large cities. Cook served as director of the Office of Economic Development in the United States BIA during 1970-71; as president of the National Congress of American Indians from 1971-73; and for several years as a member of the Board of Directors for the Kateri Tekakwitha Conference.

Cook attributes much of his dedication to the concerns of his people to the Benedictine influence he received during his early years as a student at the Mission School. He writes:

> *I had become part of the Benedictine community at Red Lake . . . . It was [this] sense of community with each other and us that motivated and influenced me to go to work for my Indian community and to commit myself to it.* [25]

Since 1960, another program has gained success on the reservation. This is a home-construction program known as the Red Lake Builders or Mutual Help-Housing. The program is unique in that tribal members themselves build the homes while the U.S. government grants approval and funding. This money becomes "seed" for further building. Celestine Maus did much of the initial work on this program.

As changes and commitments grew throughout the 1960s and '70s, the spirit of community continued to blossom at St. Mary's. Sister Adelma organized a group of women of the parish to help clean the church on Saturdays. She visited the homebound and those in the hospital – this, attests Brother Gregory, "long before it was the fashionable thing to do." Other sisters became involved as well. This stalwart woman also kept charge of the store until she left the Mission in 1974 at age seventy.

Sister Thea, still going strong at age seventy, began taking lessons on a guitar which Father Cassian bought her in order to accompany the congregational singing in church. "Sister Thea was my best 'mentor,'" adds Sister Jean Schwartz, OSB, second grade teacher. "She taught me much about Indian ways and how to work with the students and parents."[26] Sister Thea directed the church choir and played the organ until 1972, when she left the Mission. This choir sang for special occasions and continued the long tradition of singing Ojibwe hymns on Christmas Eve and at wakes.

Sister Benet Frandrup, OSB, became the school principal and eighth grade teacher in 1968. Around this time, the first lay teacher, Mrs. Matt Vorderbrugger, was hired to teach fourth grade. The school included more study of Ojibwe language and art, and several sisters took courses at BSU (Bemidji State University) in Indian culture or studied the language from local teachers.

In 1970, Patrick DesJarlait, a renowned Indian artist with roots at Red Lake, visited St. Mary's Mission School to teach Indian ways and to show his work. DesJarlait portrays, in a distinctive style, the culture of the Ojibwe people, which for him includes ". . . the dances, the work and play that he remembers from growing up on the Red Lake Reservation . . . the wild rice harvest, the blueberry harvest, the making of maple sugar. . . ."[27] Patrick DesJarlait's two grandsons, Chris and Michael, recently graduated from St. Mary's Mission School.

Brother Samuel Lickteig, OSB, spent 1970-71 at the Mission and taught seventh and eighth grade math on an individual basis. "He was very good," affirms Sister Madonna Niebolte, the sixth and seventh grade teacher. Brother Michael and Father Ignatius both continued the tradition of boys' basketball at the school, coaching excellent junior high squads which practiced every day and competed against nearby schools.

Brother Gregory Eibensteiner, OSB.
[Photo: Julius Beckermann, OSB]

In 1970, Brother Gregory Eibensteiner, OSB, returned to St. Mary's to serve as teacher's aide in grades four, five, and six, as school-bus driver, farmhand with the chickens, teacher of carpentry, and carpenter. He built new cabinets for the priests' dining room in the convent, completely renovating the room with carpeting and a sink. He painted the convent and changed all the windows in both school and convent buildings. Over the summers, other brothers and clerics from St. John's, as well as sisters from St. Benedict's, continued to help out on the Mission. Food still "fell from heaven"; that is, as forty ducks or so, a hundred gallons of smelt, or several squirming turtles, were deposited "miraculously" on the convent doorstep by faithful hunters. Sister Benet attests that on some Saturday afternoons, they cleaned as many as a hundred or more chickens.

There was, besides, much fun to share on the Mission. It was created, spontaneous fun, for in those days, as Brother Gregory says, "we didn't have the opportunity of going away." The sisters tell about collecting driftwood on Sunday afternoons along the lake, riding bike around town, and even snowmobiling. One year, Father Cassian received a snowmobile from a friend. It was often seen (or not seen, as the case might be) flying with a well-bundled sister or monk pilot over the frozen expanses of "Lake Borgerding" or Red Lake itself.[28] In the summertime, two Honda motorbikes brightened the road adventures of the brothers. There were, in addition, always rousing pinochle games, popcorn parties, or entertainment provided by Sister Delphine Heier, OSB, and her jolly puppets: Howdy-Doody and a pair of Mexican dancers.

In July 1971, Father Cassian wrote to Abbot Baldwin Dworschak, OSB, Abbot of St. John's, and to the Catholic Indian Bureau since they held the land title, stating that he wished to transfer several acres of property at the east end of the Mission to the Tribe for building a Law

Patrick DesJarlait displays his painting "Red Lake Fishermen." [Photo: Charmaine Branchaud]

"Fish in Birchbark Basket," by Patrick DesJarlait.

Enforcement Center. Meanwhile, the Bureau had decided that all land titles still held on reservations be transferred to the respective dioceses in which they were located. Father Cassian believed that the land in question here, no longer used for educational or religious purposes as originally specified, be given back to the Tribe. After visiting Red Lake in July, Bishop Kenneth Povish of the Diocese of Crookston granted permission to go ahead with the land transfer. In November 1971, 4.65 acres became available for the building of the new Center.[29]

In 1972, Father Cassian remodelled and painted the church and built a recreational den with a fieldstone fireplace in the rectory. He also added a kitchen. Brother Gregory says that until then, "We couldn't even cook a cup of coffee in our house!"

By the end of the year, St. Mary's 245-acre Mission complex presented a thriving appearance, with its neat frame buildings, its farm and egg business, and its school, still privately funded, providing state-accredited education to 180 youngsters, grades one through eight, along with a state-sponsored hot lunch program.

However, in the spring of 1973, word was out that Father Cassian would be leaving St. Mary's for the small mission of Naytahwausch near White Earth. He would be exchanging places with Father Adrian Foxxe, who would return to Red Lake as pastor. Brother Julius Beckermann, OSB, from St. John's would also be arriving to join Brothers Mike, Greg and Dunstan.

Thus St. Mary's bid farewell to Father Cassian with a special feast. Sister Benet remembers waking up at 3 a.m. one fine spring day as the sounds and smells of food preparation rose to her window from near the grotto. Here, a lamb and a pig, basted with "gallons of white wine," were roasting on a spit over an open fire. "It seems the whole town turned out for him," she recalls.

As a special gift, Father Cassian received lifetime privileges to hunt and fish on the reservation from the Red Lake Tribal Council. As for the independent and spirited man himself, Father Cassian reported, "I left part of my heart at Red Lake." Later, he confided that his favorite assignment had been St. Mary's Mission among the Native American people of the Red Lake Reservation.

Sister Benet also left that summer. Sister Patricia Wallis, OSB, came to take her place, her second time at the Mission. But financial worries and a shortage of teaching sisters prompted a "hard look" at the feasibility of maintaining the seventh and eighth grades. Difficult times lay ahead once more.

CHAPTER 9

CRISIS (1974-1980)

T HE DECISION TO CLOSE the seventh and eighth grades was not made lightly. Father Adrian, whose task it was, cared deeply about the children and their future. Only after several meetings with Abbot John Eidenschink of St. John's Abbey, Bishop Kenneth Povish of Crookston, and Sister Evin Rademacher, prioress of St. Benedict's Convent in St. Joseph, did the work of closing these grades begin.

Many were saddened. Parents, both Catholic and non-Catholic, regretted the loss of choice they now had on the reservation to send their young people to a school they felt offered a superior educational system. Yet it was difficult for most of them to financially support the school. Many were on a low level of economic stability.

Therefore, the spring and summer of 1974 continued goodbyes and hellos – to students, parents, and personnel.

Sister Elizabeth Theis, OSB, came to replace Sister Patricia as principal; Father Ignatius left; and a new pastor, Father Jordan Stovik, OSB, arrived. He joined Father Adrian for the next year in a "shared" pastorate of the parish.

"Financially, the parish was just about broke," Father Jordan recalls. "There were very few people in church on Sundays. This was discouraging. There was no profit from the chickens, and no money to work with in school."[1]

Brother Dunstan had begun closing off the chicken business the year before because it was not paying off. He, too, left St. Mary's in the spring of 1974. A year later, the chickens would be either sold, given away, or butchered and the farm closed.

Brother Placid returned over the summer of 1974 to help repair and paint the steeple of the church. He remembers being hoisted up in a bucket! As it swung around, he says, he'd slap on the paint. He added a new gold-plated cross to the steeple – one from the old St. John's Abbey twin towers.

Another difficult situation was pending in the parish in 1974, left over from the school year before when a seventh grader, Luanne Sigana, was struck in the head by a ball and died. Litigation continued for several years until the case was finally settled out of court.

While coping with these several anxieties, St. Mary's opened its school doors to the 1974 school year, albeit on a shoestring and counting as usual on its donors, benefactors, and sponsors. With the loss of the seventh and eighth grades, however, enrollment dropped from 186 to 150. Sister Elizabeth took up the task as the school's first full-time principal. Many items awaited addressing: financial support, school policies, an updated curriculum, and student discipline, a serious concern at the time.

Sister Jean Schwartz, OSB, who taught second grade, remembers the mood: "Teaching was hard. There were hard things happening on the reservation: alcohol, gambling, violence, even murder. Mondays were especially hard days when the children returned after a weekend of some kind of violence in the community or at home. But they were eager to learn, and I tried to make my classroom a happy and safe place for them."

Sister Elizabeth organized the first St. Mary's School Board with the hope that cooperative study and relationship might begin to remedy student problems. In a letter dated December 1975, to Sister Evin Rademacher, OSB, prioress, Stephanie Hanson, chairperson for the new School Board, summarized the necessity and significance of this organization: ". . . to share in the decision and policy-making for the Mission

School for the first time in its history." Other Board members were Judy Roy, Steve Cobenais, Charles Blanchard, Allen Lussier, Ellen Thunder (bookkeeper), and Lorena Cook.

"I also had a wonderful staff to work with," Sister Elizabeth explains.[2] Everyone worked together, becoming as involved as possible in diocesan meetings and policy-making. Some Indian culture and arts were taught with the help of Indian people; Sister particularly remembers Willa Beaulieu, who was an excellent teacher and served as a counselor in the Mission School.

Father Jordan taught religion in the first three grades and Father Adrian in the upper three. Father Jordan and Sister Jean also began teaching CCD (Confraternity of Christian Doctrine) to public school youngsters grades one through six on Thursday evenings. Father hoped to initiate an adult Bible study class as well, but this venture did not "take wings." An attempt to form a parish council was made, and those participating included Betty Beaulieu, Lucy Barrett, Joe Johns, Darlene Staberg, Jim Eisenrich, Jenny B. Hollis, and Melvina Johnson.

Confirmation was held each year for the sixth grade. Sister Dominica Freund, OSB, who taught fifth and sixth grades from 1973-1984, says, "It was a joy for me to work with the people. They were generous and kind. It was, in fact, a *privilege* to be with them!"[3]

Sister Marlene Schwinghammer, OSB, who taught first grade, adds that she enjoyed the children very much as well as the home visits she made because "people were very welcoming."[4]

Father Adrian's gentle style with the youngsters is reflected in his "Message from Father Adrian" which appeared in the November 1974 issue of *Indian Drum Beats*, the Mission School newspaper:

> We are hoping to get some paving and sidewalk work done this coming spring and summer. We have ample playground space, quite a few beautiful trees, lots of good fresh air. The great outdoors is all around us here at the Mission School and we strive to keep it beautiful and useful. . . .
>
> A great part of our education is to appreciate nature, the outdoors, whether at school, at home, or anywhere along the road. If we do our little part in keeping the world clean, it will always be beautiful for us.

Early in the summer of 1975, fire destroyed Christ the King Church at Redby. The group who attended Mass there had grown smaller over the years. Several months previously, Father Adrian had closed the church down and taken out the furnishings. After that, attempts were made by vandals to burn the building. But for those who loved Christ the King, the loss was great.

With the chickens gone and the farm machinery sold, Brothers Michael and Gregory left the Mission in 1975, returning to St. John's. Father Adrian also left. "Those were sad years," he reported. Brother Julius, who remained at St. Mary's, agrees. "It was a stormy time."

Brother Stephen Thell, OSB, joined the staff that summer as general maintenance man or "jack-of-all-trades." But in the words of Sister

Stephen Thell, OSB.

Elizabeth, Brother Stephen was "a calming and steady asset to the Mission." His workshop was in the old boys' building which was in the process of being torn down. Along with general maintenance, Brother Stephen repaired and built furniture. He made regular trips to the Twin Cities and to St. John's to pick up loads of clothing and furnishings for the Mission store. But a couple of big things, he said, stuck in his mind, like cleaning 400 fish one weekend until his fingers were sore; and watching the old barn (built in 1890) burn (by arson) several times until it was finally taken down, board by board.

Despite the difficulties of school and parish, community building continued to grow among the men and women Benedictines serving the Mission. Outside of work time, there was time taken for fun together: fishing, berry picking, volleyball, parties. Sister Marlene says, "I guess because we didn't have many other outside activities, we had to make our own fun. Our parties were the best!" Sister Jean recalls the fun of biking around town just to meet people, walking with Sister Adelma to visit patients in the hospital, or polishing up the driftwood pieces she'd collected along the lake.

"We had our own community here," Brother Gregory adds. "The

Indian people were here. We lived a very 'real' lifestyle. And the longer we stayed, the less 'different' things and people became. It was home."

An important addition to the staff in 1975 was Sister Jane Weber, OSB. She took charge of the kitchen for the year, and then began a ministry to the elderly and sick which she accomplished with great compassion and faithfulness – in addition to helping in food service – for the next thirteen years. "My best preparation for Red Lake," she says, "was my experience in Japan. I went there in 1962 not knowing the language, but I did learn enough of it *not* to impose on them but to listen."[5]

Meanwhile, Sister Elizabeth continued her search for adults from the Indian community to become involved in the school. Two lay people joined the classroom teaching staff for 1975-76: Miss Rosie Swenson in grade three, and Mr. Mike Scott in grade five. Three lay aides also worked under the Title I government program. Sister Marlene remembers Bernadine "Deanie" Bailey, her classroom aide who, she says, was "so responsible and a real role model for me." It was St. Mary's hope that more teachers would come prepared with backgrounds in human relations and an interest in working with Indian students.

Celestine Maus, 1978.

Celestine Maus, Superintendent of the BIA, Red Lake Agency, maintained a position as liaison for the Mission School. He was successful, with much work on the part of the School Board and faculty, in securing financial assistance for the school from foundations and grants. Many letters were written. With a special grant from the McKnight Foundation of $30,000 received in 1975, the school was able to buy new textbooks and build its curriculum. The grant paid for a physical education teacher, a librarian, and a teacher aide. "We could even get fun-stuff for our classes!" Sister Jean adds.

To help reduce the operating costs of the school, families not eligible for free lunch were asked to pay twenty-five cents per day. There was still no tuition charged for the children's education. The problem of financial support of the school remained.

Then, beginning in January 1976, a group of concerned parishioners organized a "Save the Mission Committee" to help sponsor fund raising activities such as weekly bingo and a fall carnival to support the school. Officers of the committee were Stephanie Hanson, chairperson; Celestine Maus, vice-chair; and John and Isabelle Hanson, co-treasurers. Members included Alma and Hubert Roy, Duane and Dorothy Cobenais, Leland Lussier, Kathleen Dudley, George Jones, Frank Lajeunesse, Betty Beaulieu, and Paul "Snuffy" Smith. Members continued to solicit funds to help the school for several years.

Other good things were taking place in the Mission School. As a result of Sister Patricia's field study dissertation done in 1973-74, students were benefiting from a holistic approach to learning based on experience and environment. Teachers focused on establishing a broader cultural atmosphere. A study of Ojibwe arts and crafts, music and language continued, and Indian adults were invited to share their teaching with the children. Students enjoyed participating in the traditional maple syrup gathering activities in spring and powwow dancing on their Indian Heritage Day. Mini courses of specialized study were also introduced in school for the first time in February 1976.

That summer, Father Jordan left St. Mary's. He was replaced by Father Peter St. Hilaire, OSB. The plague of financial and other parish worries prompted Father Peter to share his frustrations with the prior at St. John's: "Red Lake is an island and St. Mary's Mission is an island on the island," he wrote.[6] Father Peter felt that unless the people took on more financial responsibility for the operation of the school, it would have to continue being subsidized. This could be a long struggle.

At one time, during the financial crisis, Roger Jourdain, Tribal Chairman and advocate of education, offered to take the school over, but this did not meet with the approval of St. Mary's School Board, the diocesan superintendent, or the Red Lake community who wished to continue providing a Catholic environment for the education of their youth.

Father Peter did believe in the presence of the Benedictines at Red Lake and further wrote: "I am totally convinced that the Catholic school at Redlake is of more influence in the cause of Christ at this time than any other institution."[7]

The school year of 1976-77 opened with an enrollment of 141 students. Special services were offered under Title I, including that of a psychologist and community health and drug awareness programs. Cooperative relationships in several areas, including bussing, were continued with the Public School Board and the State Department of Education. Through the National School Lunch Program, children eligible for free lunch were served breakfast in school. Sister Jane and Sister Elizabeth coordinated this service, followed later by Sister Dorothy Ann Marx, OSB, and Sister Emerentia Fleischhacker, OSB.

In October 1976, the Mission School held its first Marathon for Catholic Education. Contributions were solicited from everyone. It was a fund raiser of pure profit. Sister Marcella Weber, OSB, fourth and fifth grade teacher, remembers "tackling" her friends, family, and even her doctor and dentist for dollar pledges. Brother Julius wrote to his old high school classmates. Sister Barbara Zinzer, OSB, who taught special reading classes, says that even the bears got caught up in the spirit and were seen lumbering along ahead of the walkers on the Marathon route!

Other new faces appeared at the Mission during the 1976-77 school year. Sister Gretchen Yanz, OSB, served as school secretary and as a resource person for helping locate sources of income. She made an 8mm. movie of the apostolate at the Mission. Sister Loretta Rothstein returned for a second time to the Mission to take charge of the store.

Sister Kayleen (Sharon) Nohner with CCD class. Early 1980s. [Photo: Julius Beckermann, OSB]

"One day," she laughs, "Duffy Fuller came in and asked me, 'Whatever happened to Sister DePorres? We liked her so much.' So I told her . . . I had changed my name and my headdress. It was quite a joke!"

Sister Kayleen (Sharon) Nohner, OSB, also came in 1976 to teach second grade. During the 1977-78 school year, she began setting up a released-time religious education program, funded by the Diocese of Crookston, for public school youngsters, kindergarten through ninth grade. The children were bussed to and from public school by Mission bus. Classes first met in the church basement and then in the choir loft. "It was a struggle to start," she recalls.[8]

Sister Kayleen is considered the first full-time religious education coordinator for youth in the parish. While engaged in this work, she also taught the religion classes of the lay teachers at St. Mary's School. In 1978, she expanded her ministry to include other social services on the reservation, such as AA, the Rehab in the hospital, and a women's support group. She felt it important to speak to the spiritual needs of the people, especially adults, and to address such topics as stability, responsibility, and identity. Just to be present in the significant parts of people's lives, she says, "to walk with them in their pain" was important to her. That is why she chose to broaden the concerns of the parish to include health and other issues.

When the school children began eating their lunch in school in 1982, Sister Kayleen transformed the vacated student dining room in the convent building into a religious education room. The program then took on a feeling of permanence.

A significant auxiliary to Sister Kayleen's staunch teaching efforts for all the released-time students was the bus driving of Brother Julius, who some days might have felt that he wore out the road between the

Sister Patricia Wallis, OSB, with students Desmond and Rhonda (1980),

Sister Delphine Heier, OSB. [Photo: Julius Beckermann, OSB]

1978. (Left to right): Row 1: Sisters Delphine Heier, Jane Weber, Lucy Revering; Row 2: Caroline Eckroth, Marlene Schwinghammer, Dominica Freund; Standing: Dorothy Ann Marx, Loretta Rothstein; Row 3: Emerentia Fleischhacker, Elizabeth Theis, Constette LeFevere, Marcella Weber.

Sisters Jean Schwartz, Dominica Freund and Elizabeth Theis share a lighter moment. (1975). [Photo: Michael Laux, OSB]

"We hold its future in our hands."

(Left) Religious Education coordinators: Sisters Annette Fernholz, SSND, and Laurita Wydra, SSS. (Right) Sister Mary Minette ("M&M"), OSB, with a sweet treat!

public school and the Mission on his shuttle runs.

Other full-time religious education coordinators followed Sister Kayleen: Sister Regina Haag, OSB (Watertown, SD) from 1982-84; Sister Nancy Boushey, OSB (Crookston) from 1984-86; Sister Laurita Wydra, SSS (Los Angeles, CA) from 1987-1990; Sister Annette Fernholz, SSND (Mankato) from 1990-1993; Ms. Bonnie Moen of nearby Kelliher, 1993-94; and Mrs. Anita Wheatley (Golden Valley, Minneapolis) 1996-97.

As Sister Jane (and Brother Julius) began doing more home visiting and tending to the spiritual life of the parish, Sister Lucy Revering, OSB, came aboard to acquaint herself with the kitchen work. She stayed from 1976 to 1982. Several women from Red Lake helped her in the kitchen with the hot lunch preparation. These included Theresa Lussier, Vange Donnell, Helen Greene, and Patsy Blue. Food was prepared for about 150 students and the staff of priests, brothers, and sisters.

Sister Lucy loves to tell many "hare-raising" stories about life at the Mission. However, not all involved rabbits – though she prepared several of these for meals. There were porcupine and the usual deer, moose, bear, turtle, and fish. But one PIG story begs to be repeated:

> One day a Red Lake man told me, "I can get you a pig real cheap." "Good," I said and we went out to a farm in his van. I thought the pig would be all ready to take home and freeze. Well, we looked at all the pigs hoofing around in the pen and he said, "Which one do you want?" I was flabbergasted, so I just pointed anywhere. The farmer shot the pig, and since my friend had a bad back and couldn't lift it into the van, I did, and off we went. I butchered that big pig on our kitchen counter – my friend told me what to do. It was awful. It stunk up the whole convent and the sisters were so mad at me![9]

Brother Gabriel Bieniek, OSB, also came to lend his services at the Mission from 1976 to November 1978. He tended a very good garden as well as doing custodial work in school and church.

Father Peter began inviting Indian culture and tradition into the life of the church. He asked "Sonny" Green to build an Ojibwe "crèche" for Christmas. This birchbark lodge, covered with fresh cedar and evergreen boughs each Christmas, continues to be a familiar and beloved

St. Mary's Christmas crèche

sight with its Holy Family (Indian figures), animals of the surrounding woodland (bear, deer, rabbit, etc.), and Wise Men (Chiefs).

In February 1977, the Mission School received $5000 for operating expenses through the Tribe. But funds were still low. Tuition was not charged, but a dollar a month was suggested and a tuition scale was arranged for those who could pay more. Both St. John's and St. Benedict's were asked to increase their stipend for personnel and to make a monetary contribution.

May 1977 saw another change of pastors with Father Patrick Okada, OSB, taking over for Father Peter, who was not well. One of the first tasks of the new pastor that September was to deed over, along with the Diocese of Crookston, approximately sixty acres of shoreline property no longer used for agriculture by the Mission, to the Tribe for the construction of the new hospital and related facilities. Groundbreaking for the hospital took place on October 17, 1977, with Governor Rudy Perpich and Senator Wendell Anderson present.

Father Patrick also liked to garden and did it in Japanese fashion with the vegetables growing on poles. He may have given Brother Gabe some friendly competition as both produced bountiful harvests. Father also liked to go mushrooming and often took Indian people along, teaching them about his method and process.

With both Sister Jane and Sister Kayleen often "on the road" because of their ministries, it became necessary to buy a car and to replace the old station wagon with a new one. These purchases were financed through the Mission.

Three lay persons were on the teaching staff for the 1977-78 school year: Sam Wilkes, grade two, Suzanne Kemp, grade three, and Mike Scott, grade five. Four aides, hired by the district under Title I, also worked at the school. Arts and crafts, especially beading and some language, were taught once a week by Tina Stately, Tom Stillday, and Jeff Zeller of Red Lake through Title IV, a special government program for Indian students. In November, the former "bunkhouse" for employees was converted – after much discussion regarding "legal" space and location – into a classroom for special education students taught by a teacher provided by the public school board.

At this time, a tuition policy was suggested of $54 a year for one child, $36 for the second, and $18 for the third. Most families paid $108 total. Results were quite positive, Sister Elizabeth reports.

The observance of Indian Heritage Day at St. Mary's enhanced and celebrated the children's native roots. A further activity for older students was the monthly 4-H program provided by the local Extension Office. This included trips to wildlife and forestry areas on the reservation.

Some disturbing "rumors" were heard, however, that St. John's planned to withdraw its personnel from Red Lake at the end of the 1977-78 school year. But Abbot John Eidenschink hastened to set the record straight in a letter to Sister Elizabeth: "I have not heard any such rumors nor have I thought about or discussed . . . the questions of our withdrawing from Red Lake next year. We want to continue our work there as long as possible."[10]

More good news followed. In December 1977, the school received an increased stipend from the Tribe of $5000 to $10,000 a year.

Another significant development in the parish which the monks and sisters became involved in at this time was the Tekakwitha Conference, and several attended the national meeting at Rapid City, South Dakota, in 1977.

The Tekakwitha Conference, first known simply as the Catholic Indian meeting, had its beginning in 1939 when Aloysius J. Muench, Bishop of the Fargo Diocese, invited twenty-three missionary priests from the Dakotas and Minnesota to come together and be a support to one another in their missionary endeavors among the Native Americans.

Over the years, the organization grew from this handful of men to include women religious engaged in similar work, then to lay ministers, both men and women, and, finally, most importantly, to the Indian people themselves. Today, the Conference, under the patronage of Blessed Kateri Tekakwitha (Algonquian Mohawk, 1656-1680), is fully directed by Indian people with input from religious and lay people, both Indian

Deacon John Spears

and non-Indian. John Spears of Red Lake, the first Indian permanent deacon for the Archdiocese of Minneapolis/St. Paul, was very active in Tekakwitha as was Leon Cook, who served for a time on the Board of Directors. Over 100 Kateri Circles exist around the country today. A National Conference is held annually in regions from coast to coast, hosted by local tribes.

Goals of Native peoples and friends of Native peoples who participate in the Conference include continued growth in Native and Catholic traditions and in the spiritual quest for healing, respect, hospitality, and love; building self-esteem and appreciation for Native cultures and gifts; becoming more actively involved in the life of the Church; strengthening commitment and responsibility to family, youth, ministry, and social/economic/ecological issues.

Sister Gilmary Kempf, OSB, who taught at the Mission in the 1980s observes:

> *The Tekakwitha Conferences are one of the best things that has happened for the people. Father John Hascall, OFM, Cap., an Ojibwe Medicine man and Catholic priest from Wisconsin, took the leadership at the Conferences. He was able to bring our two cultures together. The Conferences also promote intertribal unity. There's always a big powwow. It's definitely a spiritual renewal.*[11]

Jane T. Beaulieu, still active in her eighties, also participated in the Tekakwitha Conferences, where both her Indian tradition and her Catholic faith were nourished. "Jane T," as she was fondly called, stood out among parishioners of St. Mary's as one of its "pillars." She seemed able to successfully integrate both the Indian and Christian spiritualities. She was active in all church events, especially the choir, where she faithfully taught the traditional Ojibwe Christmas hymns each year. "Jane T" believed it was vitally important for the people to maintain the Ojibwe language.

Today, many of the staff at St. Mary's continue to participate in the

BLESSED

KATERI

TEKAKWITHA

LILY

OF THE

MOHAWKS

Betty Beaulieu and Thern Hegstrom with John Hascall, OFM Cap., at the 1986 Tekakwitha Conference in Montana. [Photo: Julius Beckermann, OSB]

Douglas Mullin, OSB. Mission school principal, 1986-89.

Sister Mary Lou Carlson, OSB (granddaughter of Peter Graves).

Cultural Exchange with volunteers from South Bend, IN (1992).

Riho Yamaguchi from Japan with St. Mary's school children (1994). [Photos: Sister Mary Minette Beutz, OSB]

National Tekakwitha Conferences, along with a group, or "circle," of dedicated parishioners, including Thern Hegstrom, Betty Beaulieu, Melvina Johnson, Marcella and McKinley Auginaush, Kathy Anderson, Mary Johnson, and Mildred Sumner. To attend the Conferences each summer the group raises its own funds by sponsoring bake sales and special dinners. Sister Mary Minette Beutz, OSB, who taught first grade at the school from 1987-1995, remembers staying up into the "wee hours" of the night baking cakes, breads, and candies for these sales.

In the summer of 1978, a pastoral change brought Father Meinrad Dindorf, OSB, to the Mission to replace Father Patrick, who was appointed pastor of the Catholic parish in Albany, Minnesota. These were rapid changes in leadership at St. Mary's: five changes of pastors between 1973 and 1978. Brother Gregory once said that stability was one of the most necessary ingredients of mission life at Red Lake.

Meinrad Dindorf, OSB.
[Photo: Meinrad Dindorf,
OSB]

Brother Stephen also left that summer as did Brother Julius; they were replaced for one year by Brother David Manahan, OSB.

Father Meinrad served the parish faithfully for eight years. He found evidence of a parish council having been initiated, and called a meeting as winter came on. Only a couple of people responded, and he later learned that there was a good bit of uneasiness about meetings around the reservation that winter.

One of his concerns was to support the efforts being made to involve both the people and the customs of the place in the liturgy. He recalls an incident in his first weeks at Red Lake when two of the local women came to the rectory and asked to have their children's beaded dance clothing blessed. "I agreed," he says, "and we went over to church, spread out the garments in the sanctuary, and they knelt for the blessing prayer. Afterwards, one of the women told me, smiling, that it had really been a test to see whether I would be amenable to something like this!"[12]

Father began attending the annual Tekakwitha Conferences and found hopeful the often repeated keynote, that Native Americans can be truly Catholic and truly Indian; he made efforts to re-enforce that message.

Early in his pastorate, he began a "Christmas gift" of proclaiming the gospel of the Nativity in Ojibwe (having studied the basics at BSU and with an elder in Cass Lake). He meant this as a symbolic action of respect, and, some years later, was pleased to listen to this same Ojibwe Christmas gospel proclaimed by parishioner McKinley Auginash.

Other Christmas customs fostered by the sisters, pastor, and people over preceding years included the dance up the aisle, at a signal of the drum, by parishioners bearing the figure of the Infant Jesus, gifts of rice, fish and furs, to a place of honor in the birchbark and fir bough crib.

At the Good Friday liturgy, Brother Placid's twelfth-station icon of the Indian Christ was used during the Veneration of the Cross. Father Meinrad also remembers the Easter Vigils where he felt a real sense of "keeping watch" as the people listened to one Old Testament story after another being told by Red Lake lectors. These were followed by the baptism of children of catechetical age who had been prepared by the religious educators.

Father tried to involve more parishioners as lectors for Sunday Mass. Judy Roy and Veronica Hegstrom were two of a goodly number who participated. On occasions such as graduation, honor drum songs were sung in church. Drum songs would sometimes be sung at wakes in the community centers or at the cemetery. At confirmation, the Thunder Bird symbol often had a place of honor.

Father Meinrad says he gained some awareness, through powwows and through study, of the honored role of elders, and began inviting elders, two at a time, to place the blessed ashes on the foreheads of the school children during the Ash Wednesday service. Some of these elders were Jane T. Beaulieu, Eliza Lussier, Sam Colhoff, and McKinley Auginash.

During his first year at the Mission, Father Meinrad and Brother David sought the advice of one of the foremen of Red Lake Builders and "walked through" the whole physical plant operation of the Mission.

There were some ten buildings in all. It was acknowledged that immediate response to emergencies should be available and that the adoption of some basic principle of stewardship for the mostly old frame buildings should be put in place.

Upcoming events soon proved to be of crisis proportion, however, at both the Mission and on the reservation, and Father Meinrad found himself ministering to many cases of tragedy and death, often related to chemical abuse. In addition, major political unrest was mounting among the people.

In the spring of 1978, Stephanie Hanson had been elected, in a very close election, to the office of tribal treasurer. She was installed on November 9, 1978. Stephanie investigated possible misuse of tribal funds, and because of her allegations against Tribal Chairman Roger Jourdain, was suspended from her office by the Tribal Council on February 28, 1979. The suspension became permanent on May 18 when Stephanie was fired. The political situation grew serious.

Early the next day, May 19, disaster and tragedy struck, the effects of which long reverberated within the community. Stephanie's husband, Harry Hanson, and several other men from the reservation began an angry confrontation at the police complex regarding Stephanie's firing. When some of the men broke into the new jail, where confiscated guns, drugs, and liquor were stored, all control was lost and violence broke out.

What happened in the next several hours around the Mission, which was adjacent to the site of the turmoil, is here pieced together from several witnesses who were among the staff at the Mission at the time:[13]

> On Saturday morning, the sisters were awakened by shooting outside the convent. There was fear and confusion as Father Meinrad held a hasty communion service instead of Mass because they did not know what might happen next.
>
> The sisters went to the basement for safety. Here, Sister Delphine led the rosary. Upstairs, unintentionally, stray bullets flew through the children's dining room. Everyone was tense and frightened.
>
> Some lawmen were in the convent building but were asked to respect

the building as church property and not use it as a target. The sisters recalled that before the outbreak, the Mission held a position of neutrality as it served the children and people from both sides of the political issue.

By this time, the jail was burning and the situation had grown worse. At mid-morning, the sisters were asked to leave. They hardly knew what to take with them. In minutes, they walked over to school where some bullets also had hit, got into cars, and were escorted by police off the reservation to Bemidji. Father Meinrad and Brother David chose to stay on at the Mission. It seemed the right thing to do. Mass was celebrated as usual that night. Two people came in from Redby along a circuitous route. A few more attended the Sunday Mass. Afterwards, a parishioner paused to thank Father Meinrad for staying.

The sisters returned to the Mission on Monday. They packed up the children's belongings from their desks in paper bags and closed school for the summer. Several sisters stayed on. They felt it was important to do so and the people seemed happy, too.

As this tragic summer went on, some random burning of buildings and shootings continued. It was an uneasy time. No powwows were held for awhile. "We felt sad," states Sister Marlene, "because of all the damage, but even more so because it affected relationships among the Indian people."

In a homily preached by Father Meinrad at the funeral Mass and a funeral service for two young men shot and killed in the general turmoil of May 19th, he said in part:

. . . People are not objects. And if a person can sometimes be a symbol, then it is, maybe, as a symbol not of one side versus another side, but a symbol of all the little people in every time and place who accidentally get in the way of . . . causes and get crushed by the spinoffs from . . . events. It is not this cause or that which has any right to claim these little people. It is not one cause or another that we are here to blame. We gather . . . not to ascribe guilt for a death that all lament. We gather to extend compassion to parents, to a family, whose son and brother died tragically not for this one's victory or that one's defense, but from the accidents that haunt the human condition; the accidents that are made easier by the moods and tempos set loose in the wake of causes that cannot ever control all their effects . . . .

Throughout these days, St. Mary's remained keenly aware of family fragmentation. The staff, in its ministry, tried to bridge the difficulties. The school saw a change among the children: best friends regarded one another with distrust and fear not of their own making as the following conversation overheard between two youngsters bears out:

"Go riding with me."
"I can't. Don't you know your father burned our house down?"[14]

During this time of upheaval within the community, there was opportunity for growth for those who were willing and able to get involved. Construction of the new hospital continued throughout the summer, new homes went up, new jobs became available, and a new Humanities Center was underway near the powwow grounds on the east side of Redlake. At the Mission, Father Meinrad had all the buildings checked, and major repairs were begun on the convent.

Sister Elizabeth, after the unforgettable weekend of May 19, which was to have been her "farewell" celebration, welcomed the return of Sister Patricia Wallis, OSB, as the new principal of St. Mary's Mission School. Brother Julius Beckermann, OSB, also returned at this time to serve the Mission for the next twelve years.

"The Mission School is such a neat place to be," affirm young Lotoya Schoenborn and Michael Thunder (ca 1992).

CHAPTER 10

TRANSITION (1980-1991)

HOPE REMAINED AN IMPORTANT INGREDIENT in the everyday lives of the people of St. Mary's following the political uprising on the reservation in 1979.

The Mission School continued as a place of neutrality where efforts were made for all to come together in peace to listen to each other. The school believed in its children and hoped to insure a continuum of learning into the future.

Principal Sister Patricia Wallis saw the importance of cultural integration. As a result of her study in curriculum methodology, she realized that the students at St. Mary's definitely did better in school using learning methods specific to their own background and needs.[1]

In order to lay a firm foundation for this methodology, St. Mary's considered opening a kindergarten for the 1980-81 school year. Diocesan approval was received but the kindergarten was not able to get underway.

Tribal funds had been "frozen" after the uprising and the Mission School received no assistance from the Tribal Council. But because the CETA (Comprehensive Employment Training Act) was already in place and was federally funded, these monies were still available to the school.

In 1979, Mary Lou Carlson, the granddaughter of Peter Graves, was hired as the eleventh Title I aide for the district. She was placed, along with Bernadine Bailey, at St. Mary's Mission School. This was a happy coincidence for Mary Lou. Not a Catholic, she nevertheless loved teaching with the sisters and even joined them for early morning prayer in the convent. Her attraction to prayer, to the Eucharist, and to the community life she experienced here eventually led her to be received into full communion with the Catholic Church in Advent, 1981.

But that was not the end of Mary Lou's story. She taught as an aide at the Mission until 1983. She then decided to become a Benedictine sister and was professed in 1993 at St. Benedict's Monastery in St. Joseph, Minnesota. Today, Sister Mary Lou works as an LPN at St. Scholastica's, a retirement home for the Benedictine sisters in St. Cloud, Minnesota. She returns regularly to visit her family in Redby, and, of course, the sisters at St. Mary's.

In the early months of 1979, the Diocese of Crookston inaugurated an annual appeal, and asked that parishioners be organized as visitors to present the appeal to their neighbors face-to-face. Sister Elizabeth and Sister Jane were invaluable helpers in tapping likely visitors. A great effort was made by some two dozen Red Lakers in going house-to-house on these calls, with the result that diocesan offices were much impressed.

At the Mission, major repairs were underway on the convent. "It was a very visible sign of the Church's intent," Father Meinrad explains, "to invest itself in the Red Lake community." The huge old convent had gone unrepaired for many years; rot was eating through a few sections of exterior wall; rolled roofing on the south end had taken hits from high winds; some windows had storms and some hadn't. The scaffold rigging around this building through the summer and fall of 1979 and the siding work of Dan Duerst, craftsman and artisan, and his crew definitely gave visibility to continued presence.

This project was made possible by the Catholic diocese of Crookston which, never blessed with deep pockets or much of a pocket at all, went out and borrowed $45,000 for St. Mary's Mission, "trusting that they would find benefactors later," Father Meinrad says, "so that this work could be done not only when it was needed physically, but when it would offer most hope to community morale."

Father Meinrad gratefully recalls the support and encouragement received from Bishop Victor Balke and the diocesan financial managers. He remembers, too, how Bishop Balke came to ask each parish to have an annual collection to help St. Mary's Mission School. Going beyond its borders, the diocese invited Father Meinrad to write up needs that the diocese would incorporate into its requests to such organizations as the Bureau of Catholic Indian Missions, the Catholic Church Extension Society, and the American Board of Catholic Missions. Father Meinrad says he felt that it helped in the case with BCIM that he once managed to "spirit away" Msgr. Paul Lenz, longtime director, from a clergy conference in Thief River Falls, so that Lenz could actually see St. Mary's Mission.

In 1980, an energy audit was done of all the existing buildings at the Mission. Sister Patricia wrote up an application for a government grant for financial assistance, and in October 1980, an energy conservation grant of $10,130 was received. With grant funds and contributions from Msgr. Lenz, the school was insulated and rewired, new storm windows installed, asbestos removed, and siding put on. The primary wing was reroofed and stuccoed. One summer, Father Robert Pierson and Brother Paul Richards from St. John's came to help. Brother Kevin Ludowese gave two summers; he and Allen Branchaud took down the old boys' building at this time with money made from the removal of two old Quonsets. Volunteers from the Diocese of Crookston and men from Indian Action, a vocational training school in Redby, also helped with work around the Mission.

In January 1981, the Benedictines of St. John's and St. Benedict's declared that St. Mary's Mission School indeed filled a "vital place in the community" but added that "tribal support was necessary."[2] A sum of $10,000 was received that same month from the Tribal Council. In this way, the financial struggle of the school was shared between the Red Lake community and the Benedictine institutions.

During this time, Sister Patricia attended a Basic Skills Program financed by the State of Minnesota. She returned to implement a comprehensive basic skills program of excellence in the school.

Three lay teachers were again hired in 1981 as well as a recess

Jim Needham adorned the Mission School walls with stenciled design. [Photo: Placid Stuckenschneider, OSB]

supervisor and custodian, Jim Needham. Over the years that Jim worked at the school, he also did some physical education teaching and coaching. One year, Sister Patricia asked him to paint Ojibwe designs and figures on the walls of the hallways. Jim, still employed at the Mission School as custodian and all-around assistant, reports that the children have always respected these paintings and never defaced them. He preserves a great love for the school and the children, evidenced by the care he provides.

In 1981, Sister Constette LeFevere, OSB, took on the position of secretary and bookkeeper at the Mission School – a service she performed faithfully for eleven years.

A custom that has continued with great enthusiasm for many years at the Mission School is the annual Christmas play. From first grader to bus driver, everyone gets involved. Sometimes the stage in the gym is transformed into the birthplace of Jesus, which, in this case, is an Indian lodge for the Holy Family. Jesus Himself is often represented by

someone's little brother or sister. The
Wise Men from the East appear in traditional powwow dress. Parents and grandparents love these performances and
eagerly watch as their little ones interpret
the ageless story anew.

In other locales on the Mission, the
store continued to do well. It changed
hands in 1981 after Sister Emerentia
Fleischacker, OSB, broke her ankle.
Then Sister Ansgar Willenbring, OSB,
took over – her second time on the
Mission – with Sister Delice Bialke, OSB,
joining her in 1982. "The store made

*"Joseph, Mary, and Baby Jesus"
with Brother Julius.*

approximately $10,000 a year," Sister Delice reports. The sisters contin-
ued their post here until 1991, when Billy and Helen Green were hired.
In 1993, the position was filled by Billy and Millie Sumner. Today, Millie
continues to "keep" the store for several hours each weekday.

"When I worked in the store," Sister Delice recalls, "I got to know
the people well. They'd come in often just to talk. 'Blush' (Margaret
May) would come in every day. Rachel Barrett, who bought a fan for
the store, loved to talk. She said that when she went home afterwards
she always felt good. People liked to talk on a one-to-one and would
wait around until others left."[3]

Another friend of the Mission was Laurentia Colhoff, a former graduate of St. Mary's, who had attended the University of Minnesota/
Duluth and become a nurse. After the new Red Lake Indian Hospital
opened in the spring of 1981, she served here as Director of Nursing.

Laurentia's father was a familiar sight around the Mission also,
faithfully ringing the bell for Mass and helping out where needed.
Laurentia is remembered for her kindnesses to the sisters, taking them
on many cultural excursions. Today, she continues to influence the Red
Lake community and the Mission through the activities she initiates,
such as the "Kitchen Warming" held in the new Kapsner Center in
1994, and a Thankgsgiving feast here in 1995. Laurentia appropriately
chairs the parish hospitality committee.

During the school year of 1981-82, the school board adopted a new plan for hot lunch. Since the government program had been cut, lunch was now handled by the public high school. This meant that food was no longer prepared in the convent but had to be picked up from the high school. Sisters Jane and Dorothy Ann boarded the school station wagon to do this chore each school day and served the meal as usual. They were paid by the public school for these services.

Since lunch was no longer prepared and served in the convent, Sister Lucy was out of a job. She left St. Mary's greatly moved and influenced by her life there. "It was actually a culture shock for me to leave," she reflects. "The white world is so extravagant. At Red Lake, community and sharing meant so much."

In December 1981, Robert Pierson, OSB, produced a paper in which he examined the immediate effect of the uprising upon the parish and presented a view to its future. The needs, as he assessed them through the eyes of several interviewees, were for a parish council (a board of trustees was already in place) and regular social and spiritual activities for youth and adults. There was still a weekly bingo, the proceeds of which went to the Mission School, and volleyball once a week in the school gym. But Pierson saw that continued outreach was very important: home visiting and ministering to the spiritual, emotional, and physical needs of the people which would also help them stay in touch with the life of the parish. This all required personnel – already being stretched – and finances. One of Pierson's recommendations called for an additional brother to teach in the school who could also serve as a male role model for the children.[4] This recommendation was filled in the fall of 1982 when Brother Douglas Mullin, OSB, arrived to teach sixth grade, a position he held until 1986, when he became principal of the school.

"In spite of the difficulties with each other in the wake of the uprising," Brother Doug later stated, "we continued to insist that this place, the Mission, was a place where all could come together in peace, where we would listen to each other without fighting."[5]

The challenge of the ongoing years remained as to how best empower people to grow into the future with respect for traditional values. In addition to excellence in education for the children, the faculty placed this challenge at the top of a list of items to be taken up in the Mission School's self-study begun in 1988. Children were encouraged to respect their own culture and that of others. The staff, particularly Brother Doug and Sisters Ruth Ann Schneider, OSB, and Gilmary Kempf, OSB, who were involved in the sacramental programs, visited the homes of their students to become better acquainted.

Inviting Indian elders into the classrooms to teach Ojibwe and traditional crafts remained a successful and important way of reaching the roots of the people and helping preserve a heritage. Because Red Lake is a closed reservation and shares a commonality of land and heritage, it is observed that many people tend to live their culture here at a deep level.

"It is the land and the people themselves, more than anything else, that give the people their identity," Brother Doug has observed. And Vickie Graves, a parent at Red Lake, adds, "Red Lake is one of the last places in the United States where Indians can be themselves."[6]

Many Indian traditions continue to be observed at Red Lake today. These include powwows, the use of drums and dance and traditional dress, name-giving ceremonies, the sweat lodge, blessing with tobacco and sage, feasts and honor-songs. But many elders regret the loss of the language, especially among the younger people. Sister Mary Lou Carlson contends that for many, the Ojibwe language is no longer an intregal part of the culture the people are presently living. "It has to be spoken in the homes to be really learned,"[7] she adds.

The language is the "backbone" of the people's culture, Brother Julius agrees. Having lived among the people at Red Lake for some sixteen years and learned to speak Ojibwe, he feels that without this spoken word, the whole meaning of the people's traditional way of life could be in jeopardy. For example, the names of the months of the year, which the people marked as "moons," indicate the kind of work the people did in the past: September, WASE BUGO-GIIZIS, "shining leaf month (moon)" when the people picked cranberries, harvested gardens and medicinal plants, hunted and trapped and stored up game for feasts; January, GITCHIE-MANIDOO GIIZIS, "Great Spirit month (moon)" when crafts and storytelling took place. Sister Ruth Ann recalls that during her years at the Mission in the late 1980s, Donny Applebee from Red Lake came to the Mission School to teach Ojibwe stories. "He always came when the snow was on the ground," she says, "during storytelling month, January."[8]

Having taught Ojibwe to youth in the Red Lake Public School, Melvina Johnson continues today to teach the language and Ojibwe heritage to three-and four-year-olds at Red Lake Headstart, where she has worked for sixteen years. Here, the little ones learn some of the old stories and how to count and name animals and colors in their own language. Melvina received her BA in the 1990s to teach a special Ojibwe Immersion Language Program. She is a member of St. Mary's and also believes that both traditional ways and the Catholic religion can be harmonized.

Sister Mary Lou sees the Tekakwitha Conference as an important movement among the Indian people toward this harmonization. "The people feel more 'free' to integrate now," she says. "Old rules and laws have become more flexible and open in the Church."

In 1985, Father John Hascall, OFM, Cap., visited St. Mary's. He was instrumental in helping the Red Lake people feel more comfortable in using Indian traditions such as the drum in church, use of the sweat lodge, and blessings with sweet grass. "I think the Church as a whole has a lot to learn from traditional Indian spirituality," Brother Doug asserts. "We need to understand that the experience of true faith can take place in many ways and have diverse expressions."[9] Sister Patricia Wallis suggests that the people will come to a fuller understanding of God's love by more deeply understanding their own Indian identity. She adds, "The biggest aim of the Mission is to form such a love community."[10]

Christopher Vecsey, in his book *Traditional Ojibwa Religion and Its Historical Changes* (1983), writes: "Ojibwe today stand between their collapsed traditional religion and Christianity, embracing neither." This presumption does not apply to all Ojibwe people, however. Many of the people of St. Mary's have made strong efforts to preserve and harmonize their traditional ways and the Catholic faith. An example in point is the life and death of parishioner Jane T. Beaulieu.

When this revered woman died on the evening of November 7, 1984, at the new Red Lake Indian Hospital, St. Mary's bell tolled 88 times, marking her passing and her years. A large wake was held at the Redby Center, and on November 10th, the funeral Mass and burial took place at St. Mary's with Deacon John Spears of the Archdiocese of Minneapolis/St. Paul assisting. (That same day, ironically, Jane's house burned down along with all her beloved Ojibwe hymn books!)

Bishop Victor Balke of the Crookston Diocese was not able to be present for "Jane T's" funeral but sent his condolences and the following message to the people of St. Mary's:

Jane T. Beaulieu, 1981. [Photo: Sister Patricia Wallis, OSB]

> *When I was ordained bishop of Crookston, Jane T. Beaulieu came to the ceremony and presented me with a beautiful beaded medallion; I still treasure that gift. She also took part several times in our ceremony in which we bless the Oils to be used in the Sacraments of Baptism, Confirmation and Holy Orders; in fact, she received these oils in the name of all the people of Red Lake Reservation. I also remember meeting her at several of the Tekakwitha Catholic Indian Conferences around the country.*
>
> *Jane T. Beaulieu was proud to be a member of the Red Lake Community and of the Red Lake Band of Chippewa Indians. She was a high credit to her family, to her Church, to her community, and to her Tribe. May her spirit continue to live on in all your hearts.*[11]

Several months before her death, in January, Jane had accepted the honorary chair of the RENEW program at St. Mary's. In an article from *Our Northland Diocese* she received this tribute: "A recent book, called *Finding a Way Home*, seeks to show the compatibility of Indian and Catholic spiritual paths. Jane T. Beaulieu's faith journey pursued that way, and in doing so, undergirded much of the life of the Red Lake Catholic Community. That community knows that it stands in need of her still."[12]

The same article pointed out "Jane T's" outstanding memory of the early days of this century (1910) when ". . . friendly Sioux from Fort Totten came to Red Lake to acquaint the Chippewa with the work of the St. Mary and St. Joseph Societies and Catholic Indian Congresses." Her recollections honored another era. For example, "it was the time of year when we were in berrypicking camp over towards Bagley. . . ."

The desire to do well, to persevere, to build upon faith and tradition

Olympic gold medal win-
ner, Billy Mills, with
Father Meinrad, OSB.

was also exemplified in the early 1980s when St. Mary's Mission School was honored by a visit from Olympic gold medal winner, runner Billy Mills, a model for youth in achievement and Indian pride. He brought with him the movie made of his life, "Running Brave." Billy returned for a second visit in 1990.

Interest in sports has remained high at the Mission. Red Lake youth enjoy playing basketball in the school gym and have been willing to pay a small fee, beginning in 1984, for the use of the facility in the evenings. It continues to be a busy and exciting gathering spot.

In 1984, Sister Marion Zimmerman, OSB, returned to St. Mary's as resource coordinator (librarian) at the Mission School, replacing Sister Caroline Eckroth, OSB. Sister Marion was instrumental in acquiring many good books and periodicals. For several years after she left, Sister continued returning a day here and there to "put the library in order."

The growing problem in America of alcohol and drug consumption also continued to influence the lives of everyone at Red Lake, including the monks and sisters who remember attending many wakes and funerals resulting from alcohol-related deaths. Issues were dealt with seriously. Ronald Head of Red Lake, a program planner in the chemical dependency division of the Minnesota Public Welfare Department, offered his reflections on the difficulties in an article from the *St. Paul Sunday Pioneer Press*, February 26, 1984: "Drinking is a learned behavior among Indian children. That cycle has got to be broken." Head recalled that the cycle began when white Europeans introduced alcohol to the Indians. From 1832 to 1953, when it was illegal for Indians to be served liquor, it was smuggled onto reservations and consumed privately. "Reservation drinking," Head observed, is still practiced and the style passed on to youngsters. By observing the adults around them, Indian youngsters are often taught that drinking is a way to deal with stress. For those living in the city, peer pressure also pushes them into drinking.

Programs today are especially designed to help Indian children with chemical problems. Renee Senogles, a family counselor in a Minneapolis treatment program and a member of the Red Lake Band, encourages families to become involved in their youngsters' treatment. She has worked to build up children's self-esteem (especially those living in the city, where there is no extended family to help instill values as on a reservation) by inviting Indian spiritual leaders to talk to the children about their culture, about traditions such as the use of the drum and dance, and to participate in powwows. As a family counselor, she helps parents regain their authority, draw boundaries for their children, and work on solving problems one at a time. "Indian kids need to have their spiritual identity addressed," Senogles offers. "If they get a solid spiritual and cultural base at home, that would be enough to ensure their success."[13]

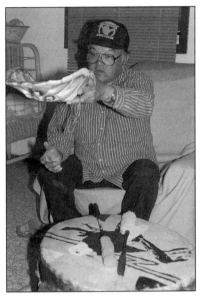

McKinley Auginash demonstrating a ceremonial.

In the early 1980s, a policy was put in place at St. Mary's regarding the use of alcohol or drugs on the school premises. As principal, Sister Patricia believed that parents and students alike required meaningful employment, and the hope of meaningful employment, to increase their self-esteem in overcoming addiction.

Over all these challenging years, the financial picture of the Mission continued to be a fragile one. It was not a matter of commitment; both the Benedictine personnel and the people of St. Mary's felt "committed" to a certain faithfulness after ninety-seven years of working and praying together. But given the condition of unemployment and other difficulties that existed on the reservation, along with a growing demand for human and financial resources in the ministry, staff and administration faced a constant reality check: "Can we provide the resources necessary? Should the school be closed?"

Brother Doug addressed the question in a paper destined for consideration by both Benedictine communities, St. John's and St. Benedict's.[14] In it, a plea was made for the Church's "preferential option for the poor" voiced in the American Bishop's Pastoral, *Catholic Social Teaching and the U.S. Economy,* and for the continued sharing of the unique monastic community life lived out at St. Mary's for so long a time by the sisters and monks who had helped shape the heart of the Mission.

Not only the religious personnel, but all the successive religious education coordinators worked to involve Red Lakers particularly in the baptismal preparation process. Infant baptism remained an important contact with the young people. An encouraging moment for all came when in June 1986, Sister Nancy Boushey, OSB, of Crookston, Father Meinrad, Lois Lussier and Kathy Anderson were able to participate together in a workshop at St. John's on the Rite of Christian Initiation of Children, under the sponsorship of Christianne Brusselmans.

Another instance of participation by parishioners in adult faith formation was in the Native American Marriage Encounters. Father Meinrad learned of a presentation being given by Sister Charles Palm, OSB (Watertown), with couples from the Sisseton area and went there to confer with her. On a cold weekend in January 1983, three couples from Red Lake joined several others at one of these marriage encounters that had been set up at Mt. St. Benedict in Crookston.

Also in fellowship with the diocesan community, Red Lakers received the Holy Oils from the bishop at the Chrism Mass in Crookston each Lent. They participated in the national RENEW program when it was held in six six-week "seasons" during 1984-86. Thern Hegstrom served as coordinator of this program which brought parishioners together in small groups for scripture reflection and faith sharing. Lent 1985 had as many as forty participants.

These events all pointed toward future parish development. St. Mary's had also been blessed over the years with various volunteers coming for some months or a year. Some of the young men who came in Father Meinrad's time were Cliff Cotter, who kept his connections to

Red Lake when he married a local woman, Paula Smith; Doug Gould, Tom Connally, and Joseph Pounder.

From 1986 to 1989, Brother Doug assumed the responsibility as principal of the Mission School following Sister Patricia's tenure and a one-year term by Mr. Gene DeYoung. Both St. Benedict's and St. John's re-affirmed their commitment to Red Lake, and three monks and ten sisters served the needs of the parish during the 1986-87 school year. A new pastor, Father Aelred Tegels, OSB, arrived in August 1986.

Media coverage of the Mission was also given that fall by the Saint Cloud Diocese in its diocesan newspaper, the *Visitor*. Photos and story attempted to capture the life of the people of Red Lake in their struggles and pains as well as joys and hopes. The issue proved controversial, however, among Red Lakers by alluding insensitively to difficult issues on the reservation. In the article, Vernon Whitefeather, a member of the Red Lake Band and teacher in the Red Lake Public School, spoke toward the tension of these post-uprising years: "Somewhere you have to have hope for the situation, but as far as having the answers to the problem, I don't know what the answer would be."[15]

Aelred Tegels, OSB, and Rachel Donnell (far right) at a Baptismal celebration.

Approximately 1,500 of the 4,000 Ojibwe living on the reservation at this time were baptized members of St. Mary's parish. Father Aelred estimated that 75-100 participated in the regular Sunday liturgy. He realized that adult evangelization apart from the school was necessary, and he attempted to re-activate the parish council and the liturgy committee, and to develop hospitality groups.

Some customs begun by Father Aelred helped to bring people together. For example, on Ash Wednesday, after the distribution of ashes, bread and soup were served in the school gym. On the eve of All Souls' Day, the dead were remembered in church by name as family members lighted candles in their honor. Other traditions continued among the children and the sisters including the display of art work done during the school year and produce harvested from the Mission garden at the Red Lake Fair. The arrival of the fall and winter holidays also brought particular joys for the children. "We usually had over two hundred children come to the door for treats on Halloween," Sister Delice reports. Brother Julius gave his little visitors oranges and carameled apples.

In April 1988, with finances barely reaching, Brother Doug, along with the Mission School Board and others, developed a Five-Year-Plan for the school to increase its funding. "Those who are concerned . . . must accept the responsibility to plan now for the future of the school . . . . Not to plan . . . means there will be no future," he said.[16] The focus of this plan targeted three sources of income: tuition (raised to $170, first child), fundraising (grants and beneficiaries), and the Red Lake Tribal Council.

Meanwhile, the school planned to celebrate its 100th anniversary on July 3, 1988. Lorraine Kingsley, a member of the School Board, organized volunteer alumni for a committee to plan the events. Leonard and Vi Donnell spearheaded much of the work. The festivities began with an outdoor Mass celebrated near the grotto by Bishop Victor Balke of the Diocese of Crookston. Roger Jourdain gave a welcoming address, and Roger Head and Lorena Cook served as masters of ceremonies for the afternoon's program.

But tough times still lay ahead. Teachers' salaries could not be assured that fall, and it was only with the financial aid of the Diocese of Crookston that the Mission School was able to open. The lack of operational finances prompted a hard look at the reality of closing. The Tribal Council again offered to take over the school. But the problem, Brother Doug reiterated, was not just lack of dollars, but of shouldering responsibility for the distinct goals and objectives of St. Mary's School. The challenge of survival depended upon community commitment toward self-sufficiency and not Church subsidy, he urged. This could translate into an increase in tuition and in teachers' salaries but would guarantee high educational standards. Unless these competitive markets were met, he maintained, St. Mary's School would continue to have a high turn-over among teachers and personnel – none of which would help the stability of the school.

In 1989, the principalship of St. Mary's School changed hands as Brother Doug returned to St. John's to work at the preparatory school. A lay woman, Jean Thompson, took up the challenge for the next two years. Ms. Thompson lived with the sisters in the convent.

Other changes and transitions occurred on the reservation. On May 1, 1989, following a community leaders' forum retreat for Tribal Council representatives, members shared their dreams for the future of their community. These included, through a grant request, a bank, more small businesses, expanded gambling operations on ceded lands (a reality in 1991 with the "Lake of the Woods" Casino at Warroad and "River Road" at Thief River Falls), a shopping mall, farming to raise trout and other fish, a tribal economic development corporation (a reality in 1991), and even a tribal college.

The new Humanities Center, which opened around 1977 near the powwow grounds, had first been used to exhibit Ojibwe heritage and to host such events and activities as indoor powwows, basketball, hockey, and swimming. Headstart also moved into this facility from the public school and remains there today. In 1985, tribal bingo was held in the Center, and, later, a small casino which continues to be operated by and for the Tribe. Since 1996, Americorps also has its headquarters there.

The Chippewa Trading Post opened its doors October 22, 1986. It continues to be a major business place for Red Lakers today. The complex includes a grocery store, video store, laundromat, gas station, and bank, a branch office from Plumber, Minnesota. A hardware store nearby completes this business section of Red Lake. Other government, federal, state, and tribal agencies continue to be major employers on the reservation. Health care (through the hospital and extended care facility) offers professional and service opportunities. Logging and fishing remain important occupations, and the lake continues to be the largest producer of walleye in the United States.

Among the many fine features of the Red Lake Hospital is a series of paintings along the lobby skylight by Duanne Johnson Loud, Jr., an Ojibwe Episcopal priest, illustrating traditional Indian life for each of

Red Lake Hospital lobby painting. Early Objibwe life in winter.

the four seasons. Above the main nurses' station in the *Jourdain/Perpich Extended Care Facility* (added in 1989), bright bold paintings by the same artist illustrate the clan or family systems of the Red Lake Ojibwe: bear, turtle, bullhead, mink, eagle, pine marten (sable), and kingfisher.

Roger Jourdain's term as tribal chairman ended in the spring of 1990, when Gerald "Butch" Brun was elected to this office. Brun served a four-year term and was succeeded by Bobby Whitefeather, the present tribal chairman.

Care of youth remains an important concern of Red Lakers, and teen-age pregnancy is a problem that worries many, especially elders and grandparents who often shoulder the responsibility of rearing the "children-of-children." Elders are anxious about the future of traditional Ojibwe family life.

Red Lake logo.
[Used with Tribal permission.]

Aloysius Thunder believes that the Indigenous Games (comparable to the Olympics) originating in 1990 at Edmonton, Canada, and the Tekakwitha Conferences do much to provide Indian people, young and old alike, with strong values and voices. "We must come forth ourselves," he insists.[17] The Indigenous Games are sporting events that only the best and most disciplined athletes compete in. In 1995, Peter

Neadeau was bearer of the Sacred Lance from Red Lake to Cass Lake for the opening ceremonies in St. Paul. Thunder himself plans to carry the Eagle's Staff of the Indigenous People of North America during a "link" of the 1997 ceremonies from a site in the western states to Victoria, British Columbia.

Father "Bill" Mehrkens

In 1991, Father Aelred left St. Mary's. He was replaced on July 1 by Monsignor William Mehrkens of the Diocese of Crookston. Monsignor Mehrkens, or "Father Bill," as he is more commonly known, had just completed fourteen years at Moorhead State University as university campus pastor for the Catholic Church at Newman Center. Father Bill's arrival at St. Mary's Mission marked the end of the Benedictine pastorate here, which had spanned 108 years.

Father Bill brought with him not only his many years' experience in parish ministry and work with youth, but a great eagerness to serve the Indian people. A strong advocate of peace and justice, he is known for his consistent dedication to the "Anawim" or little people often left on the margins of society. He is credited with several ongoing programs in Moorhead including The Dorothy Day House, Churches United for the Homeless, and local chapters of Amnesty International and Bread for the World. Father Bill is also the co-founder of the Laketrails Base Camp on Lake of the Woods for the wilderness experience of youth.

Shortly before Father Bill arrived at St. Mary's Mission, Brother Julius returned to St. John's to pursue further studies. In a letter to Abbot Jerome Theisen, OSB, in September 1991, Father Bill stated that he hoped Brother Julius would be able to return to Red Lake some day, where his reputation was "outstanding" among the people. Five years later, in 1996, Brother Julius did return and today continues his ministry as pastoral assistant.

In 1991, Father Bill appointed Sister Philip Zimmer, OSB, principal of St. Mary's School, where she had already served four years as fifth grade teacher.

The number of sisters serving the Mission from St. Benedict's dropped from eight in 1989-90 to four in 1990-91 and to two in 1991-92. Sister Philip and Sister Mary Minette held the big convent together that year along with Sister Annette Fernholz, SSND, religious education coordinator.

It was indeed a transitional time; a new "beginning" time; a time of rekindling and reshaping.

CHAPTER 11

ON THE THRESHOLD (1991-1997)

ESPITE THE SMALL NUMBER OF PERSONNEL at St. Mary's that fall of 1991, there was much determination to continue a viable ministry among the people. Father Bill was intent and eager to take up pastorship. His work for peace and non-violence represented deep personal convictions and took high priority. At Red Lake, there were many opportunities for commitment to these issues.

Outreach among the people and ministry to the homebound, the sick, and the elderly was the new pastor's first and major thrust. During his first six months at the Mission, he visited many of the parishioners, accompanied by Sister Laurita Wydra, SSS, who stayed on briefly to be of assistance, and then by Leonard Donnell. He mailed out requests for help in the parish with this priority in mind. People volunteered in several service-oriented capacities, including help in the cleaning of the cemetery, which had become overgrown.

A second priority in the parish at this time was the continuing effort to integrate Ojibwe tradition. Bringing people together in cultural exchange had already become a custom – since about 1980 – in the parish with the visit of Father Paul Lippstock from the Dubuque Diocese and his group of Catholic high school students for volunteer service. Today, Father Paul continues leading young people from Iowa to Red Lake from his new location in Waterloo.

This kind of cultural exchange and dialogue has grown at St. Mary's. Since 1991, six college students from the College of St. Benedict and St. John's University have regularly spent their January interim on the Mission. In conjunction with the Japanese International Internship Program, Riho Yamauchi spent four months at the Mission in 1994-95 sharing her Japanese culture and tradition. Volunteers from the Newman Centers of Bemidji State and Moorhead State Universities, where Father Bill served as campus pastor for many years, have also shared time and talent on the Mission. In 1995 and 1996, respectively, seminarians Allen Larson and Sean Dulay from the Crookston Diocese lived at the Mission for several months, giving service and receiving invaluable experience.

In 1993, spurred on by other parishes expressing interest in becoming "sister parishes," Father Bill wrote invitations to every Catholic parish in Minnesota. The major thrust, of course, was cultural exchange. Sister Philip says that as a bonus, groups are treated to some major sight-seeing events when they come, such as observing bears and eagles in their natural habitat, witnessing the beautiful sunsets over Red Lake, and visiting the source of the Mississippi River at Itasca State Park.

The Mission staff works together to plan for these groups, which sometimes total fifteen or twenty individuals. Groups provide their own food and food preparation. Their usual stay is four days, most often during the summer months. Women and girls are housed in the large dorm on the third floor of the convent, and men and boys in the parish house.

Father Bill took an educative stance while supporting these groups of young people. He maintains, "There is an unconscious and hidden racism in our society and it is very difficult to counter this unless a personal encounter is made with the people."[1] As pastor, counselor, and writer of the official justice and peace column in the Crookston diocesan paper, *Our Northland Diocese*, Father Bill was eager to broaden this scope dedicated to experiences of cross-cultural immersion.

The number of groups who arrive yearly at St. Mary's for this purpose continue to develop. They include:

1) St. Francis Cabrini Parish in Minneapolis which assists with financial and material benefits. Families stay a weekend.

2) St. Elizabeth Ann Seton Parish of Hastings, MN, come as families and also give financial and material assistance. Some material accomplishments over the years include painting of several classrooms, repair of playground equipment, and the installation of eaves on the church. Hastings' offshoot became Cretin-Durham High School in St. Paul, whose representatives first came in 1995 and worked in the small tree nursery on Mission grounds.

3) Sts. Peter and Paul in St. Cloud, MN. These youth groups began in 1995 for inculturation and work on the cemetery.

4) Particularly noteworthy are the forty to fifty members of three parishes from South Bend, Indiana, whose big project was the east section of the cemetery. They prepared new crosses for those that were broken off or weathered; they prepared the central monument for this restored section of the cemetery with large stones collected by Father Bill, and planted flowers on the four sides. They worked on stripping and refinishing the church pews and left materials for parishioners to continue the work. Though the groups came for only two years, 1992-1994, four women continue to come for an annual visit and enjoy gardening, painting, etc.

5) In the winter of 1966, Father Nic Dressen brought eight youths from Big Lake, MN, and plans to return.

6) Joan of Arc Parish in Minneapolis has sent two youth groups.

After an initial orientation meeting, programs and tours are conducted by the staff and local people, including elders who provide cross-cultural experiences to help visitors become more aware of traditional ways. These resource people include Judy Roy, Thern Hegstrom, Melvina Johnson, Ennis Johnson, Betty Beaulieu, and McKinley Auginash. Al "Wishy" Thunder and Bill May conduct tours to the lake, to meet Tribal Council members, and to a sweat lodge. In addition, tours are taken of the fishery and forestry departments, the powwow is

*Working in the tree nursery: Sister Philip Zimmer, OSB, with
volunteers from Joan of Arc parish, Minneapolis: Kevin Kelly and
children Colin and Sarah (1997).*

explained and sometimes attended, beading classes are held, and feasts
are shared.

An important document issued on September 21, 1992, by Bishop
Victor Balke of the Diocese of Crookston lent a supporting voice to
those involved in such cross-cultural encounters. The document, a public declaration to all Indian people of northwestern Minnesota, contained, first of all, an apology by the Church for past violations of dignity and respect, especially in regards to the people's traditional ways.
It affirmed the people's rights in light of the Church's teaching and of
the American Religious Freedom Act (P.L. 95-134, 1978). The document
further called upon all Catholics of the diocese to commit themselves to
seeking this peace and justice and righting previous wrongs.
Specifically, the document affirmed the Indian people's right to practice
traditional ceremonies and rituals, to be assured protection of their
sacred places, and to use their religious symbols (feathers, tobacco,
sweet grass, etc.) for traditional ceremonies and rituals. (This document in its entirety can be found as Appendix C.)

Another aspect of "building up the Church" among the people, of retaining and recording the old with the new, blending, expanding, and incorporating, emerged in two projects begun in 1992: an updated history of the Mission, and the building of a parish center, including a remodelling of the church. In January 1992, arrangements were made with Sister Owen Lindblad, OSB, of St. Benedict's Monastery in St. Joseph, Minnesota, to update the written history of St. Mary's Mission. Completion of the book was planned to coincide with the completion of the church addition and remodelling. Efforts were made to interview elders first, beginning in the fall of 1992 with Sister Adelma Roers, OSB, Frank and Julia Lajeunesse, George Head, Mary Ann Aitken, and Agnes and Jim Roberts.

Plans for the new addition had been discussed as early as the 1980s with funds, totalling $55,000, donated by former employee Joseph Kapsner. Upon completion, the Center was named in his honor. The remainder of funds needed were available through the Catholic Church Extension Society and individual donations. To further the building project, Father Bill revived a parish council and established finance and building committees which met monthly in preparation. Members were

Parish Council	Finance	Building
William & Joan Strong	William Strong	Philip Johns
Marcella Auginash	Marcella Auginash	Henry Donnell
Joyce Roy	Henry Donnell	Roman Stately
Betty Beaulieu	Leonard Donnell	Joyce Roy
Priscilla Stately		Harold Donnell
		Leonard & Violet Donnell

By spring 1992, drawings for the new addition were complete. Father Bill sent letters to parishioners asking for suggestions and inviting them to meet with the architect. In September, the basement of the structure was dug, extending the church to the north. The contractor engaged was Lindow Construction of Bemidji.

The number of sisters increased to four in January 1992 when Sister Teresa Duerr, OSB, arrived to serve as pastoral minister of the parish.

In June she organized a parish liturgy committee and served as its chairperson. This committee continues to meet monthly, and since 1996, when Sister Teresa left the Mission, Thern Hegstrom and Priscilla Stately act as co-chairs. The group prepares the church environment for the liturgical seasons and organizes parishioners for participation as lectors, communion ministers, gift bearers, etc. Advent is a particularly exciting time as a "Giving Tree" is set up and the crèche prepared for Christmas.

With the return of Sister Ansgar Willenbring later in 1992, the little group in the convent increased to a stalwart five. The next year, Sister Marina Schlangen returned for a second time. Mission thrust remained constant, emphasizing community and hospitality. The big white house opened itself to cultural exchange and diversity among those who shared its roof regularly or those who were privileged to spend either days or months in its shelter. Recently, at least one lay teacher and/or volunteer at the Mission also help make up the population of this household. Dedication to liturgy, prayer, hospitality, community, good cheer, and Benedictine peace all remain characteristic of this group of dedicated women. Perhaps *presence* is the best word to describe the missioners' lives here, and it is deeply communicated. There is an ease and graciousness with which each day and its unforeseen circumstances are met that seem to turn ordinary lives into extraordinary ones. This unique spirit overflows into each person's relationships, and any guest staying for either a few minutes or a few days is immediately touched by it. A particular custom shared with guests when they leave the Mission is a blessing at the front door by all in the house.

The convent has also continued the tradition of having a dog. In this case, two, Tigger and KoKo, who arrived in 1994 and 1995 respectively. Each has her own story to tell, and there are no better dogs than these to welcome and entertain visitors.

As life moves on a day-by-day basis, 1991 found the sisters without regular kitchen personnel after the departure of Sister Dorothy Ann Marx, OSB. So talents were combined and the sisters began preparing their own meals. Sister Marina took up bread baking with great energy, and St. John's famous bread recipe with cracked wheat flour (also from the Abbey) continues to offer luscious loaves for hearty eaters.

(Above left) The Christmas crèche and Giving Tree. St. Mary's Mission Church. (Above right) "Tigger" greets the author (December 1994). (Below) Always room for one more! (l to r): Millie Sumner, Sister Teresa Duerr, Pamela Ettiene-Planche, Sister Philip Zimmer, Sister Ansgar Willenbring, Melvina Johnson, McKinley Auginash, Phyllis Gurno, Thern Hegstrom and Marcella Auginash.

(Left) Preparing the foundation on the new Kapsner Center (1992).

(Right) First Summer School of Religion (1995) with Sue Eschenbacher of Hastings, MN.

(Left) Sister Priscilla Sullivan "reaches out" to Delores Neadeau at the 1993 Indian Congress. (Right) Betty Beaulieu and Thern Hegstrom display the 100th Anniversary cake of St. Mary's Church.

At school, local women, instead of the sisters, serve the children's hot lunch which is still brought from the high school, where it is prepared. Theresa Neadeau of St. Mary's has helped prepare these meals for the past twenty-one years.

Sister Ansgar, completing her twenty-third year at the Mission, brings the wisdom and experience of many years of service. She can as easily fix a radiator leak as a headache; tell you why the BIG BOY washer isn't working; how best to remove fruit stain from a white blouse. She is receptionist, laundress, hospitality person; she can do electrical and plumbing repair; knows remedies for aches and pains; is historian, caretaker, convent sacristan, and church organist. In short, the big white house couldn't run without her.

Sister Ansgar Willenbring, OSB

The 1992-93 school year began with the hiring of a full-time school counselor, Ms. Eleanor Swanson, and the opening of a kindergarten for about twenty-five students, boosting the total enrollment that year to 160. Hopes ran high. The convent dining room, now too big for the sisters, was painted and decorated brightly to welcome the little ones. Small desks, tables, chairs, toys, and learning tools acquired from a variety of suppliers, filled the room. Mrs. Candace "Candy" West was engaged as kindergarten teacher. But, due to lack of funding, this venture sadly had to be discontinued at the end of the year. September 1997 finds this room in "full swing" again as Sister Stephen Kurpiers, OSB, engages St. Mary's students in a new "Writing to Read" program financed by the Riordan Foundation, Graham Foundation, and Peter Weller.

The counseling services are highly necessary and valued by the school. Ms. Swanson continued to serve in this capacity, working individually with students and in classroom settings with self-esteem activities. With much individual attention, patience, love, and the cooperation of parents and often other students, problems can be worked out.

Sister Philip, with her long background in teaching and administrative experience in Catholic grade schools, was aware of the particular needs at St. Mary's. She began efforts at building personal pride and

Sister Philip Zimmer, OSB.

self-esteem, mutual respect, cooperation, a sense of reverence for all creation, dedication to God, and enthusiasm for life – all of which serve to bolster the spirit of the school and draw parents, students, and teachers closer together. Since 1991, staff meetings are held every two weeks. Sister Philip maintains personal interaction with the students and classrooms daily by also teaching science in grades four through six. Her active interest in rural living and the issues of the land and environment helped launch the yearly observance of Earth Day, begin a small tree nursery at the Mission, and re-activate a small "kitchen garden." Sister Philip's thrust of reclaiming nature and the ways of the earth are echoed by Bishop Balke of Crookston in his reflection on rural living published in *America*, May 15, 1993:

> *[people] . . . need to have a "sense of the sacred" about the land and the lakes, the forests and the pastures and the air we breathe. This "sense of the sacred" ought to be the primary attitude of soul before the world "charged with the grandeur of God" (Gerard Manley Hopkins). Without this, there will be little or no love for the environment, and all the gifts of God in and through nature will be merely things to be used, commodities.*
>
> *The Red Lake Reservation is holy land, too, where the Great Spirit of God and His Christ breathes through the trees and over the water . . . for here, too, there is a big lake where simple fishermen make their living.*

Sister Philip stresses sensitivity toward and integration of the Ojibwe culture and spiritual values. Each school day begins in the "sacred circle" as a total school with prayer and with the encouragement to live the day as responsible, dedicated people, true to the Christian and Indian heritage. Each week begins with smudging ("cleansing" oneself with the smoke of burning sweet grass or sage) by local personnel, e.g., Georgia Downwind, the school secretary.

It is the aim of the school to offer a safe and nurturing environment for learning and for expressing social skills as well as to maintain a supportive spirit among the staff. One of Sister Philip's first projects was to update the school curriculum and to introduce a total reading program in grades one through three. Good working relationships are encouraged with the public school (where events and even materials are shared) and with the Tribal Council which continues to support the Mission with significant annual contributions.

With the building of a new public elementary school in the "backyard," so to speak, of the Mission (forty acres returned to the tribe in July 1994), concentration on excellence and values dominated the theme of St. Mary's Mission School. A brochure issued in 1995 following the school's accreditation contains a revised Mission Statement. The recent achievement (1996) of membership in the Minnesota Non-Public Accrediting Association has affirmed the credibility of the Mission School.

When Sister Marina returned to the Mission as an aide in school and as librarian, the school installed several computers, and Sister taught computer keyboarding. In order to assist the Mission financially, Father Bill also asked her to begin writing grants. "I never did anything like that before," she says. "But Sister André Marthaler, OSB, from St. Benedict's helped me a lot. She edited what I wrote and suggested helpful persons and organizations to contact."[2]

Operating funds had again fallen dangerously low. Since 1991, the Bureau of Catholic Indian Missions cut its subsidy to the school by over $3000. In the fall of 1993, money even had to be borrowed to pay salaries, and cuts were made in non-academic and non-parish ministry areas. Father Bill realized that income needed to be increased or the Mission could be in serious financial trouble within the year. He posed some recommendations for the people to consider:

1) Increase donations, especially the Sunday collections.
2) Cooperate in paying the new tuition of $350 a year.
3) Support the cemetery plan and fund.
4) Institute an "Adopt Our Mission" project throughout the state.
5) Request an increase in monies from the BCIM.
6) Rethink the stewardship attitude.
7) Continue writing requests for grants (over the summer of 1993,

Sister Marina Schlangen, OSB.

about sixty had been written). Small returns began to flow in, including some from grant requests. Sister Marina acquired a Macintosh computer and set up an office in the convent, thus launching a serious development program. She works constantly to build up a secure financial base. By January 1996, Sister had written many grants and received over $400,000.

Mailings to donors are done twice a year; benefactors are remembered daily in prayer and at the Eucharist. A special Mass on the first Tuesday of each month is offered for the intentions of benefactors. Many of these, in turn, have become particular devotees of the needs and of the people of St. Mary's. For example, the retired Benedictine Sisters at St. Scholastica Convent in St. Cloud and the Poor Clare Sisters in Sauk Rapids pledge daily prayer for the needs of the Mission.

During the summer of 1993, it was Red Lake's turn to host the Indian Congress. Guest speaker for this weekend in June was an Ojibwe woman religious, Sister Priscilla Sullivan, from Sudbury, Ontario, who addressed the topic of masculine and feminine energies. A Pipe ceremony was held at the cemetery and a healing service at church. The evening Eucharist included the traditional smudging of the people, Indian dance, and drumming. A parish potluck dinner was held on Sunday. According to the fifty or so participants from around the state – including White Earth, Cass Lake, Duluth, Minneapolis, and Net Lake – a great feeling of peace pervaded the entire weekend.

That fall, a new religious education director, Ms. Bonnie Moen, was hired at the Mission, replacing Sister Annette Fernholz. Preparations for Confirmation scheduled for the following March were soon underway.

(This sacrament is held yearly for grades six through eight.) Ms. Moen lived with the sisters and was a great asset to the community here. However, at the end of the school year, she married and moved to Norway! A replacement was not found until 1996, with the hiring of Mrs. Anita Wheatley. During the two interim years, Father Bill and Sister Marina "filled in." Father prepared the Confirmation classes, and met with youth groups throughout the school year. Sister Marina prepared the children for First Penance and First Eucharist. A two-week "summer school" was also held in 1995, taught by Sister Rose Mary Cramble, OSB, of Crookston, assisted by Sue Eschenbacher of St. Mary's sister parish, Hastings, Minnesota. Sue returned in 1996 along with Linda Anderson. This summer religion program continued in 1997.

September 29, 1993, marked the 100th Anniversary of St. Mary's Church. Though observance was made of the occasion at the Sunday Mass on October 3, "a bigger celebration will be held in a few years as part of the dedication of the Kapsner Center when we finish remodelling the church," Father Bill announced in his Sunday, September 8, bulletin.

October 3rd was also a red-letter day for St. Mary's in another important way. That afternoon, under a clear autumn sky, Bishop Victor Balke of Crookston and Abbot Timothy Kelly, OSB, from St. John's Abbey officiated at the rededication of the old east section of the cemetery and blessed the new stone monument (see pp. 135-137).

Father Bill was intent upon being personally present to the people in the events of their lives. His care was demonstrated in his availability for emergency help, providing, he says, as much as "$12,000 annually for food, transportation, and medicine not covered by inadequate salaries nor by welfare." A special Emergency Fund was tagged for this purpose. Concern for oppression and indignity among people remained a strong priority.

Sister Teresa worked as a co-partner in these ventures, making her daily rounds among the people in their homes, at the nursing home, in the hospital. Both she and Father presided at wakes and funerals, with Sister Teresa doing follow-up grief work with home visits, telephone calls, and cards. "I became friends with the sick," she says, "and to lose them was personally very painful."[3]

Sister conducted Baptism classes for adults of new infants or young

Tekakwitha Conference, Bemidji, MN (1994). (L to R): Sister Teresa Duerr, OSB, Melvina Johnson and Mildred Sumner.

children, and for adults as well. In 1994, she initiated a Befrienders class, helping to train individuals to minister to others in need. She considered enabling others in leadership roles an important aspect of her ministry.

In other leadership positions, the Kateri Circle continued to meet regularly for prayer and Bible study, led by Thern Hegstrom. The group is made up of some eight to ten members. In 1994, the annual Tekakwitha Conference was held in nearby Bemidji, August 3 – 7, giving more Red Lakers the opportunity to attend. Brother Julius Beckermann, though still engaged in studies elsewhere, was invited to give a presentation on family spirituality. He was pleased to do so, stating that the sixteen years he had spent at Red Lake were "the best years of my life." He addressed the topic of Native American spirituality with examples from his own experience among the people of Red Lake, who, he said, are a "very sensitive and thoughtful people" and from whom he learned that his spirituality and the Native American spirituality, though different, were both of value for his own spiritual growth. Brother Julius believes that both spiritualities have value in the eyes of the Creator.

Meanwhile, Father Bill was open to new ideas regarding the parish. Thern Hegstrom, present member of the parish council, says, "Whenever I'd ask him about something, he'd say, 'Go ahead and do it.'" Thern continues to offer generous service to the church. In addition to her work with Tekakwitha, with the liturgy committee, and the inculturation groups, she has served on the Board of Education and helps with traditional meals. Her generous service, she acknowledges, may be an inherited trait from her mother and aunt, who, along with several other families, were active in the church at Redby during the 1950s and 1960s. Thern hopes that younger people today will become involved in church and community activities. She is happy that Father Bill and Father Mark McDonald, the neighboring Episcopal pastor (appointed Episcopal Bishop of Alaska in 1997), worked so well together with teens.

The first meeting of the teens group was held on January 10, 1994. Present to share ideas were also Father Johnson Loud, Bonnie Moen, Joyce Roy, Evelyn and Nick McKenzie, and four junior high boys: Peter McKenzie, Chris Roy, Jessie Smith, and Justin Neadeau. Today, teenagers, grades seven through twelve, continue to gather on Wednesday evenings for socializing, recreation, and faith development.

In 1995, Ms. Beth Loftus, sixth grade teacher at the Mission School, joined the teens group for basketball. She built a fine reputation as coach in the Mission School for fourth through sixth grade boys and girls. During the 1995-96 season, the boys were undefeated and participated in a tournament against teams including Bagely, Cass Lake, Bemidji, and Leech Lake. In the 1996-97 season, the Red Lake High School basketball team, including several graduates of the Mission School, went on to the state tournaments played at the St. Paul Civic Center. It was a "first" for Red Lake, and Indian people, not only from Red Lake, but from neighboring states, were in attendance to "cheer" the team on. The boys lost, 113 to 117, in an intensely exciting and overtime game with Wabasso of southeastern Minnesota, and received an honorable 4th place in their division. Basketball will always remain a favorite sport among Red Lake youth.

As the Kapsner Center neared completion, parish activities began in the new environs. A "kitchen warming" was held in the fall of 1994, and donated utensils, dishes, and appliances were placed on new shelves. Michael Fairbanks presented a Blessed Virgin statue for the gathering area. The image combines Indian materials with biblical and Christian faith expressions.

As time went on, the Center became a true "gathering space" for people to meet and socialize, and, of course, to prepare for liturgies and

Blessed Virgin and Kateri Tekakwitha Shrine in the new Kapsner Center. [Photo: Placid Stucken-schneider, OSB]

other religious events. An ecumenical Thanksgiving service held in the church on November 20, 1994, joined Catholic and Episcopal pastors and parishioners. The Ojibwe singers provided reflective song, while Verna Graves and Judy Roy presented reflective messages. A collection was taken up for the poor. Another service between the two churches, called a Day of Healing, was held in 1995 and again in 1996. The event, initiated by Vi and Leonard Donnell, hopes to promote unity among Christians through common prayer.

The 1995 Thanksgiving dinner held in the Center (organized by Laurentia Colhoff, her sister Tillie, and their extended family) was very successful, according to Priscilla Stately, who helped serve hot dishes, fry bread, and cut up many donated turkeys and pies. A large crowd gathered, and the PTL (Praise the Lord) Club from the reservation entertained.

Another project that grew with the remodeling of the church was a suggestion by Father Bill for a new backdrop to hang behind the altar. A design of an 8-pointed star encircled by rainbow colors was subsequently found and was beautifully quilted by Alice Benais. Sister Philip further suggested that the piece be quilted onto a larger white

A Kapsner Center gathering. (L to r): Bill Strong, Melvina Johnson, Joan Strong, Ashlyn Charnoski (child), Leonard Donnell, Henry Donnell and Betty Beaulieu.

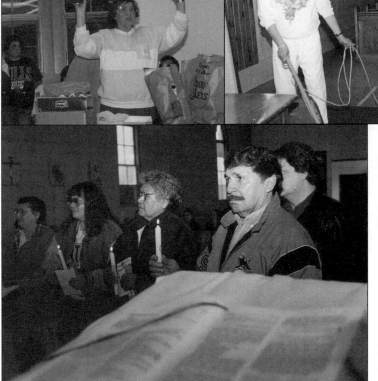

(Above left) Vi Donnell displays new wares at the Kapsner Center Kitchen Warming (1994). (Above right) Joyce Roy helps with the "clean up" detail.

(Left) Witnessing to the Light of Faith. (L to r): Thern Hegstrom, Marlene Thunder, Millie Sumner, Jim Brun.

(Right) Servers (L to R): Dylan Lussier, Toby Donnell, Chris Branchaud (ca 1992).

(Right) 1993. Down with the old backdrop and...

(Above) The Blessed Virgin Mary clothed with an Indian shawl. [Photo: Placid Stuckenschneider, OSB]

...up with a new quilted backdrop to enhance the altar where the Christ-Star leads all to prayer and unity. (Contrast with 1940 view on p. 104.)

background. This work was done at a fabric shop in Blackduck. As Christmas 1993 approached, the old backdrop was removed and the quilt hung in position. It seems particularly significant that such a symbol be raised in St. Mary's Mission Church at this time. A sign of unity, inner light, and fidelity, the radiant star reminds parishioners of another rainbow-circled light that once shone over Red Lake many years ago during this church's infancy, and witnessed by Father Francis X. Pierz, first minister to the Catholic Ojibwe of this place. Then, as now, that supernal light pointed out, "Here is a blessed place. Here is where Christ's love is revealed to all. Here is where God's people come together to worship."

St. Mary's liturgy committee has also provided prayer wheels for either side of the sanctuary. Other contributions include an Indian shawl from Sister Teresa for the statue of Mary, and an Indian blanket from the Kateri Circle for St. Joseph. When Sister Jose Hobday, OSF, nationally and internationally known teacher, writer, and lecturer of Native American spirituality, saw these at an Indian-Religious retreat held at St. Mary's in 1994, she was delighted.

"We try to integrate the Native tradition with the Catholic liturgy," Sister Teresa explains. "Though many people struggle today with what it is to be Indian, they continue to be faithful to the Church."

Indian leadership, especially among women, is an important phenomenon today. Phyllis DeCory, director of Native American ministry in the Diocese of Rapid City, South Dakota, stated in an opening address to a group of the world's religions gathered at the Vatican on September 21, 1994:

> *We are on a threshold of a new era among our people. Women are taking on responsible leadership roles. The women of our nations see and are saddened with what is happening to our youth, how western influences have destroyed their sense of respect, their self-esteem, their pride and hope. We are angry because of the oppression and racism that is prevalent in the United States against our people.*
>
> *We are still a very proud people and hope that somehow God will see fit to rectify the situation.*

Judy Roy, a leader in the Red Lake community as well as the

Judy Roy with Distinguished Graduate Award from St. Mary's School (1997).

church, takes this role seriously. She became Executive Director of Administration for the Tribe in 1990 to 1994, supervising programs and coordinating the administrative activities for Chairman Gerald "Butch" Brun. In June 1994 Judy was elected the first woman Tribal Secretary, a position she holds today with Tribal Chairman, Bobby Whitefeather.

Judy says there are other very good leadership roles emerging from the community today and points out those in the Substance-Abuse Prevention Program and Juvenile Justice Program, as well as in the role of Chief of Police which was filled by Joyce Roy from 1989 to 1994. Joyce was the first woman to hold a supervisory position within the ranks of tribal police. She also continues as lector at St. Mary's and is active in parish activities.

In 1995, Judy Roy formulated a reservation-wide campaign to deal with non-violence. With the support and cooperation of the Tribal Council, who organized district meetings to explore ways of responding to the question, "What can we as a community do to end the violence?", a community unity process was established to carry out the recommendations made by the districts when they came together for discussion. Hundreds of people became involved including Chairman Whitefeather and the representatives from the respective districts.

In the late summer of 1996, Judy helped to organize another movement aimed at stamping out diabetes, one of the major causes of illness and death among the Indian people. Called A MILLION MILES AGAINST DIABETES, this exercise program involves the whole community. Everyone who can, gets out and walks daily, wearing a little mile counter which adds each step to a million-mile goal. The Mission School, both faculty and students, also participate, walking briskly around the playground even on cold winter days.

Because of her generous and peaceful efforts in serving others, Judy has been identified as "a catalyst toward unity."[4] Her many contributions to church and school, to Red Lake, and to the United States, prompted Sister Philip to submit Judy's name to the NCEA (National Catholic Education Association) in 1996. On January 30, 1997, Judy received a special honor as Distinguished Graduate of the Mission School. Present for the celebratory dinner at St. Mary's were her colleagues from the Tribal Council and other guests of the community.

Meanwhile, in the late summer of 1996, Sister Teresa left St. Mary's Mission, and Brother Julius returned. Because of the vacancy left by

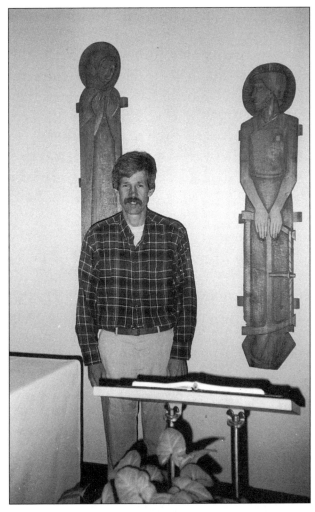

New pastor: Father Patrick Sullivan (July 1997). Wood carvings by Placid Stuckenschneider, OSB (convent chapel).

Sister's position, Brother Julius took up the work. He is happy to be back and is busy using his many gifts of care, counseling, and companionship – often in conversational Ojibwe, which he has "polished up." He also assists, when requested, in the Twelve-Step Program with those on the fifth step.

In the spring of 1997, Father Bill announced his retirement, but happily for St. Mary's, his retirement will be spent at the Mission. St.

Mary's new pastor, Father Patrick Sullivan, took office in July. He brings his youth and energy to serve not only Red Lake and Nebish, but the parish at Wilton. Upon arrival from his parish at Warroad, Father Pat announced, "It will be good to live on the south end of the lake and to share in the tradition of the Tribe, the Church and the Mission. I pray with all my being that Jesus and the Great Spirit may draw us deeper into the mysteries that were, are and will be."

Thus, between these two priests, a wise-ordering of ministry is underway this fall of 1997 after Father Bill's well-earned "sabbatical" spent at his favorite wilderness spot: Laketrails Camp on Lake of the Woods.

Present trustees, William "Bill" Strong and Marcella Auginash, serve as a bridge for the smooth transfer of pastoral administration which took place on July 1. Bill and his sister, Melvina Johnson, descend from a long line of both Traditional and Christian witness. Both their paternal and maternal grandfathers (Sumner) were Catholic; their great-great-grandfather was Chief Meskokonaye (Red Robed), one of the seven chiefs who signed the land treaty of 1889. Bill, a graduate of St. Mary's Mission School and of Whittier College in California, speaks both English and Ojibwe. Along with Melvina, Bill agrees that the Ojibwe language is important to preserve though it is a difficult language to learn. "It is very descriptive," Bill says, "and very discriminate. One must *think* in Indian to teach the language. Humor is built in because many phrases or words are 'turned around' from the way they are in English and become really funny."[5]

Bill's wife, Joan, though non-Indian, has been accepted by the people. She speaks about the early creation stories of the Indian people and how these are a symbolic parallel of the Christian story of the exodus, the entry into the promised land, of the prophets, and even of Christ.

Bill's father worked at the early saw mill (later moved to Redby) at Pike's Creek. Here, he says, the people gathered annually on July 6 to hold their traditional powwow in honor of their independence as a nation. It is an historic place. The Treaty of 1889 had been signed here on the west side of the creek by the lake. Later, Indian Congresses were held here. This writer is given to believe from research that this historic spot may have received its name from Lieutenant Zebulon Pike,

(Above, Top Row, L to r): Natalie Kantor, Jim Needham, Beth Goodwin, Brother Julius Beckermann, OSB; Middle Row: Father Bill Mehrkens, Sister Marina Schlangen, OSB, Colleen Crowell, Barbara Scherber, Neoka Donnell; Bottom Row: Sister Philip Zimmer, OSB, Eleanor Swanson, Mary Luethmers, Rene Lushko, John Eklund. Not pictured: Georgia Downwind, Secretary.

(Above) Terry Harris, Assistant Custodian (1997).

(Left) Diana Mystic, Mission School Secretary (1997).

Dan Needham in traditional Ojibwe pow-wow outfit: beaded leggings and arm bands; porcupine and eagle feather roach. [Photo: Sister Mary Minette Beutz, OSB]

who was in the Upper Mississippi region around 1806 exploring the source of the Mississippi River for the U.S. Government. Later, by an Act of Congress dated May 26, 1824, Indian agents were allowed to locate traders at a Fort Pike on Red Lake.[6] Earlier still, of course, the Ojibwe had already settled at this south side of the lake.

Today, a much smaller Pike's Creek still meanders through the ravine designated as Pike Park, created in 1989 when Red Lake commemorated the signing of the 1889 treaty.

Powwows are held near the Humanities Center today, on pow-wow grounds high above the lake, east of Pike's Creek. In addition to the four-day July powwow, at which dancers from around the nation and Canada compete, several other powwows are held in the course of the season, including the August powwow to choose the new Brave and Princess, a Labor Day pow-wow, and a Sovereignty powwow in October. Many Indians still bead their own outfits, and many treasure outfits that have been handed down from generation to generation. Participation in the powwow brings into the sacred circle family, friends, comfort, and the vitality of Ojibwe culture.

Red Lake itself, on whose banks the people dance, remains a powerful symbol and reality. Glacial in geologic history, it once formed part of the great Lake Aggaziz. Visible from many vantage points, this vast, shallow lake continues to play a prominent part in the lives of the people. Commercial fishing remains a major industry, and fishermen still pay their respect to the lake, offering tobacco to its spirit for protection and success in their endeavors. Many come to its shores to gaze at the incredible beauty of sunsets. Sometimes in the spring the great ice-covered lake is swept by powerful winds that crack up the ice and heave tons of it over the shores, crushing trees and even buildings in its path. These thick chunks of ice creep like ancient glaciers up and over roadways, eventually bringing traffic to a halt.

The power, the beauty, and the resources of this lake have historically given life to the people of Red Lake. But the water holds still further significance, and we have come full circle in the telling of its story. It was the water of rivers and lakes and streams that first brought the Ojibwe people to this place. For the Catholics of St. Mary's, it was also the waters of Baptism which their ancestors encountered on their westerly route, first at Madeline Island with missioner Father Frederic Baraga; then at Red Lake itself, journey's end, with Fathers Francis Pierz and Lawrence Lautischar.

These life-giving waters continue to call many born anew in Christ to ongoing transformation in love. The faith journey of the people of St. Mary's will always be one interconnected to this earlier migratory journey. But the challenge remains in these days to frame new visions where HOPE persists as the expectation of renewal of all things in Christ. For the past, the present, and the future are all bound up in the radiant revelation of the haloed Cross of Christ appearing over this place on a cold Epiphany night, 1855.

Now, on the eve of a new millennium, poised on the threshold of new dreams, the Christ-Light shines afresh and joyfully over a "handsome Christian congregation" where a foundation, once firmly laid in faith, observes its life and growth, the Church of St. Mary, "full of fair hope."

Red Lake at sunset and at the spring thaw

...one Lord,

one faith,

one baptism;

BIND US TOGETHER

*one God
and Father
of all...*

Eph. 4: 5, 6.

BIBLIOGRAPHY

Ahern, Patrick H. *Catholic Heritage in Minnesota, North Dakota, South Dakota*. St. Paul, MN: H.M. Smyth Company, Inc., Book Publishing Division, 1964.

Barry, Coleman J., O.S.B. *Worship and Work*. Collegeville, MN: St. John's Abbey Press, 1980 & 1994.

Benton-Benai, Edward. *The Mishomis Book*. St. Paul, MN: Indian Country Press, 1979 & 1981.

Berg, Carol, O.S.B. *Climbing Learners' Hill: Benedictines at White Earth, 1878-1945*. University of Minnesota, 1981.

Bowden, Henry Warner. *American Indians and Christian Missions*. University of Chicago, 1981.

Brill, Charles. *Indian and Free*. University of Minnesota, 1971, 1974 & 1991.

Brown, Joseph Epes. *The Spiritual Legacy of the American Indian*. New York, 1982.

Burnquist, Joseph A. *Minnesota and Its People*. Vol.1. Chicago: S. J. Clarke Publishing Co., 1924.

Burnside, Ed (1986) and Paul Buffalo (1968). Redlake, MN: Red Lake Archives. (Audio cassette).

Coleman, Bernard, O.S.B., Ellen Fragner and Estelle Eich, *Objibwe Myths and Legends*. Minneapolis, MN: 1961.

Coleman, Bernard, O.S.B. and Verona LaBud, O.S.B. *Masinaigans: The Little Book*. St. Paul, MN: North Central Publishing Co., 1972.

Collections of the Minnesota Historical Society. Vols. V & IX. St. Paul, MN: 1901.

Crawford, Dean A. *Minnesota Chippewa Indians*. St. Paul, MN: 1967.

Densmore, Frances. *Chippewa Customs*. Minnesota Historical Society Press, 1979.

Duffy, Consuela Maria, S.B.S. *Katharine Drexel*. Cornwells Heights, PA: 1977.

Folwell, William Watts. *A History of Minnesota*. St. Paul, MN: 1956.

Fruth, Alban, O.S.B. *A Century of Missionary Work Among the Redlake Chippewa Indians*. Collegeville, MN: St. John's Abbey, 1958.

Furlan, William P. *In Charity Unfeigned*. Paterson, NJ: St. Anthony Guild Press, 1952.

Hickerson, Harold. *The Chippewa and Their Neighbors: A Study in Ethnohistory*. Holt, Rinehart and Winston, Inc., 1970.

Hilger, Inez, O.S.B. *Chippewa Child Life and Its Cultural Background*. Washington D. C., 1951.

Holcombe, R.I. *Minnesota in Three Centuries 1655 – 1908*. New York: The Publishing Society of Minnesota, 1908.

Lass, William E. *Minnesota*. New York, 1977.

McDonald, Grace, O.S.B. *Minnesota – Its History and People*. New York, Chicago, 1941.

McDonald, Grace, O.S.B. *With Lamps Burning*. St. Paul, MN: The North Central Publishing Company, 1957.

Mittleholtz, Erwin F. *Historical Review of the Red Lake Indian Reservation*. Beltrami County Historical Society, Bemidji, MN, 1957.

Morrison, John G. Jr. *My Forebears and the World They Lived In*, 1955. (Private collection).

Tekakwitha Conference. National Center, Great Falls, MT (Program notes: 1987, 1989, 1990-1992).

Treuer, Robert. *Voyageur Country – A Park in the Wilderness*. University Of Minnesota Press, Mpls., 1979.

Trigger, Bruce G. *Handbook of North American Indians*. Vol.15. Washington D.C., 1978.

Vecsey, Christopher. *Traditional Ojibwa Religion and Its Historical Changes*. Philadephia, PA, 1983.

Verwyst, Rev. Chrysostum. *Life of Bishop Baraga*. Milwaukee, WI: M. H. Wiltzius & Co., 1900.

Vizenor, Gerald. *The People Named the Chippewa*. Minneapolis, MN: University of Minnesota Press, 1984.

Warren, William W. *History of the Ojibway Nation*. Minneapolis, MN: Ross & Haines, Inc., 1853 & 1970.

Washburn, Wilcombe E. *Handbook of North American Indians*. Vol.4. Smithsonian Institute, Washington D.C., 1988.

Weatherford, Jack. *Native Roots*. New York: Crown Publishing, Inc., 1991.

Winchell, N.H. *Aborigines of Minnesota*. Vol. II. St. Paul, MN: Minnesota Historical Society, 1911.

Wright, H.E. Jr., Barbara A. Coffin, Norman E. Aaseng. *The Patterned Peatlands of Minnesota*. Minneapolis, MN: 1992.

APPENDICES – DOCUMENTS

APPENDIX A

(1892 Church Circular)

Red Lake Reservation, Minn., May 20, 1892.

CIRCULAR OF INFORMATION.

N. B.—PLEASE FILL OUT BLANK PLAINLY AND CONCISELY.

1. Name of Church. *(Old church, St. Ignatius of Antioch) Present church, Immaculate Conception*

   Diocese *Duluth*

   City or Town *Red Lake, Minn.*

   County *Beltrami*   State *Minnesota*

2. Location *NW quarter of NE quarter, Section 29 Town 157 N. Range 34 W.*

   Dimensions *25 x 41*

   Material *Logs*

   Value *$700.00*

   Date of placing the cornerstone *About Aug. 5, 1890*

   Date of ~~consecration~~ or dedication *Dec. 8, 1891*

   Change of location *The church of St. Ignatius of Antioch, a mile west of*

   Improvements *the present church, served from Dec. 25, 1879 to Dec. 8, 1891.*

3. Date of organization *This place had resident missionary from Aug. 14, 1858, to Dec. 31, 1858; from March 7, 1879, to June 1883; and from May 15, 1888 up to date.*

   First pastor *Laurentius Lautizar, who resided and held services at the house of Peter Jourdan (about two miles east of present church) where services*

   Incorporation *continued to be held at distant intervals up to the year 1879.*

   Limits *Red Lake Indian Reservation.*

   Nationalities *Chippewa Indians, and a few white men on or near the limits of the Reserve*

4. List of pastors, with dates *Laurentius Lautigar (Aug. 14, 1858 till Dec. 3, 1858),*
   Franciscus Pierz (visited 1858, 1865, 1866), Joseph F. Buh (visited 1867,
   1869, 1871, 1872, 1873, 1874). Ignatius Tomazin (visited 1875, 1878,
   and resided 1879 till 1883), Aloysius Hermanutz O.S.B. (visited 1883, '84, '85, '86, '87, '88)
   Thomas Borgerding O.S.B. (resided from 1888 till date), Simon Lampe (resided 1888 till date)

5. Present status: Number of families *120 (not including stations visited.)*
   Communicants *About 150* Baptisms in '91 *Red Lake H., Leech Lake & Lake Winibigosh*

6. Church privileges *None*
   Indulgences *n*
   Privileged altars *n*

7. Cemetery, area *About two years acres, near old church*

8. Schools, parochial or district *Catholic Industrial Boarding School*
   Teachers *4 Benedictine Sisters* Attendance *About 50 (average)*
   Religious instruction how provided for *By priests and Sisters*
   Length of school term *10 months*

9. Parish house; dimensions *16 x 22'*
   Cost and date of erection *About $625.00 Erected 1889*

10. Church societies for religious and charitable purposes *None*

    Church or school libraries *None*

11. Principal incidents: Missions *Bishop Seidenbush visited 1882, accompanied by Rev. Jos. Buh.*
    Accidents *Rev. Laurentius Lautigar froze to death on Red Lake, Dec. 3, 1858.*
    Difficulties *Most of the people partly retain their nomadic habits.*

    Thomas Borgerding O.S.B.
    Simon Lampe O.S.B. RECTOR

APPENDIX B
(Text of Land Grant)
1912

Filed for record October 15 A.D. 1912, at 3 P.M.
J.O.Harris Register of Deeds.
Act of May 29, 1908 (Pub. No. 156.)
409 86

THE UNITED STATES 0F AMERICA,

To All to Whom these Presents shall come, Greeting:

Whereas, There has been deposited in the General Land Office of the United States an order of the Secretary of the Interior directing that a patent issue to "The Bureau of Catholic Indian Missions" according to Section 20 of the Act of Congress of May 29, 1908. (Public No. 156) for the

Southwest quarter of the Southeast quarter of Section twenty-six, the Northwest Quarter of the Northwest quarter, and the Lots, Two, three, and four of Section thirty-five The Northeast quarter of the Northeast quarter of Section thirty-four and the southeast quarter of the southeast quarter of Section twenty-seven in Township one hundred forty-two north of Range forty-one west, the South-east quarter of the northwest quarter and the northeast quarter of the southwest quarter of Section ten in Township one hundred forty-four north of Range forty-two west, and the Lots one, two, and twelve of Section seven in Township one hundred forty-four north of Range forty west of the fifth Principal Meridian, on the White Earth Reservation, Minnesota, containing four hundred twenty-seven and sixty-five hundredths acres, and the Lots two and three of Section twenty and the west half of the northeast quarter and the east half of the northwest quarter of Section twenty-nine in township and hundred fifty-one north of Range thirty-four west of the Fifth Principal Meridian on the Red Lake Indian Reservation, Minnesota, containing two hundred forty-five and forty-hundredths acres, and containing, in the aggregate, six hundred seventy-three and five hundredths acres .

Now Know Ye, That the United States of America, in consideration of the premises, Has Given and Granted, and by these presents Does Give and Grant, unto the said The Bureau of Catholic Indian Missions, and to its successors, the lands above described:

To Have and to hold the same, together with all the rights priviledges, and immunities, and appurtenances, of whatsoever nature thereunto belonging, unto The said The Bureau of Catholic Indian Missions, and to its successors and assigns forever.

IN TESTIMONY WHEREOF, I, Theodore Roosevelt, President of the United States of America, have caused these letters to be made Patent, and the seal of the General land Office to be hereunto affixed.

Given under my hand, at the City of Washington, the seventeenth day of September, in, the year of our Lord one thousand nine hundred and eight, and of the Independence of the United States the one hundred and thirty-third,

By the President: Theodore Roosevelt
By M. W. Young, Secretary.
H. W. Sanford Recorder Of the General land Office,
(U. S. General Land Office Seal) Patent Number,
Recorded 14117. Vol. page.

APPENDIX C

A PUBLIC DECLARATION
TO THE TRIBAL COUNCILS, TRADITIONAL SPIRITUAL
LEADERS,AND TO ALL INDIAN PEOPLE
OF NORTHWEST MINNESOTA

Dear Brothers and Sisters,

The Second Vatican Council, enlightened by the Holy Spirit, declared "that the human person has a right to religious freedom." It went on to say that all persons "are to be immune from coercion on the part of individuals or of social groups and of any human power, in such wise that in matters religious no one is to be forced to act in a manner contrary to his [her] own beliefs. Nor is anyone to be restrained from acting in accordance with his [her] own beliefs, whether privately or publicly, whether alone or in association with others, within due limits."

In light of this, I wish to apologize for those times when the Catholic Church violated your freedom of conscience, showing little or no respect for your dignity as human persons, for the dignity of your sacred places and ceremonial objects, and for the traditional ways in which you live and worship.

I call upon all Catholics within this Diocese not only to recognize and respect, as a matter of justice, your sacred dignity as persons, but also, as a matter of justice, to recognize and respect the many aspects of your Indian culture: language, chants, sweat lodges, powwows, to mention just a few.

More specifically: in light of the Church's teaching and in light the American Religious Freedom Act (P.L. 95-134, 1978), I want to go on record as affirming the following:

1. The right of Indian People to practice and participate in traditional ceremonies and rituals with the same protection offered all religions under the Constitution;

2. The right of Indian People to have reasonable access to and protection of sacred places and public lands for ceremonial purposes;

3. The right of Indian People to use their religious symbols (feathers, tobacco, sweet grass, etc.) for use in traditional ceremonies and rituals.

The Church of Crookston commits itself to join with you in seeking justice and in the righting of previous wrongs, for we are all called to be doers of justice and makers of peace.

May the Spirit of the living God, the Great Spirit blowing over the waters and in the forests, over the land and in our hearts, grant us that joy which comes from doing justice and making peace.

Sincerely Yours,

✠Victor H. Balke
Bishop of Crookston

Crookston, Minnesota
September 21, 1992

APPENDIX D

RELIGIOUS SERVING ST. MARY'S MISSION, RED LAKE, MINNESOTA

MISSIONARIES

Lawrence Lautischar	1858
Visited by Francis Pierz from Crow Wing	1858 – 1867
Visited by Joseph Buh from Belle Prairie	1867 – 1875
Visited by Ignatius Tomazin from White Earth	1875 – 1879

PASTORS

Ignatius Tomazin	1879 – 1883	
Aloysius Hermanutz, OSB,	visited from White Earth	1883 – 1888
Thomas Borgerding, OSB	1888 – 1923; 1942 – 1948	
Simon Lampe, OSB	1888 – 1896; 1923 – 1940	
Felix Nelles, OSB	1898 – 1899; 1900 – 1901	
Corbinian Hermanutz, OSB	1901 – 1906	
Julius Locnikar, OSB	1906 – 1907	
Florian Locnikar, OSB	1915 – 1941	
Francis Bernick, OSB	1928 – 1929	
Egbert Goeb, OSB	1940 – 1951; 1954 – 1955	
Leo Hoppe, OSB	1941 – 1947	
Timothy Majerus, OSB	1941 – 1942	
Benno Watrin, OSB	1947 – 1952	
Omer Maus, OSB	1951 – 1954	
Columban Kremer, OSB	1952 – 1955	
Alban Fruth, OSB	1955 – 1960	
Cassian Osendorf, OSB	1956 – 1973	
Adrian Foxxe, OSB	1960 – 1965; 1973 – 1975	
Maurice Hurrle, OSB	1965 – 1968	
Ignatius Candrian, OSB	1968 – 1974	
Jordan Stovick, OSB	1974 – 1976	
Peter St. Hilaire, OSB	1976 – 1977	

Patrick Okada, OSB   1977 – 1978
Meinrad Dindorf, OSB   1978 – 1986
Aelred Tegels, OSB   1986 – 1991
Msgr. William Mehrkens   1991 – 1997
Patrick Sullivan   1997 -

BENEDICTINE BROTHERS

Joel Blekum   1948 – 1950
Felix Nuessendorfer   1950 – 1952
Placid Stuckenschneider   1951 – 1956
Jerome Zeleznikar   1952 – 1954
Elmer Cichy   1954 – 1956
Michael Laux   1954 – 1972; 1974 – 1975
William Borgerding   1955 – 1966
Gregory Eibensteiner   1957, 1970 - 1975
Dunstan Nordick   1958 – 1959; 1967 – 1974
Samuel Lickteig   1970 – 1971
Julius Beckermann   1973 – 1978; 1979 – 1991; 1996 –
Stephen Thell   1975 – 1978
Gabriel Bieniek   1976 – 1979
David Manahan   1978 – 1979
Douglas Mullin   1982 – 1989

BENEDICTINE SISTERS

Amalia Eich   1888 – 1890
Evangelista McNulty   1888 – 1898
Marciana Horn   1889 –   ?
Alphonsa O'Donnell   1889 – 1890
Augustine Terhaar   1889 – 1890
Euphrasia Hirtenberger   1889 – 1895; 1898 – 1906
Nepomucene Chalupsky   1890 – 1891
Ambrosia Rettenmaier   1890 – 1893
Eusebia Merten   1891 –   ?
Emilia Sehr   c.1891 – 1894
Blasia Bollig   1892 – 1893

Caroline Albers	1894 – 1895
Basilia Cosgrove	1898 – 1899
Leocadia Vanderlinde	1899 – 1903
Sienna Baumgartner	1901 – 1903
Leonissa Dorfner	1902 – 1904
Beatrice (Richard) McGuinn	1902 – 1905
Helena Hansen	1902 – 1907
Carmelita Schlosser	1903 – 1904
Raphael Kohler	1904 – 1905
Renilda Muggli	1904 – 1911
Emma Schwieters	1905 – 1906
Corbinian Bukoski	1905 – 1907
Desideria Winkels	1906
Columbina Adrian	1908 – 1909
Altonia Schiesser	1908 – 1910
Firmina Robeck	1909 – 1911
Hyacinthe Simmer	1909 – 1931
Bathildis Griese	1910
Frieda Kraemer	1910 – 1913
Claudina Locnikar	c.1910 – 1916
Tharsilla Weinans	c.1910 – 1916
Agnella Schmitt	1911 – 1912
Aegidia Braegelmann	1911 – 1920; 1921 – 1928
Octavia Roth	1912 – 1913; 1914 – 1916; 1917 – 1920; 1934 – 1937
Lina Braun	1913 – 1914
Sylvina Ettel	1913 – 1921
Florian Weis	1914 – 1917; 1927 – 1928
Mercedes Praml	1915 – 1917
Hildeburg Dehmer	1916 – 1919
Jovita Wagner	1916 – 1922
Heliodora Wensmann	1916 – 1928
Liberia Weinans	1918 – 1919
Erasma Pachel	1919 – 1920; 1928 – 1935
Emerine Zerr	1919 – 1920
Laura Hesch	1920 – 1921; 1934 – 1939
Hilberta Ludwig	1920 – 1921
Petra Mayer	1920 – 1922

Winefride Linhoff	1921 – 1923
Arleen Jundt	1921 – 1924
Mariola Schwartzbauer	1921 – 1927
Ortrude Nester	1921 – 1928
Alban Ruhland	1922 – 1924
Benette Bursey	1922 – 1929
Mona Schroeder	1923
Emil Schmuck	1923 – 1927; 1930 – 1932
Hildine Mischke	1923 – 1937; 1971 – 1975
Anselma Hunder	1924 – 1926
Leo Boller	1924 – 1929
Cornelia Geschwill	1926 – 1927
Roselma Roers	1926 – 1927; 1948 – 1949
Xavier Hens	1927 – 1929; 1932 – 1935
Ermin Pohlkamp	1927 – 1930
Cordella Goertel	1928 – 1929
Celestia Lauerman	1928 – 1930
Verna Viktor	1928 – 1930
Mary Edgar Feist	1928 – 1931
Clarona Wetzstein	1928 – 1933; 1937 – 1938
Tilberta Goertel	1928 – 1937
Meinulpha Hassing	1929 – 1931
Villanova Bise	1929 – 1932
Gisella Moudry	1929 – 1934
Seraphica Kennedy	1929 – 1935
Reingardis Kramlinger	1929 – 1940
Severine Sand	1930 – 1935; 1936 – 1937
Eucharia Koltes	1930 – 1954
Adelphia Fitterer	1931 – 1937
Almeda Schroeder	1931 – 1942
Valois Barthe1	1932 – 1960
Hugo Huck	1932 – 1934
Georgella Sickler	1933 – 1936
Jucunda Sickler	1933 – 1937
Adelma Roers	1933 – 1952; 1956 – 1974
Sidonia Zeug	1935 – 1942
Rudolphine Traeger	1936 – 1937
Mary James Emter	1936 – 1939

Rhabana Scheuren	1936 – 1948
Baldwin Dworschak	1937 – 1938; 1949 – 1955
Leopoldine Schwahn	1937 – 1938
Noel LeClaire	1937 – 1939
Veronette Schramel	1937 – 1940
Aniceta Drontle	1939 – 1946; 1962 – 1968
Ethelbert Krenik	1939 – 1946
Annina Zierden	1940 – 1941
Rosabel Schweitzer	1940 – 1943
Alonzo Winkelman	1940 – 1946
Delora Schweitzer	1941 – 1943
Adella Winkelman	1941 – 1945
Adolphine Kahl	1942 – 1944
Edwina Bromenshenkel	1942 – 1947
Mary Ida Klehr	1942 – 1952
Cleta Kurth	1943 – 1944
Doloria Goeb	1943 – 1954
Gudilia Duclos	1943 – 1955
Philothea Hondl	1944 – 1947
Theodora Nelson	1944 – 1949
Annetta Osendorf	1945 – 1946
Amata Sieverding	1946 – 1947
DeAngelis Vasquez	1946 – 1947
Clementine Kahl	1946 – 1953
Roman (Genevieve) Leuer	1946 – 1954
Rhoda (Mary Jane) Hunkler	1947 – 1949
Mary Louise Walz	1947 – 1950
Martel Greeninger	1947 – 1955
Felicia Stager	1949 – 1950
Aaronette Herzog	1949 – 1953
Alvina (Anna) Blumhoefer	1950 – 1951
Lourdette Bogner	1950 – 1951
Gordian Miller	1950 – 1951
Elmer (Marie) Reisinger	1951 – 1957
Eulalia Siebels	1951 – 1957
Patricia Wallis	1951 – 1958; 1973 – 1974; 1979 – 1985
Debora Herda	1952 – 1954
Rosaria Zenner	1952 – 1956; 1969 – 1972

Angelita Hooley	1953 – 1954
Teresita Sand	1953 – 1958
Karen Nordick	1953 – 1964; 1989 – 1990
Areta (Cecelia) Yanta	1954 – 1955
Joachim Leifeld	1954 – 1963
Thea Grieman	1954 – 1972
Maristelle Pick	1955 – 1956
Zitella Ruprecht	1955 – 1956
Erna Miller	1955 – 1958
Elaine Schindler	1955 – 1959; 1967 – 1970
Herbert Dehler	1955 – 1962
Redempta (Louise) Koltes	1955 – 1962; 1970 -1973
Loretta (Catherine) Ludwig	1956 – 1959
Caedmon Kessler	1957 – 1958
Merle Maerz	1957 – 1963
Frances Lorraine Eisenschenk	1958 – 1962
DePorres (Loretta) Rothstein	1958 – 1963; 1976 – 1979
Egene Wicker	1958 – 1964
Mardelle LeDuc	1958 – 1970
Mary John Sweeney	1959 – 1960
Jocile Robinson	1959 – 1963; 1985 – 1986
Mary Agnes Wantoch	1960 – 1961
Engelbert Suek	1960 – 1968
Florine Schoemer	1961 – 1962
Marina Schlangen	1962 – 1964; 1993-
Rosaire Pratschner	1962 – 1967
Josina Ann Holdvogt	1963 – 1964
Johnette Kohorst	1963 – 1975
Clara (Marion) Zimmerman	1963 – 1967; 1984 – 1987
Edna Rader	1963 – 1969
Maura (Joyce) Willenbring	1964 – 1965
Josephine Witzmann	1964 – 1966
Victoria (Rose) Schindler	1964 – 1968
Madonna Niebolte	1965 – 1974
Beata (Geraldine) Zierden	1966 – 1968
Norma Meyer	1967 – 1970
Benet Frandrup	1967 – 1973
Emerentia Fleischhacker	1968 – 1969; 1978 – 1981

Mary Neil Notch	1968 – 1970
Rose Michaelis	1968 – 1974
Ansgar Willenbring	1968 – 1976; 1981 – 1991; 1992 –
Delphine Heier	1968 – 1989
Beatrice Eiynck	1969 – 1971
Lynette Primus	1970 – 1974
Alice Alquin Deutsch	1970 – 1975
Jean Schwartz	1970 – 1976
Marla Maus	1972 – 1973
Ronald (Alice) Ethen	1973 – 1974
Leona Caspers	1973 – 1975
Dominica Freund	1973 – 1984
Anselm Hiltner	1974 – 1976
Leodette Hiltner	1974 – 1976
Elizabeth Theis	1974 – 1979
Marcella Weber	1974 – 1985
Felicitas (Barbara) Zinzer	1974 – 1989
Jane Marie Barlage	1975 – 1976
Marlene Schwinghammer	1975 – 1982
Jane Weber	1975 – 1989
Gretchen Yanz	1976 – 1977
Dorothea Lenz	1976 – 1978
Kayleen (Sharon) Nohner	1976 – 1982
Lucy Revering	1976 – 1982
Caroline Eckroth	1977 – 1979, 1982 – 1984
Constette LeFevere	1977 – 1990
Dorothy Ann Marx	1978 – 1991
Delice Bialke	1981 – 1991
Gilmary Kempf	1983 – 1990
Ruth Anne Schneider	1985 – 1989
Mary Minette Beutz	1987 – 1995
Philip Zimmer	1987 -
Teresa Duerr	1992 – 1996
Stephen Kurpiers	1997 –

NOTES

Chapter 1

1 Ron Libertus, "An Essay Building on the Past," *Minneapolis Tribune*, October 28, 1972. "The Ojibwa or the Chippewa exist in the minds of the dominant society, while the Anishinabe exist in the souls of 'the people.'"

2 *Handbook of North American Indians*, ed. Wilcombe E. Washburn, (Washington D.C., 1988), Vol.4, "History of Indian-White Relations."

3 William W. Warren, *History of the Ojibway Nation* (Minneapolis, Minnesota: Ross & Gaines, Inc., 1853; reprinted, 1970), pp. 404,405. The chapel was called the Chapel of the Holy Spirit, or LaPointe du St. Esprit located on the west shore of Chequamegon Bay. A map of Lake Superior was attached to the *Jesuit Relations of 1670-71* which was an annual report published during the 17th and early 18th centuries by the Jesuit missionaries in New France.

4 William Watts Folwell, *A History of Minnesota* (Minnesota Historical Society, 1956), Vol. 1.

5 Even in the late 20th century, Ojibwe elders remember and pass on lessons of gratitude. Paul Buffalo, Oral History, (Red Lake Archives, Redlake, Minnesota, 1986), tapes #344, #348. "Never forget, never forget, never forget what you receive."

6 Edward Benton-Banai, *The Mishomis Book* (Indian Country Press, Inc., St. Paul, Minnesota, 1979), p. 106: "If they did not accept these teachings, they would not pass on to join their ancestors in the Spirit World to the West. Instead, they would burn forever in a place under the ground! This idea was terrifying to many Native people." It is understandable that resentment might build around just this issue by those Indians who, according to the Traditional way, wanted to be buried on elevated or sightly elevated places, facing west, the direction of their soul; or to have low structures (houses) built over the graves at which food was placed to aid the spirit.

7 Jody Beaulieu, Archivist, Red Lake Archives, Red Lake, Minnesota, 1992.

8 Robert Treuer, *Voyageur Country* (University of Minnesota Press, Minneapolis, Minnesota, 1979), p. 45.

9 *Handbook of North American Indians*, ed. Wilcombe E. Washburn (Smithsonian Insitute, Washington D.C., 1988), Vol.4, p. 529.

10 Thomas Borgerding, OSB, Red Lake St. Mary's Mission Memoirs (St. John's Abbey Archives, Collegeville, Minnesota, 1949), p. 1. "A village of Sioux lived on the shores of Red Lake between the mouths of Big Stone River and Sandy River. . . . The reason this was called Red Lake is due to an actual historical event. A company of Sioux Indians were surprised early one morning by some Chippewa Indians. The Sioux tried to flee from the Chippewa Indians on the frozen lake. The ice was honeycombed at the time, and the Sioux were barefooted. In the course of their flight, the ice became red with the blood from their feet. . . ."

11 William P. Furlan, *In Charity Unfeigned* (St. Anthony Guild Press, Paterson, N.J., 1952), p. 120. Letter from Pierz to Baraga's sister in Carniola (Austria).

12 Benno Watrin, OSB, Red Lake Memoirs (St. John's Abbey Archives, Collegeville, Minnesota, 1949), p. 9. The story is told that Lautischar had forgotten the only overcoat he had on Mackinaw Island during his trip from Michigan to St. Paul, and was probably unprepared for the rigorous winters of northern Minnesota. A donation of 57.55 guldens was later sent him from a priest in Slovenia "for the forgotten overcoat."

Benno Watrin, OSB (Photo 1985).

13 Msgr. Z.L. Zaplotnick, *Acta et Dicta* (St. John's Abbey Archives, Collegeville, Minnesota, 1934), Vol. 6, No.2 – pp. 271, 272, 274, 275, 277.

14 *Ibid.*, p. 280.

Chapter 2

1 Amalia Eich, OSB, Interview (St. Benedict's Monastery Archives, St. Joseph, Minnesota, 1940), p. 2.

2 Msgr. Z.L. Zaplotnick, *Acta et Dicta* (St. John's Abbey Archives, Collegeville, Minnesota, 1934), Vol.6, No.2 – p. 281.

3 Charles Vandersluis, *Source Books*; 1954 (St, John's Abbey Archives, Collegeville, Minnesota). Josepha, the daughter of Josens Jordan (spellings vary), was born in this house. Josepha became the mother of

Father Bill Mehrkens, pastor, 1991-1997, at old Military Marker (see p. 16).

Mrs. Roy Bailey of Redby. This house stood on a bank rising 20 feet above shore about 12 miles east of the first agency site; or 2.3 miles east of the present St. Mary's Mission Church. In the 1950s, a stone marker of a sailor was observed here and an Indian grave. Today, only one marker in an upright position remains among the trees and brush covering the site. It is a stone military marker which reads:

> Captain Robert Aitken
> Co. C Ninth Division
> Minn. Inf.

Thomas Borgerding also says in his 1952 memoirs, page 33 (St. John's Abbey Archives): "Formerly the Catholics had had a cemetery about a mile and a half east of the agency near the lake shore. There one can still see graves – those which have stones. Robert Aitken, a civil war veteran, is buried there. There are a few more crosses but no names."

4 According to a letter written by Father Lautischar, in his haste to depart on the steamer across Lake Michigan enroute to Minnesota, he forgot his overcoat (brought from Carniola) at the rectory on Mackinaw Island. He writes, "…I shall miss it very much during the winter because I shall not be able to buy me a new one. However, I did not worry in the least about it; God clothes the birds and the beasts, and He will clothe me also." *Acta et Dicta* (St. John's Abbey Archives, Collegeville, Minnesota, 1934), Vol.6, No.2, p. 267.

5 Following the abandonment of the Crow Wing Mission and Cemetery, Lautischar's remains were removed to Calvary Cemetery in Duluth, Minnesota on September 22, 1892. Here a grey granite marker stands in memory of the first resident pastor of the Diocese of Duluth (at the time).

In 1929, Abbot Alcuin Deutsch had a bronze memorial tablet to Lautischar erected near the entrance of St. Mary's Mission Church at Red Lake. It is said the Indians themselves collected the money to erect this memorial. With the building of the new addition on this church in 1992, the memorial was moved closer to Highway 1 (see p. 93).

6 Erwin F. Mittelholtz, *Historical Review of the Red Lake Indian Reservation* (Beltrami County Historical Society, Bemidji, Minnesota, 1957), pp. 116-128. Bill Strong and Melvina Johnson's great-great-grandfather was Chief Meskokonaye, or Red Robe, who was sixty-four years old at the time of the treaty signing. He was chief of forty-three families near Thief River, west of Red Lake, and wished to keep, he said, this "swamp land valueless to the whites but of some value to the Indians as there was much wild game on it which could be used for subsistence."

7 "Chippewa Indians of Minnesota," House of Representatives, Ex. Doc. 247; 51st Congress, 1st Session; 1889 (St. John's Abbey Archives, Collegeville, Minnesota).

8 Thomas Borgerding, OSB, Red Lake St. Mary's Mission Memoirs (St. John's Abbey Archives, Collegeville, Minnesota, 1949), p. 10. Also, it was later added, ". . . excavations could still be seen of these buildings which were just north of the cemetery cross in the depression for the larger building and beside it for the house . . . ." (1952), p. 13.

9 Frederic Baraga composed an Ojibwe grammar and dictionary, a catechism and prayer books. Limited copies are still extant today.

10 Thomas Borgerding, OSB, Red Lake St. Mary's Mission Memoirs (St. John's Abbey Archives, Collegeville, Minnesota, 1949), p. 13.

11 According to a statement by Allen A. Jourdain, subscribed and sworn to at Washington D.C., March 7, 1883, and signed by notary public Geo. M. Lockwood, artifacts such as medicine bags were taken by Tomazin from converts with the intention of burning but were brought East for exhibit and for collecting money. "Red Lake Manuscripts" (St John's Abbey Archives, Collegeville, Minnesota).

12 Thomas Borgerding, OSB, Red Lake St. Mary's Mission Memoirs (St. John's Abbey Archives, Collegeville, Minnesota, 1949), p. 14.

13 Statements by Allen A. Jourdain, March 7, 1883; Archives of the Bureau of Catholic Indian Missions and the Catholic Indian Bureau, Washington D.C.; "Red Lake Manuscripts" (St. John's Abbey Archives, Collegeville, Minnesota).

14 Letter of Archbishop Gibbons regarding Tomazin to Charles Ewing, Commissioner of the Bureau of Catholic Indian Missions, March 20, 1883

(St. John's Abbey Archives, Collegeville, Minnesota).

15 Benno Watrin,OSB, Red Lake Memoirs (St. John's Abbey Archives, Collegeville, Minnesota, 1949), pp. 12-15.

16 Original letter available: "Red Lake – Abbatial Correspondence" (St. John's Abbey Archives, Collegeville, Minnesota).

Chapter 3

1 Colman Barry, OSB, *Worship and Work* (Collegeville, Minnesota: The Liturgical Press, 1980), p. 479.

2 Consuela Marie Duffy, SBS, *Katharine Drexel* (Cornwall Heights, Pennsylvania: Sisters of the Blessed Sacrament, 1966; reprinted, 1977), p. 100. Katharine Drexel founded the Sisters of the Blessed Sacrament for Indians and Colored People in 1891.

3 Inez Hilger, OSB, "Memoirs of Amalia Eich" (St. Benedict's Monastery Archives, St. Joseph, Minnesota, 1940), p. 1.

4 Thomas Borgering, OSB, Letter to the Abbot (St. John's Abbey Archives, Collegeville, Minnesota, 1888).

5 Amalia Eich, OSB, written interview (St. Benedict's Monastery Archives, St. Joseph, Minnesota, 1937), p. 19.

6 Benno Watrin, OSB, Red Lake Memoirs (St. John's Abbey Archives, Collegeville, Minnesota, 1949), p. 18. Father Thomas Borgerding adds later in his memoirs of 1952 that this cemetery ". . . had grown to 2,200 graves with more than half of them unnamed."

7 Thomas Borgerding, OSB, Letter to the Abbot (St. John's Abbey Archives, Collegeville, Minnesota, 1888).

8 Thomas Borgerding, OSB, Red Lake St. Mary's Mission Memoirs (St. John's Abbey Archives, Collegeville, Minnesota, 1949), p. 43.

9 *Ibid.*, 1952 Memoirs.

10 Thomas Borgerding, OSB, Letter to the Abbot (St. John's Abbey Archives, Collegeville, Minnesota).

11 T.J. Welsh, "Indian Mission – Red Lake Interviews" (St. John's Abbey Archives, Collegeville, Minnesota, 1895). Welsh was a logger and historian who wrote about his visit to Red Lake in his book, *Early Minnesota Logging Days*.

12 "Laws Relating to Indian Affairs," 60th Congress, Sess. 1, Ch. 216, 1908; p. 367.

13 Fr. Robert Pryor, *Our Northland Diocese*, Sept. 1956: "Miss Drexel made provisions for the building of a new log church at Red Lake with logs she

bought while visiting there."

14 Inez Hilger, OSB, "Memoirs of Amalia Eich" (St. Benedict's Monastery Archives, St. Joseph, Minnesota, 1940).

15 Ambrosia Rettenmaier, OSB, Memoirs (St. Benedict's Monastery Archives, St. Joseph, Minnesota, 1890).

16 Thomas Borgerding, OSB, Letter to the Abbot (St. John's Abbey Archives, Collegeville, Minnesota, 1890).

17 Alban Fruth, OSB, *A Century of Missionary Work Among the Redlake Chippewa Indians* (Collegeville, Minnesota: Order of St. Benedict, 1958), p. 41. This may or may not accurately reflect the source of the money which appeared to have accrued from land ceded to the government and deposited for the benefit of all Ojibwe Indians in Minnesota.

18 Benno Watrin, OSB, Red Lake Memoirs (St. John's Abbey Archives, Collegeville, Minnesota, 1949), p. 25.

19 *Ibid.*, p. 26.

20 Thomas Borgerding, OSB, Letter to Mother Katharine Drexel (St. John's Abbey Archives, Collegeville, Minnesota, 1892).

21 Erwin F. Mittelholtz, *Historical Review of the Red Lake Indian Reservation* (Bemidji, Minnesota: Beltrami County Historical Society, 1957), p. 31.

22 Thomas Borgerding, OSB, Letter to Mother Katharine Drexel, St. John's Abbey Archives, Collegeville, Minnesota, June 26, 1893).

23 *Ibid.*

24 Thomas Borgerding, OSB, Red Lake St. Mary's Mission Memoirs (St. John's Abbey Archives, Collegeville, Minnesota, 1949), p.25.

25 Thomas Borgerding, OSB, Letter to Abbot Bernard Locnikar (St. John's Abbey Archives, Collegeville, Minnesota, November 15, 1893).

26 On May 6, 1889, Katharine Drexel entered the novitiate of the Sisters of Mercy at Pittsburgh, Pennsylvania. On February 12, 1891, she made her profession as the first sister (and foundress) of the Sisters of the Blessed Sacrament for Indians and Colored People. M. Katharine Drexel died March 3, 1955. *The Record* (student newspaper of Saint John's University), Vol. 6, p. 216; October, 1893.

27 Benno Watrin, OSB, Red Lake Memoirs (St. John's Abbey Archives, Collegeville, Minnesota, 1949), p. 27.

Chapter 4

1 Frederic Baraga, *Otchipwe Grammar* (St. John's Abbey Archives, Collegville, Minnesota, 1850), p. 211.

2 Clifford P. Hooker, "Concerning Education on the Red Lake Reservation (1890 – 1946)." (St. John's Abbey Archives, Collegeville, Minnesota, January 1988).

3 U.S. Government Statement (St. Benedict's Monastery Archives, St. Joseph, Minnesota), Box 15, 24-3-2.

4 Thomas Borgerding, OSB, Memoirs (St. John's Abbey Archives, Collegeville, Minnesota, 1952), p. 42.

5 Basilia Cosgrove, OSB, Interview (St. Benedict's Monastery Archives, St. Joseph, Minnesota, 1941).

6 Felix Nelles, OSB, "Thirty Years on the Missions" (St. John's Abbey Archives, Collegeville, Minnesota, 1930), p. 4.

7 Education Circular No. 62; Dept. of the Int., January 17, 1902 (St. John's Abbey Archives, Collegeville, Minnesota).

8 Thomas Borgerding, OSB, Letter to Mother Katharine Drexel (St. John's Abbey Archives, Collegeville, Minnesota, 1904).

9 M. Katharine Drexel, Letter to Thomas Borgerding (St. John's Abbey Archives, Collegville, Minnesota, 1904).

10 Benno Watrin, OSB, Red Lake Memoirs (St. John's Abbey Archives, Collegeville, Minnesota, 1949), pp. 31, 32.

11 Thomas Borgerding, OSB, Letter to Abbot Engel (St. John's Abbey Archives, Collegeville, Minnesota, Dec. 12, 1905).

12 *Ibid.*, August 3, 1908.

13 George Head, Interview notes, September 21, 1992, Red Lake, Minnesota. The stone foundation for the Church of the Immaculate Conception was built in 1911 during remodeling. Up to this time, the building rested on wooden posts.

Chapter 5

1 Letter from Thomas Borgerding, OSB, to Mother Katharine Drexel, June 19, 1911 (St. John's Abbey Archives, Collegeville, Minnesota).

2 Letter from Thomas Borgerding, OSB, to Abbot Peter Engel, OSB, February 28, 1913 (St. John's Abbey Archives, Collegeville, Minnesota).

3   Octavia Roth, OSB, Interview, 1989 (St. Benedict's Monastery Archives, St. Joseph, Minnesota).

4   Letter from Sister Hyacinthe Simmer, OSB, to Abbot Peter Engel, OSB, November 14, 1913 (St. John's Abbey Archives, Collegeville, Minnesota).

5   Letter from Claudina Locnikar, OSB, to Florian Locnikar, OSB, April 17, 1911 (St. John's Abbey Archives, Collegeville, Minnesota).

6   Ortrude Nester, OSB, Interview, 1989, (St. Benedict's Monastery Archives, St. Joseph, Minnesota).

7   *Ibid.*

8   Ervin "Tippie" Branchaud, Interview, August 18, 1993, Red Lake, Minnesota.

9   Leo Desjarlait, Interview, June 15, 1993, Red Lake, Minnesota.

10 Frank and Julia Lajeunesse, Interview, September 21, 1992, Red Lake, Minnesota.

11 Ed Lussier, Interview, June 16, 1993, Red Lake, Minnesota.

12 Mary Ann Aitken, Interview, September 22, 1992, Red Lake, Minnesota.

13 Thomas Borgerding, OSB, Memoirs (St. John's Abbey Archives, Collegeville, Minnesota, 1952), pp. 52-54.

14 *Ibid.*

15 Albert Drouillard, Interview, August 19, 1993, Red Lake, Minnesota.

16 Alban Fruth, OSB, *A Century of Missionary Work Among the Chippewa Indians* (Collegeville, Minnesota: Order of St. Benedict, Inc., 1958), p. 72.

17 *Ibid.*

18 Benno Watrin, OSB, Red Lake Memories (St. John's Abbey Archives, Collegeville, Minnesota, 1949), p. 36.

19 Erwin F. Mittelholtz, *Historical Review of the Red Lake Indian Reservation*, (Bemidji, Minnesota: Beltrami County Historical Society, 1957), p. 111.

20 Letter from a Committee of Indian Catholic Mothers at Red Lake, Minnesota, April 8, 1929, to Msgr. Wm. Hughes, BCIM, Washington, D.C. (St. John's Abbey Archives, Collegeville, Minnesota).

Chapter 6

1   There was only one power washing machine for the whole school, and much of the washing was done by the older girls on washboards.

2   Delphine "Duffy" Fuller, Interview, June 16, 1993, Red Lake, Minnesota.

3   Betty Beaulieu, Interview, June 15, 1993, Red Lake, Minnesota.

4 Adolf "Punce" Barrett, Interview, March 10, 1994, Red Lake, Minnesota.

5 Albert Drouillard, Written Account, February 4, 1994, Wildomar, California.

6 Frank "Farmer" Donnell, Interview, March 9, 1994, Red Lake, Minnesota.

7 Leonard Donnell, Interview, March 9, 1994, Red Lake, Minnesota.

8 St. Mary's Mission Edition of *The Indian Sentinel*: Winter 1929-30 (St. John's Abbey Archives, Collegeville, Minnesota).

9 A bronze memorial tablet, first planned for the Lourdes Grotto, was erected by Abbot Alcuin in memory of Rev. L. Lautischar on June 3, 1929, in front of St. Mary's Church.

10 Letter from a Committee of Indian Catholic Mothers at Red Lake, Minnesota, April 8, 1929 (St. John's Abbey Archives, Collegeville, Minnesota).

11 Agnes and Jim Roberts, Interview, September 22, 1992, Red Lake, Minnesota. It was customary in all consecrated Catholic cemeteries at this time to have a section for those who were not baptized. This did not mean, however, that the unbaptized were not "saved."

12 Violet "Vi" Donnell, Interview, March 9, 1994, Red Lake, Minnesota.

13 Letter from Ermin Pohlkamp, OSB, to Bishop Timothy Corbett, 1930 (St. John's Abbey Archives, Collegeville, Minnesota).

14 Adelma Roers, OSB, Interview, 1989, St. Benedict's Monastery Archives, St. Joseph, Minnesota).

15 Ruth Jourdain-Fevig, July 19, 1996, Red Lake, Minnesota.

16 Agatha Starkey, Interview, September 25, 1995, Red Lake, Minnesota.

17 Alban Fruth, OSB, Interview, September 15, 1994, St. John's Abbey, Collegeville, Minnesota.

18 Veronette Schramel, OSB, Interview, June 8, 1993, St. Scholastica Convent, St. Cloud, Minnesota.

19 Alban Fruth, OSB, *A Century of Missionary Work Among the Redlake Chippewa Indians* (Collegeville, Minnesota: Order of St. Benedict, 1958), p.97.

Chapter 7

1 Wilfred McGraw, Interview, March 10, 1994, Red Lake, Minnesota. Francis Blake is a writer today. There were three other Thunder children at the boarding school: Joseph, Genevieve, and Imogene.

2 Egbert Goeb, OSB, "Redlake Benedictine," St. Mary's Mission, Red Lake, Minnesota, Vol.1, No.1, 1955 – p. 4 (St. John's Abbey Archives, Collegeville, Minnesota).

3 Mary Ida Klehr, OSB, Interview, February 1, 1994, St. Benedict's Monastery, St. Joseph, Minnesota.

4 Genevieve Leuer, OSB, Interview, January 27, 1994, St. Raphael's Convent, St. Cloud, Minnesota.

Sister Mary Ida Klehr, OSB

5 "Golden Age." So designated by the Bemidji *Pioneer Press*, May, 1950, to describe this period in the history of St. Mary's School.

6 Gudilia Duclos, OSB, Interview, February 17, 1994, St. Benedict's Monastery, St. Joseph, Minnesota. Sister Louise Koltes, OSB, reports the same kind of teasing by Father Egbert when she came to the Mission in 1955. This time he stopped at an old abandoned farmhouse and quipped, "This is the Mission."

7 Aaronette Herzog, OSB, Interview, January 27, 1994, St. Raphael's Convent, St. Cloud, Minnesota.

8 Debora Herda, OSB, Interview, January 27, 1994, St. Raphael's Convent, St. Cloud, Minnesota.

9 Eulalia Siebels, OSB, Interview, January 26, 1994, St. Scholastlca's Convent, St. Cloud, Minnesota.

10 Elaine Schindler, OSB, Interview, February 7, 1994, St. Benedict's Monastery, St. Joseph, Minnesota.

11 Marie Reisinger, OSB, Interview, February 15, 1994, St. Benedict's Monastery, St. Joseph, Minnesota.

12 Thea Grieman, OSB, Interview, January 26, 1994, St. Scholastica Convent, St. Cloud, Minnesota.

13 Mary Rose Skinaway, Interview, March 9, 1994, Red Lake, Minnesota.

14 Thomas Borgerding, OSB, Memoirs are available at the St. John's Abbey Archives, Collegeville, Minnesota. Dr. Charles Vandersluis published his interviews with Thomas Borgerding in weekly articles of the Bemidji *Northland Times* from January to June, 1954.

15 Placid Stuckenschneider, OSB, Interview, February 15, 1994, St. John's Abbey, Collegeville, Minnesota.

16 William Borgerding, OSB, Interview, March 6, 1994, St. John's Abbey, Collegeville, Minnesota.

17 Omer Maus, OSB, Interview, February 3, 1994, St. John's Abbey, Collegeville, Minnesota.

18 Alban Fruth, OSB, *Redlake Benedictine*, (St. Mary's Mission, Redlake, Minnesota), Vol.4, No.4 – December 1956.

19 Stephanie Cobenais, Interview, Summer 1996, Red Lake, Minnesota.

20 Letter from Thomas Borgerding, OSB, to Alban Fruth, OSB, August 24, 1956 (St. John's Abbey Archives, Collegeville, Minnesota).

Chapter 8

1 Cassian Osendorf, OSB, Interview, February 12, 1993, St. John's Abbey, Collegeville, Minnesota. No plan was ever found showing how the graves were marked which Father Cassian refers to. There are various opinions regarding this cemetery problem and what happened. Some people say that it was customary for families to keep a grave up for only four years. After that, it was allowed to return to nature.

2 *The Native American Press*, January 29, 1993, p. 6. Refers to an address made by Donna Jean Morrison to a group at Bemidji State University.

3 Statement by Placid Stuckenschneider, OSB, December 7, 1993. On file in St. John's Abbey Archives, Collegeville, Minnesota.

4 Brother Willy Borgerding had taken prize-winning cattle to the state Jersey sale at Owatonna, Minnesota.

5 "Redlake Benedictine," Vol. IV, March 1958 (St. John's Abbey Archives, Collegeville, Minnesota).

6 Francis J. Schenk, Letter to Alban Fruth, OSB, July 1, 1958 (St. John's Abbey Archives, Collegeville, Minnesota).

7 Alban Fruth, OSB, Interview, September 15, 1994, St. John's Abbey, Collegeville, Minnesota.

8 Film available, St. John's Abbey Archives, Collegeville, Minnesota.

9 Herbert Dehler, OSB, Interview, September 7, 1994, St. Raphael's Convent, St. Cloud, Minnesota.

10 Father Alban cited an example of the kind of mission work Father Thomas engaged in which he considered "extraordinary:"

> Father Thomas was sitting at his desk one day when an Indian came in without rapping as was the custom and sat down. Father Thomas looked up at him but kept writing letters and looking in his books. After about an hour the Indian got up and said, "Father, we had a good visit." Father Thomas answered, "Yes, we sure did."

Father Thomas had a kind of "open-door" policy for the people. His sensitivity to their culture and spirituality included his acceptance of spirit houses on the cemetery – as long as the little holes in them where the people believed the spirit escaped, be changed to crosses. He told them that the food they put on the graves should be shared with the poor.

11 Louise Koltes, OSB, Interview, August 25, 1994, St. Raphael's Convent, St. Cloud, Minnesota.

12 Aniceta Drontl, OSB, "Faculty Handbook for St. Mary's Mission School," 1962-1968, St. Mary's Mission, Redlake, Minnesota.

13 Catherine Ludwig, OSB, Interview, February 7, 1994, St. Benedict's Monastery, St. Joseph, Minnesota.

14 William Borgerding, OSB, Interview, March 6, 1994, St. John's Abbey, Collegeville, Minnesota.

15 Gregory Eibensteiner, OSB, Interview, November 1, 1994, St. John's Abbey, Collegeville, Minnesota.

16 Loretta Rothstein, OSB, Interview, August 30, 1994, St. Benedict's Monastery, St. Joseph, Minnesota.

17 Letter from Abbot Baldwin Dworschak, OSB, August 26, 1960 (St. John's Abbey Archives, Collegeville, Minnesota).

18 Michael Laux, OSB, Interview, March 25, 1994, St. John's Abbey, Collegeville, Minnesota.

19 Father Cassian's words at his 1990 retirement which were later printed in his obituary notice from the Abbey, October 19, 1996 (St. John's Abbey Archives, Collegeville, Minnesota.)

20 Madonna Niebolte, OSB, Interview, August 31, 1994, St. Scholastica Convent, St. Cloud, Minnesota.

21 *Our Northland Diocese*, January 1966.

22 Maurice Hurrle, OSB, apparently died of a heart attack while on a hunting trip in November 1969, the year after he left St. Mary's. He had just celebrated Mass for the hunters of the area that Sunday.

23 Johnette Kohorst, OSB, Interview, September 7, 1994, St. Peter's Convent, St. Cloud, Minnesota.

24 Gerald Vizenor, *Crossbloods* (University of Minnesota Press, Minneapolis, Minnesota, 1976, 1990), p. 238.

25 Colman J. Barry, OSB, and Robert L. Spaeth, *A Sense of Place: Saint John's of Collegeville* (Saint John's University Press, Collegeville, Minnesota, 1987), pp. 24,25.

26 Jean Schwartz, OSB, Interview, April 25, 1995, St. Benedict's Convent, St. Joseph, Minnesota.

27 Brian Anderson, "The Present: Is There Indian Art?" *Minneapolis Tribune Picture*, October 22, 1972.

28 "Lake Borgerding" refers to the small lake or pond behind the convent. It was thus identified by the Mission in the 1950s – perhaps in remembrance of Father Thomas Borgerding.

    Sister Johnette Kohorst described an experience of hers while snowmobiling one time on Red Lake:

> I was lost on the lake. I was on our snowmobile and I loved going over the "hills" made by the snow and ice on the lake. Suddenly, the snowmobile stopped and I couldn't get it started. I was near Ponemah and it was getting dark. Then I saw a light coming toward me. It was an Indian man. He asked what was wrong and then got the snowmobile going for me again. He told me where I was at and that I should stay close to the shore line all the way back. When I saw light, I would know it was Red Lake and I should go up the hill.

    Later, neither Sister Johnette nor anyone else seemed to know who this man was who had helped her.

29 Title to the Lands at Red Lake (St. John's Abbey Archives, Collegeville, Minnesota). Bureau of Catholic Indian Missions-Land Patent Issue Act, May 29, 1908, included the name of Theodore Roosevelt, President of the United States (copy submitted by Harlan Beaulieu, Red Lake). See Appendix B for Text of Land Grant.

Chapter 9

1 Jordan Stovik, OSB, Interview, June 1, 1995, Spring Hill, Minnesota.

2 Elizabeth Theis, OSB, Interview, April 10, 1995, St. Benedict's Monastery, St. Joseph, Minnesota.

3 Dominica Freund, OSB, Interview, April 11, 1996, St. Benedict's Monastery, St. Joseph, Minnesota.

4 Marlene Schwinghammer, OSB, Letter, February 22, 1996, North St. Paul, Minnesota.

5 Jane Weber, OSB, September 1, 1995, St. Benedict's Monastery, St. Joseph, Minnesota.

6 Letter to Prior Gordon Tavis, OSB, December 2, 1976 (St. John's Abbey

Archives, Collegeville, Minnesota).

7 *Ibid.*, November 30, 1976.

8 Sharon Nohner, OSB, Interview, November 18, 1995, St. Benedict's Monastery, St. Joseph, Minnesota.

9 Lucy Revering, OSB, Interview, June 5, 1995, St. Scholastica Convent, St. Cloud, Minnesota.

10 Letter from Abbot John Eidenschink, OSB, November 29, 1977 (St. John's Abbey Archives, Collegeville, Minnesota).

11 Gilmary Kempf, OSB, Interview, May 17, 1995, St. Raphael's Convent, St. Cloud, Minnesota.

12 Meinrad Dindorf, OSB, Interview, September 29, 1996, St. Benedict's Center, St. Cloud, Minnesota.

13 Interviewees: Father Meinrad Dindorf, OSB, and Sisters Elizabeth Theis, Loretta Rothstein, Lucy Revering, Dominica Freund, Marlene Schwinghammer, Emerentia Fleischhacker, Barbara Zinzer, and Marcella Weber, OSB.

14 Patricia Wallis, OSB, Interview, May 19, 1995, St. Benedict's Monastery, St. Joseph, Minnesota.

Chapter 10

1 Unpubl. study (St. Cloud State University, 1977) by Patricia Wallis, OSB, "Field Study: A Study to Compare the Difference in Background of Elementary Students with Curriculum Methodology."

2 St. Mary's School Board Minutes, January 1981, St. Mary's School, Redlake, Minnesota.

3 Delice Bialke, OSB, Interview, November 16, 1995, St. Benedict's Monastery, St. Joseph, Minnesota.

4 Unpubl. study (St. John's University, 1981) by Robert Pierson, OSB, "Ministry and the Rural Community," pp. 13, 15.

5 Douglas Mullin, OSB, Interview, September 4, 1995, St. John's Abbey,

Sister Delice Bialke, OSB

Collegeville, Minnesota.

6   "Indian Youth," *St. Paul Sunday Pioneer Press*, February 26, 1984, p. 10-G.

7   Mary Lou Carlson, OSB, Interview, November 15, 1995, St. Benedict's Monastery, St. Joseph, Minnesota.

8   Ruth Ann Schneider, OSB, Interview, February 23, 1996, St. Benedict's Monastery, St. Joseph, Minnesota.

9   Douglas Mullin, OSB, "Benedictine Mission to Red Lake: Nearly a Century Old," *The Saint Cloud Visitor*, October 30, 1986, p. 11.

10 *The Red Lake Times*, August 26, 1987.

11 St. Mary's parish bulletin: Letter from Bishop Balke of Crookston to the Red Lake community, November 8, 1984 (St. John's Abbey Archives, Collegeville, Minnesota).

12 *Our Northland Diocese*, November 15, 1984.

13 *The Saint Paul Pioneer Press*, February 26, 1984, p. 10-G.

14 Unpubl. (St. John's Abbey Archives, July 1985) by Douglas Mullin, OSB, "The Red Lake Question: Considerations for Recommitment."

15 "Miskwaagamiiwizaaga'iganiing 'Red Lake Reservation'," *The Saint Cloud Visitor*, October 30, 1986, pp. 11-14.

16 S. Hauser, "Red Lake Mission School: A self-sufficient future?" "The Mission School: Looking backwards and forward," *The Ojibwe News*, May 16, 1989.

17 Aloysius Thunder, Interview, September 25, 1995, Red Lake, Minnesota.

Chapter 11

1   William Mehrkens, Interview, January 15, 1996, St. Mary's Mission, Redlake, Minnesota.

2   Marina Schlangen, OSB, Interview, January 15, 1996, St. Mary's Mission, Redlake, Minnesota.

3   Teresa Duerr, OSB, Interview, May 30, 1996, St. Benedict's Monastery, St. Joseph, Minnesota.

4   *Ibid.*

5   Bill Strong, Interview, November 19, 1996, Red Lake, Minnesota.

6   William W. Warren, *History of the Ojibwe Nation* (Ross & Haines, Inc., Minneapolis, Minnesota, 1853, 1970), pp. 349, 350; 457-459.

INDEX

NOTE: Numbers *in italics* refer to pages with a photo of subject.

Prayers on the inside back cover from:

[St. John's Abbey Archives]

ANAMIHE-MASINAHIGAN.

JESUS OT IJITTWĀWIN

GAYE

ANAMIHE-NAKAMUNAN

TAKŌBIHIKĀTEWAN.

MIK' EJITTWĀWĀD
KETOLIK-ANAMIHĀDJIK.

NITTAM ANDJIBIHIGAN.

KEBEKONG ŌTENANG:
COTÉ ET CIE. MASINAHIGANIKKEWININI ENDAD.

IHIW PIPŌN—1859—KĀ AKKO NIKIT JESUS.